Health Care Issues in the United States and Japan

**A National Bureau
of Economic Research
Conference Report**

Health Care Issues in the United States and Japan

Edited by **David A. Wise and Naohiro Yashiro**

The University of Chicago Press

Chicago and London

DAVID A. WISE is the John F. Stambaugh Professor of Political
Economy at the John F. Kennedy School of Government at Harvard
University and director of the Program on Aging at the National
Bureau of Economic Research. NAOHIRO YASHIRO is professor of
economics at International Christian University and former president
of the Japan Center for Economic Research.

The University of Chicago Press, Chicago 60637
The University of Chicago Press, Ltd., London
© 2006 by the National Bureau of Economic Research
All rights reserved. Published 2006
Printed in the United States of America

15 14 13 12 11 10 09 08 07 06   1 2 3 4 5
ISBN-13: 978-0-226-90292-0 (cloth)
ISBN-10: 0-226-90292-7 (cloth)

Library of Congress Cataloging-in-Publication Data

Health care issues in the United States and Japan / edited by David A.
    Wise and Naohiro Yashiro.
        p.   cm.—(NBER conference report)
    Includes bibliographical references and index.
    ISBN 0-226-90292-7 (cloth : alk. paper)
        1. Medical care—Japan. 2. Medical care—United States. I. Wise,
    David A. II. Yashiro, Naohiro, 1946– III. Series.
    RA395 .J3H42 2006
    362.10952—dc22

                                                                2005055904

Relation of the Directors to the Work and Publications of the National Bureau of Economic Research

1. The object of the NBER is to ascertain and present to the economics profession, and to the public more generally, important economic facts and their interpretation in a scientific manner without policy recommendations. The Board of Directors is charged with the responsibility of ensuring that the work of the NBER is carried on in strict conformity with this object.

2. The President shall establish an internal review process to ensure that book manuscripts proposed for publication DO NOT contain policy recommendations. This shall apply both to the proceedings of conferences and to manuscripts by a single author or by one or more co-authors but shall not apply to authors of comments at NBER conferences who are not NBER affiliates.

3. No book manuscript reporting research shall be published by the NBER until the President has sent to each member of the Board a notice that a manuscript is recommended for publication and that in the President's opinion it is suitable for publication in accordance with the above principles of the NBER. Such notification will include a table of contents and an abstract or summary of the manuscript's content, a list of contributors if applicable, and a response form for use by Directors who desire a copy of the manuscript for review. Each manuscript shall contain a summary drawing attention to the nature and treatment of the problem studied and the main conclusions reached.

4. No volume shall be published until forty-five days have elapsed from the above notification of intention to publish it. During this period a copy shall be sent to any Director requesting it, and if any Director objects to publication on the grounds that the manuscript contains policy recommendations, the objection will be presented to the author(s) or editor(s). In case of dispute, all members of the Board shall be notified, and the President shall appoint an ad hoc committee of the Board to decide the matter; thirty days additional shall be granted for this purpose.

5. The President shall present annually to the Board a report describing the internal manuscript review process, any objections made by Directors before publication or by anyone after publication, any disputes about such matters, and how they were handled.

6. Publications of the NBER issued for informational purposes concerning the work of the Bureau, or issued to inform the public of the activities at the Bureau, including but not limited to the NBER Digest and Reporter, shall be consistent with the object stated in paragraph 1. They shall contain a specific disclaimer noting that they have not passed through the review procedures required in this resolution. The Executive Committee of the Board is charged with the review of all such publications from time to time.

7. NBER working papers and manuscripts distributed on the Bureau's web site are not deemed to be publications for the purpose of this resolution, but they shall be consistent with the object stated in paragraph 1. Working papers shall contain a specific disclaimer noting that they have not passed through the review procedures required in this resolution. The NBER's web site shall contain a similar disclaimer. The President shall establish an internal review process to ensure that the working papers and the web site do not contain policy recommendations, and shall report annually to the Board on this process and any concerns raised in connection with it.

8. Unless otherwise determined by the Board or exempted by the terms of paragraphs 6 and 7, a copy of this resolution shall be printed in each NBER publication as described in paragraph 2 above.

Contents

Acknowledgments

This volume consists of papers presented at a joint Japan Center for Economic Research (JCER)–National Bureau of Economic Research (NBER) conference held in Nikko, Japan in May 2003. Financial support to the NBER from the U.S. Department of Health and Human Services, National Institute on Aging (grants P01-AG005842 and P30-AG012810) and to the JCER from the Japan Foundation Center for Global Partnership and the Pfizer Health Research Foundation is gratefully acknowledged. Additional funding sources are noted in individual papers.

The editors wish to thank Chapin White for help in editing the papers and Richard Woodbury for his help in putting together the introduction to the volume.

Any opinions expressed in this volume are those of the respective authors and do not necessarily reflect the views of the National Bureau of Economic Research, the Japan Center for Economic Research, or the sponsoring organizations.

Introduction

David A. Wise

This volume contains papers presented at a joint JCER–NBER conference held in Nikko, Japan in March 2003. It is the fifth in a series of JCER–NBER projects comparing aspects of the economic systems and economic behavior in the United States and Japan. The previous volumes are *Aging in the United States and Japan: Economic Trends* (1994), *The Economic Effects of Aging in the United States and Japan* (1997), *Aging Issues in the United States and Japan* (2001), and *Labor Markets and Firm Benefit Policies in Japan and the United States* (2003). The papers in this volume direct attention to the health care systems in the two countries.

Recent data compiled by the Organization for Economic Cooperation and Development (OECD) in *OECD Health Data 2005* highlights significant differences in health and health care between Japan and the United States. For instance, among OECD countries, Japan spends close to the lowest percentage of its gross domestic product (GDP) on health care (7.9 percent), while the United States spends the highest (15 percent). Yet life expectancies in Japan are the longest in the world—eighty-two years (at birth), compared with seventy-seven years in the United States. Interestingly, despite its lower spending on health care, Japan has many more hospital beds per capita (8.5 per thousand population compared with 2.8 per thousand in the United States), more computed tomography (CT) scanners (93 per million in Japan compared with 13 per million in the United States), and more magnetic resonance imaging (MRI) machines (35 per million in Japan compared with 9 per million in the United States). Japan

David A. Wise is the John F. Stambaugh Professor of Political Economy at the John F. Kennedy School of Government, Harvard University, and director of the Program on Aging at the National Bureau of Economic Research.

has the lowest obesity rate among OECD countries (3 percent), while the United States has the highest (31 percent). At the same time, smoking rates in Japan are nearly double those in the United States (over 30 percent in Japan, and 17 percent in the United States). Eighty-two percent of health care spending in Japan is public spending, compared with 44 percent in the United States. These OECD summary measures, and many others, raise all kinds of questions about how the health care systems operate differently in the two countries and how these operational differences relate to health care quality, costs, and outcomes.

The goals of this volume (and the NBER–JCER project more generally) are not to replicate these comparative statistics, but rather to explore the structural characteristics of the health care systems in each country, the economic incentives underlying the systems, and how they operate in practice. In both countries the rising cost of health care presents important financial challenges. Indeed, aging populations and rising health care costs are motivating health system reform throughout the world. The intention of this effort was to begin an assessment of the health care systems in Japan and the United States, with the hope that a better understanding of elements of both systems could lead to improvements in both. The papers have not been selected to provide a systematic or comprehensive comparison of care in the two countries, although with respect to some issues such comparisons are made. Instead the goal is to explore in greater depth selected aspects of each health care system. The studies are topical investigations that can serve as background to more comprehensive and direct comparative work.

The volume is organized in three major sections. The first includes studies of the health care systems in Japan and the United States and how those systems are evolving with the financial pressures of rising health care costs. The second major section includes studies on the variations in medical practice patterns and quality of care in the two countries. A final section addresses selected other health care topics in Japan and the United States. Together, the ten studies offer valuable insight into the differences in health care systems in the two countries. This summary draws heavily on the authors' own words.

The Health Care Systems in Japan and the United States

Four papers direct attention to the structural characteristics of the health care systems in Japan and the United States, the financial challenges posed by an aging population and rising costs, and the impact of these financial pressures on health system reform. How does each country address the basic issues of health insurance coverage, access to care, and financing? And in what ways are the health systems and policies evolving in response to the common pressures of older populations and rising costs?

In "Evaluating Japan's Health Care Reform of the 1990s and Its Effects to Cope with Population Aging," Naohiro Yashiro, Reiko Suzuki, and Wataru Suzuki examine the basic structure of the Japanese medical care system, focusing primarily on recent policy issues. Their paper reviews recent demographic developments in light of policy and institutional changes in Japan's health care system in the 1990s. The authors estimate the quantitative effects of the recently proposed institutional changes in health insurance schemes and show that they have only short-term effects in improving the fiscal balances in the system.

As background, the paper discusses Japan's generous health insurance schemes, under which all citizens, including the self-employed, are supposed to have some form of health insurance. Japan guarantees patients "free access" to hospitals with no gatekeepers and provides certain medical services under a "fee-for-service" health insurance arrangement. The authors point out that such generous access aggravates the financial challenges of population aging. Thus the effect of population aging is already reflected in growing fiscal deficits in health insurance budgets that are burdened by an increasing number of elderly enrollees, who are heavy users of health resources. Given the generous access to care and the limited financial incentive for cost-effective health care decision making, the authors are surprised that Japan's national health expenditures have remained at a relatively low level.

One interpretation of the combination of low costs and generous access is that Japan has maintained relatively low physician salaries. The system also has been efficient in providing basic health care services to the population as a whole, reflecting people's strong preference for egalitarian access in Japan. With the aging of the population, however, the major burden of disease has shifted from infectious and acute diseases to chronic disease. This reduces the positive externalities of medical treatments as well as the extent of the asymmetry of information between providers and patients. Also, the preferences of patients have shifted toward better quality health services with medical information. It is against this background that changes in the Japanese health care system are considered.

The health system in Japan has many features in common with the Medicare program for the elderly in the United States. The question of how to reform the current welfarelike health scheme in Japan has much in common with U.S. Medicare reform. The major reform proposals include standardization of medical treatments, partial replacement of public health insurance with private health insurance, introduction of a partial managed care system, and introduction of for-profit hospitals to stimulate competition.

The authors find that various policy reforms introduced in the 1990s did not effectively solve the fundamental problems. For example, the expansion of long-term care insurance in 2000 was intended to move care for the frail elderly from costly hospitals to nursing homes, but the effect has been marginal, with free access to hospitals basically maintained. Another reform was raising the copayment rate and redistributing costs among various insurance providers, though the positive fiscal impacts of these reforms is projected to last only over the short run. The 2003 health insurance reform is a first step toward a more comprehensive reform of the health care services sector, the authors conclude.

The next two papers in the volume address some of the same general issues that are addressed in the Yashiro, Suzuki, and Suzuki chapter, but with a focus on the United States health care system and on the health systems of OECD countries more generally. "The U.S. Medical Care System for the Elderly" characterizes the health care system in the United States, while "An International Look at the Medical Care Financing Problem" considers the financing challenges posed by population aging and rising health care costs, how health systems may continue to evolve going forward, and the extent to which health care costs are likely to continue to increase into the future.

In "The U.S. Medical Care System for the Elderly," David Cutler and I examine the structure of the American medical care system, especially the system of care for the elderly. We focus on three sets of interactions: *coverage rules* (how people get health insurance and who pays for it), the *reimbursement system* (how providers are paid), and *access rules* (what are the financial and nonfinancial barriers to receipt of care).

We note that Medical care systems are multidimensional, and so our description must be as well. The basis for our analysis is the medical care triad. There are three participants in the medical care system: patients, providers, and insurers. Patients pay money to insurers (either directly or indirectly, as we discuss in the following) and pay for some care directly. Insurers reimburse providers for care and set rules under which the care can be provided. Providers diagnose and treat patients.

Corresponding to these three participants are three sets of interactions. The first is *coverage rules*. This encompasses the mechanisms by which people get health insurance and who pays for that insurance. The second interaction is the *reimbursement system* between insurers and providers— how is payment determined and what rates are paid? Finally, there are the *access rules*—which providers are patients allowed to see and under what circumstances? In this paper, we describe the insurance, reimbursement, and access rules in the American medical care system. We present broad outlines of the system for everyone in the United States. Because the system is so heterogeneous, we focus particular attention on the system for the elderly. We note where research has explored a link between system provisions and outcomes, but we do not take the further step of relating system provisions to health outcomes in any systematic way.

While there is variability even within the United States, we suggest the following simple summary. Coverage in the United States is spotty—excellent for the elderly, but not guaranteed for the nonelderly. Historically, reimbursement of providers was very generous, and access was open as well. Increasingly, though, the reimbursement and access routes are being restricted as insurers respond to moral hazard and the demand for cost containment.

The direction the medical system will go in the United States is not clear. Even in the past few years, reimbursement and access rules have changed, and coverage issues have dominated the public agenda. Changes along all three dimensions bear watching. We emphasize that it is also important to extend this analysis to other countries. By characterizing existing systems and comparing outcomes across countries, we can use the cross-national perspective to inform the evolution of health policy and health systems within countries. Some cross-national perspective is provided in the next chapter, which considers the challenges of medical care financing in all OECD countries.

In "An International Look at the Medical Care Financing Problem," David Cutler notes that, as populations age and medical spending rises, medical systems will account for an increasing part of economic activity. Virtually all developed countries are worried about how to finance medical care. Medical costs are increasing more rapidly than tax revenues to pay for them, and populations are aging, each of which increases the burden on the public sector. In the United States, we speak of a "Medicare crisis" and a "Social Security crisis," where the government will no longer be able to meet its health care bills. Other countries refer to "aging crisis" or an "old age insurance crisis."

Given that medical care costs are certain to rise, Cutler asks how much the increase will be and what magnitude of reform will be needed to meet the needs. To answer these questions, he develops a forecast model of medical spending in OECD countries that uses as inputs current spending on medical care and the demographic mix of the population as it stands now and as it is expected to change. The model estimates the share of medical spending in GDP in the future. Because most countries pay for the bulk of medical services publicly, this forecast is closely related to the increase in the public-sector financing burden that can be expected.

The results yield several important conclusions. First, all OECD countries can expect an increase in the cost of medical care over time. On the basis of demographic change alone, the typical country can expect medical care to increase by 2.2 percent of GDP in the next thirty years and by 3.6 percent of GDP in the next half century. Including continued technological innovation in medicine at the rate experienced in the past raises the projected increase in the next thirty years to 5.7 percent of GDP. Interestingly, the data suggest that the medical care problem is about equally split between the consequences of aging and the consequences of technological change in medical treatments.

The coming medical care burden differs substantially across countries. The countries that will be hardest hit by demographic change are Spain, Switzerland, the Czech Republic, Italy, and Greece. All of these countries have very low fertility rates and large projected increases in life expectancy. Demographic change will raise medical spending in these countries by 5 to 6 percent of GDP. Japan and the United States rank in the middle of this scale, 9th and 12th, respectively, out of twenty-nine countries (expected increases of 4.4 and 3.7 percent), while Turkey, the United Kingdom, New Zealand, and Mexico are among the countries least affected, with expected increases of 2 percent or less.

Accounting for technological change has a material impact on these rankings. Most importantly, it raises the financing burden in the United States. The United States spends more than other countries do on medical care and has the most technologically advanced medical system. Thus, if technology increases costs at the same rate everywhere, the United States will be particularly hard hit. Using historical growth rates of medical costs as a guide to the future, the projected increase in medical spending in the United States over the next thirty years is close to 10 percent. The increase in Japan will be more than 6 percent of GDP.

These are sizeable estimates, although perhaps not cataclysmic, Cutler concludes. He shows, however, that affording such increases will require reductions in the growth of nonmedical consumption, but not absolute declines in the level of such spending.

The next chapter in the volume considers the distribution of health care costs and health care use by age in Japan, the extent to which costs are cross-subsidized across age groups and across segments of the health financing system, and how recent and prospective health system reforms may affect this cross-subsidization. It enhances our understanding of the components of health care finance in Japan, and how the components interact in support of the overall health care system in Japan.

In "Removing the Instability and Inequity in the Japanese Health Insurance System" Seiritsu Ogura, Tamotsu Kadoda, and Makoto Kawamura compare Japan's current public medical insurance to an unstable two-story building, whose second floor (health insurance for the elderly) is becoming heavier each day, while its first floor is losing strength. There are three pillars in the first floor that support the weight of the whole building. These are (1) insurance programs that cover the health care costs of employees and their dependents, (2) National Health Insurance programs (NHIs)—primarily more than 3,200 municipal programs—that provide insurance to self-employed workers, retirees, and others who are not covered by employees' programs, and (3) subsidies from the national and municipal governments. Each of these supports is funded in a different way. The employees' programs charge different premiums depending on the program, but collect far more revenue than necessary to pay their benefits. The NHIs, on the other hand, are financially weak and, like the programs for the elderly, depend on generous government subsidies.

The second floor of the building consists of health care insurance for the elderly, which provides medical care benefits to those over seventy for very little cost. Because this program does not collect premiums on its own, the benefits are paid by collecting charges from the "first-floor" public insurance programs. Thus, most of the health care costs of the elderly have been shifted from the employees' health insurance programs and the national government. Under the current system, 70 percent of the health care costs of the elderly (net of their small out-of-pocket costs) are charged to these insurance programs, with each program contributing an amount in proportion to the number of its insured individuals and the average health care cost of elderly in the system. Of the remaining 30 percent, the national government contributes 20 percent and local governments contribute 10 percent.

This two-story structure, the authors say, has become very unstable for two reasons, one cyclical and the other structural. Japan's prolonged economic slump over the past decade has had a large negative effect on the revenues of all the insurance programs in the first floor. In addition, the rapid increase in the number of individuals who are reaching age seventy adds a significant weight to the second floor while removing support from the first.

Given the current two-story system, the bulk of the increase in health care costs of the elderly has been absorbed by increases in employee insurance premiums and budget deficits. Employees' out-of-pocket costs have been raised in steps, from 10 percent to 20 percent in 1997, and from 20 percent to 30 percent in 2003 for employees, and from 20 percent to 30 percent for their dependents. These changes have left employees on par with individuals covered by NHIs as far as the out-of-pocket costs are concerned, while increasing premiums by a factor of two. Similarly, the government has to deal with the swelling need for subsidies and the deepening of the budget deficit amidst a rapid decline in tax revenues.

The analyses in this paper address what the authors consider to be the two major weaknesses in the Japanese health insurance system. The authors examine the consequences of the "special" treatment of the elderly and conclude that it will be difficult to continue to support the elderly at current levels. The authors also emphasize that strengthening the financial base of the NHI system is a critical part of reforming the health insurance system for the elderly.

Ogura, Kadoda, and Kawamura's analysis is based on a microsimulation model, which is used as a tool for judging the properties of a given health insurance system. This model consists of a large number of individual households that collectively represent the economic and health statistics of the Japanese economy. The purpose of the simulations was to find a scenario under which an employee in his or her working prime (i.e., a household head age forty to sixty-four), who may be supporting children, would have a financial burden appropriate to the benefits he or she receives. The authors find systems that they believe would meet these goals. These systems would make the elderly responsible for a larger fraction of health care costs than they now pay. By replacing the current system with a consumption tax to finance health insurance benefits, it is also possible, the authors conclude, to reduce the large disparity in the contribution-to-cost ratios across different age groups and improve the vertical equity of the medical insurance system.

Practice Patterns and Quality of Care

The next four papers consider differences in medical practice patterns and quality of care issues in the United States and Japan. While the studies focus narrowly on individual diagnoses or other aspects of the health care system, rather than on broad cross-national comparative analyses of quality, they provide important insights on selected dimensions of quality in both countries. For example, the first paper looks at the effects of a hospital's volume of angioplasty procedures on outcomes among acute myocardial infarction (AMI), or heart attack, patients in Japan. The second looks at the effects of market concentration on quality among home health care delivery services in Japan. The third compares how AMI patients are treated in Japan and the United States. And the fourth looks at the dramatic variation in treatment patterns across geographic regions even within the United States and what this suggests about the quality of care in different places. Together, these studies highlight the value of studying medical practice patterns in different countries, as well as across geographic regions within countries, as a statistical basis for evaluating and improving quality.

In "The Volume-Outcome Relationship in Japan: The Case of Percutaneous Transluminal Coronary Angioplasty (PTCA) Volume on Mortality of Acute Myocardial Infarction (AMI) Patients," Koichi Kawabuchi and Shigeru Sugihara examine the relationship between the number of percutaneous transluminal coronary angioplasty (PTCA) procedures performed and negative medical outcomes among AMI patients in Japan.

A common presumption is that as the number of procedures increases, the quality will improve due to the learning-by-doing (or "practice makes perfect") effect. The authors refer to an inverse relationship between volume and negative medical outcomes as a "volume effect." Hospitals in Japan generally perform limited numbers of PTCA procedures each year. Nearly half of the hospitals performed fewer than 50 PCTA procedures per year, while only 15 percent of the hospitals performed more than 200 (the minimum number recommended by the American College of Cardiology/ American Heart Association). Hospitals with more than 400 PTCA procedures are quite rare in Japan.

This paper examines empirically the relationship between volume and quality among PTCA procedures in Japan. The authors also investigate the nature and channels of this effect, which have implications for reimbursement policy as well as competition policy. If there is a strong volume effect, policies should favor the concentration of PTCA procedures in a small number of hospitals or physicians. If this is not the case, policies favoring concentration of PTCA procedures may be inappropriate.

The main conclusions are as follows: (a) The volume effect operates not at the hospital level but at the physician level, (b) the volume effect is nonlinear. Under a specific estimation specification, volumes above a certain level result in worse outcomes, so too much is as bad as too little, (c) risk adjustment is essential for the evaluation of the quality of health care, as risk factors such as shock and multiple occlusions vary considerably across physicians and hospitals, and (d) there are virtually no spillover effects and no independent organizational influence. The implication is that physicians learn by themselves. This does not necessarily mean that there is no role for peer groups, teamwork, mentors, and so on. Presumably, the authors say, it simply means that these effects are independent of volume.

In "Market Concentration, Efficiency, and Quality in the Japanese Home Help Industry," Yanfei Zhou and Wataru Suzuki consider the effect of market concentration on the quality and cost of home help services. The authors point out that until quite recently the family network played the primary role in providing care for the frail elderly. However, changes in the social structure, such as weakening community ties, a cultural redefinition of the family nucleus, and an increasing number of women in the workforce, have raised both the financial and psychological burdens of family-based care for the aged.

In response to the expanding elderly population and the increasing demand for community-based–long-term care services, the Public Nursing Insurance Act (*Kaigo Hoken Ho*) was formally enacted in September 1997. Under this legislation, the Ministry of Health, Labor and Welfare (MHLW) introduced a new public long-term care insurance system in April 2000. This new system aims to respond to society's major concerns about aging and to assure citizens that they will receive care, if necessary, and be supported by society as a whole. According to the MHLW statistics, the supply of care services expanded after implementing the insurance system. However, the effects of market-oriented reform on service quality and efficiency are unknown. It is unknown, for example, whether introducing competition by expanding the number of providers in an area can simultaneously improve the quality of service and management efficiency.

Zhou and Suzuki use cross-sectional data to investigate the effect of market concentration on the quality and cost of home help services. They focus on home help services because the reforms in this market have been dramatic, and the proportion of for-profit providers is one of the highest among the at-home nursing care businesses. The number of home help service care providers per thousand elderly is used as an index of market concentration. To evaluate the impact of market-oriented reform on service quality and efficiency, the authors consider whether care providers in unconcentrated (i.e., highly competitive) markets have a higher level of quality and efficiency than those in highly concentrated markets. The authors note that this information is also helpful for determining the appropriate number and scale of operations of care providers in each district.

According to the Survey of Nursing Care Management (*Kaigo Jigyo Keei Jita Chosa*) 2002 by MHLW, the higher the market competition (or, the fewer users per care facility), the higher the costs per care plan. This suggests that competition among care providers may lead to higher management costs, which is reminiscent of the "medical arms race hypothesis" in hospital industry research. The paper shows that this finding does not hold in the context of the home health industry when an appropriate econometric framework is used to control for the effect of other related factors such as the quality of service.

The major findings are (a) holding constant the scale of operations, region, and ownership, there is a positive relationship between market competition and quality of services only in the case of information services. This result shows that the impact of market competition on the quality of care service, if any, was quite limited in 2000, (b) contrary to the impression created by the descriptive results from the survey by MHLW, this analysis shows that competition is associated with lower costs. In other words, market competition induces cost savings in the home help care market, and (c) there is a tradeoff between quality and cost; running a subsidiary business has few cost-saving premiums; branch offices have lower costs than headquarters; and new providers and nonprofit providers incur higher costs than their counterparts.

The authors caution against generalizing their findings beyond the home help business, but find foundation for the concern that market-oriented reforms will sacrifice quality in the name of cost savings.

In "A Comparison of the Quality of Health Care in the United States and Japan: Treatment and Outcomes for Heart Attack Patients," Haruko Noguchi, Yuichiro Masuda, Masafumi Kuzuya, Akihiko Iguchi, Jeffery Geppert, and Mark McClellan consider differences in treatment patterns and the relationship between treatment patterns and health care quality among AMI patients in the two countries.

Heart disease is the leading cause of death in the United States, and AMIs are directly or indirectly responsible for most of these deaths. In Japan, as in the United States, heart disease has become one of the significant causes of death. Perhaps more than one-third of those with heart diseases died of AMI in 1998. Though death from AMI remains less common in Japan than in the United States, the increasing incidence of AMI and the overall aging of Japanese society suggests that heart attacks may become a significant health problem in the future, much as cancer is now.

This study had several main objectives. The first was to create a data set containing information on treatments and outcomes among AMI patients in Japan, comparable to the Cooperative Cardiovascular Project (CCP) in the United States. The second objective was to investigate variation between the United States and Japan in the quality of health care for elderly patients (age sixty-five or over) with AMI, with respect to treatments and outcomes and controlling for chart-based detailed clinical information.

In this study, the authors divide medical procedures performed on AMI patients into high-tech and low-tech treatments. They define *high-tech treatments* as those with large fixed or marginal costs and *low-tech treatments* as those with relatively low fixed and marginal costs. Low-tech treatments, in principle, could be provided by virtually any medical facility. Both types of procedures are used widely enough to contribute substantially to patient outcomes and hospital expenditure.

The main conclusions are as follows. First, among elderly AMI patients the authors find significant heterogeneity both in the presence of comorbid conditions and also in the treatments received. This heterogeneity underscores the importance of utilizing a richly detailed data set when performing an observational analysis focusing on health outcomes. Second, after adjusting for chart-based patient characteristics and treatments received, the authors observe that high-tech treatments contribute significantly to improved patient outcomes and to increased hospital expenditure, but that the effects are much larger for the CCP than Japanese patients. Third, the aggressive use of intensive treatments soon after admission tends to improve patient outcomes in the short term, while it may lead to increased risks in the longer term. Fourth, a CCP patient who undergoes an intensive procedure tends to stay in the hospital longer compared to the one who does not, while a patient in Japan tends to have a shorter hospital stay, before and after, controlling for various characteristics. Finally, the CCP patients are more aggressively treated by beta-blocker use and smoking cessation than Japanese patients, but the authors observe that collaborative medical centers in the Japanese data tend to perform intensive procedures more often.

In "Geography and the Use of Effective Health Care in the United States," Jonathan Skinner focuses on the variation in medical practice patterns across geographic regions of the United States. There is a growing concern in the United States about shortfalls in health care quality. There are a wide variety of procedures that are proven to be effective yet are often used at rates as low as 50 percent. Examples of such effective treatments include the use of beta-blockers and aspirin for appropriate heart attack patients, annual eye examinations for people with diabetes, and mammography examinations for women over age fifty. On the other hand, there is evidence of overuse of procedures where they are not appropriate. For example, 20 percent of antibiotics prescribed in 1992 were used for common colds and respiratory tract infections, illnesses where the effectiveness of such antibiotics is questionable and may even be harmful. Only about one-third of angioplasties (PTCA) for cardiovascular disease are clearly appropriate, with about one-half uncertain and the remainder inappropriate. Technological advances in diagnostic methods to detect appendicitis, such as computerized tomography, have improved tremendously, but there has been no apparent decline in the rate of inappropriate surgery.

Skinner focuses on the underuse of effective procedures and, in particular, the remarkable variation across regions in the United States with regard to the use of such treatments. Geographical variation in quality of care is of interest for two reasons. First, it provides a snapshot of the degree of technological inefficiency in the health care system, that is, how much do some regions and hospitals lag behind best-practices available in other areas? It is not surprising that health care innovations take time to diffuse; physicians need to be trained in the use of new technology (perhaps through residency programs), and their use spreads as the newly trained residents diffuse to new practice areas. What is more surprising is the persistence of shortfalls in quality across regions.

To quantify the degree of technological "process" inefficiency in the United States, Skinner uses data from the *Dartmouth Cardiovascular Atlas of Healthcare* (2000) that, in turn, is based on a large detailed survey (with chart reviews) of more than 160,000 heart attack patients during 1994 and 1995. He finds that the average loss per heart attack patient, relative to best-practice care, is between $1,500 and $5,000 per year, depending on the benchmark used, the value of a life-year, and other assumptions. The measured inefficiency does not stem from specific skills of the surgeon, but instead largely reflects the use (or nonuse) of pharmaceuticals such as beta-blockers and aspirin.

Geographic variation is then used to estimate a reduced form model of technology adoption that depends on "supply" factors that might be expected to lower the cost of adapting the new technology, such as the prevalence of cardiologists—who are presumably most aware of new technologies in the use of health care innovations—and "demand" factors such as education, income, and the overall incidence of heart disease in the region. The author finds that supply factors are less important in explaining technology diffusion than expected, but estimated demand effects are significant both statistically and economically. More cardiologists per capita is not significantly associated with higher rates of beta-blocker use, nor is there an association between cardiologist supply and the *average* quality use rate for beta-blockers, aspirin, reperfusion, and angiotensin converting enzyme (ACE) inhibitors.

In conclusion, the author says, there seems to be a missing link between the potentially large benefits of effective care for heart attack patients and financial incentives to pay for them. While beta-blockers may not be reimbursed directly by the Medicare program (and indeed cost just pennies per dose), other procedures with uncertain (or potentially negative) effects on outcomes, such as nonprimary angioplasty, or angioplasty for non-Q-wave heart attacks, are paid in full by Medicare. An intriguing question that remains is why physicians working in hospital settings do not comply with quality guidelines, given the large benefits in terms of patient outcomes.

Given the significant variation in medical treatment patterns and the geographic variation from best-practices—even within the health care system of one country—continued research on the differences in health care across countries would seem extremely valuable in assessing and improving quality in all countries.

Other Topics in Health Care

The final two chapters of the volume deal with selected other issues in health care in Japan and the United States. In "Does Caregiving Affect Work? Evidence Based on Prior Labor Force Experience," Kathleen McGarry assesses the impact of caregiving on the labor force behavior of women. The United States General Accounting Office estimates that by 2040 there could be as many as 12 million disabled elderly. Based on current caregiving patterns, the vast majority of these needy individuals will receive care exclusively through informal networks of family and friends, most typically a spouse or child. Intuitively one would expect this caregiving to affect the labor market behavior of the provider; caregivers may reduce hours or exit employment entirely in response to the needs of an elderly family member. On an individual level, reductions in labor market activity would be expected to affect later financial well-being. Not only would there be the obvious decline in earnings and thus an expected decline in retirement savings, but also future pension benefits may be adversely affected as well. These adverse effects may be especially severe for women as they comprise the majority of caregivers and, perhaps for this reason, the majority of poor elderly.

However, it is not clear whether those who provide care do so because they are working fewer hours, or if they work fewer hours because of their caregiving chores. McGarry takes advantage of a longitudinal panel of observations on employment and caregiving to begin to address this issue.

She examines labor market behavior prior to caregiving and notes how it differs for those who subsequently provide care and those who do not. She looks both at short-term effects through changes in behavior over a two-year period and at more extended effects over a period of six years. Her measures of labor market attachment include employment status, hours worked, and expected retirement.

She finds surprisingly little relationship between previous employment and later caregiving. The results of her multivariate analysis show little relationship between labor market ties and caregiving later in life. Having a parent who needs care does not affect employment behavior, and lagged labor force participation does not affect current caregiving.

In "Conjoint Analysis to Estimate the Demand for Nicotine Replacement Therapy in Japan," Seiritsu Ogura, Wataru Suzuki, Makoto Kawamura, and Tamotsu Kadoda consider the demand for nicotine gum. Cigarette smoking is associated with such life-threatening illnesses as cancer, ischemic heart disease, cerebrovascular disease, and chronic lung disease. Passive smoking is also a risk factor for such diseases, and cigarette smoking is one of the most serious causes of premature mortality in Japan. It is estimated that about 95,000 Japanese die annually due to smoking-related illnesses, accounting for 12 percent of total deaths. Estimates of the annual medical cost due to smoking-related disease range from 5 to 15 percent of national medical expenditures.

In response to escalating national health care costs, particularly those of lifestyle-related diseases, smoking cessation has become one of the most important national health policy objectives. The MHLW established the "Committee on Tobacco Control for the 21st Century" in the year 2000 and was committed to a national no-smoking-week campaign. The ministry also established as an objective the provision of support to help smokers in all communities to stop smoking. The Japanese Medical Association has also conducted an antismoking campaign since 2001.

A significant proportion of smokers seriously consider quitting smoking. For example, according to the 1998 Survey on Smoking and Health Problems conducted by the Japanese government, 26.7 percent of current smokers aged fifteen and over want to quit smoking, and 64.2 percent of them want to quit smoking or reduce smoking. However, only a small fraction of them actually succeed on their own. Recently, however, smoking intervention programs, particularly those using nicotine replacement therapy (NRT), have been shown to be effective in other countries, such as the United States.

Nicotine replacement therapy is a method of treatment that helps smokers by alleviating the withdrawal symptoms associated with smoking cessation by replacing the nicotine. Two types of NRT products are available in Japan: nicotine transdermal patches and nicotine gum. Nicotine patches were approved by the MHLW in 1994, and nicotine gums were approved in

1999. Despite the effectiveness of the products, they failed to come into wide use in Japan as they were available only by prescription, and their costs were not covered by the public health insurance.

In September 2001, the MHLW approved nicotine gum (brand name Nicorette) as an over-the-counter drug. There immediately followed an extensive national campaign by the pharmaceutical company using TV, newspapers, and magazines. As a result, Nicorette is now widely recognized among smokers as well as nonsmokers.

In this paper, Ogura, Suzuki, Kawamura, and Kadoda estimate the demand for nicotine gum and examine the smoking cessation assistance policy with NRT using original survey data they gathered in late 2001. Their analysis is based on conjoint analysis (CA), a technique that is relatively new to the field of health economics.

Conjoint analysis is one of the techniques belonging to contingent valuation methods (CVM) used to estimate an individual's utilities from various choices, based on responses to hypothetical questions. Conjoint analysis was originally developed in the field of market research and psychometrics. It has been widely used in environmental economics and transportation economics, and it has been introduced into health economics. In Japan, CA has been used to estimate the demand for nursing, the choice of medical facilities, and the demand for medical care for minor illness.

The estimates obtained from conjoint analysis indicate that a 10,000 yen decrease in the price of nicotine gum (a price reduction of about 30 percent) would increase its demand by 16.5 percent, and a 100 yen increase in the price of cigarettes (a price increase of about 40 percent) would lead to an increase of 4.2 percent in the demand for nicotine gum. The analysis also revealed that if nicotine gum were sold from vending machines or convenience stores, its demand would increase by 3.3 percent. A cost-benefit analysis was conducted to estimate the consequence of a subsidy policy for nicotine gum. A 70 percent subsidy for the nicotine gum would cost the government 352.4 billion yen. The benefit of such a subsidy would be the reduction in smoking-related illnesses through successful smoking cessation. This would reduce annual medical insurance benefits by 67.6 billion yen. In five years, therefore, the government would be able to save 338.5 billion yen—almost equal to the cost of the original subsidy. A national health promotion program called Healthy Japan 21, established by the MHLW in 2000, established smoking cessation promotion as one of the most important policy objectives. The authors conclude that a subsidy for nicotine gum or insurance coverage for the gum could be a means of achieving that goal.

1

Evaluating Japan's Health Care Reform of the 1990s and Its Efforts to Cope with Population Aging

Naohiro Yashiro, Reiko Suzuki, and Wataru Suzuki

1.1 Introduction

In assessing Japan's overall health care system, it is important to balance its remarkable achievements in the past with its gloomy prospects for the future. On one hand, average life expectancy at birth, estimates of which were revised upward in early 2002, indicate further improvement relative to the highest-ranking Organization for Economic Cooperation and Development (OECD) countries. This has been achieved with a low ratio of health expenditures to gross domestic product (GDP) relative to other major OECD countries, implying to those who object to health care reform that the existing health care system is efficient. On the other hand, it is obvious that the current health system cannot cope with a rapidly aging society.

The effect of population aging is already reflected in the growing fiscal deficits in health insurance budgets. These budgets are burdened by an increasing number of elderly enrollees, who are heavy users of health resources. These effects are aggravated by features of Japan's health insurance schemes, including the following: Japan's health care system is universal, meaning that all citizens, including the self-employed, are supposed to have some form of health insurance as well as a public pension. This is based on the German social insurance model, but Japan, unlike many European countries, guarantees patients free access to hospitals with no gatekeepers. Also, once patients enter the hospital in Japan, certain medical services are provided under a fee-for-service health insurance

Naohiro Yashiro is a professor of economics at International Christian University. Reiko Suzuki is a senior economist at the Japan Center for Economic Research. Wataru Suzuki is an assistant professor in the Department of Education at Tokyo Gakugei University.

arrangement. It is surprising, given the lack of incentives for efficiency, that Japan's national health expenditures have remained at a relatively low level.

One interpretation of the combination of low costs and generous access is that Japan has practiced a policy of egalitarian renumeration, with relatively low salaries of physicians.[1] The system has been efficient in providing basic health care services, reflecting people's strong preference for egalitarianism. With the aging of the population, however, the major burden of disease has shifted from infectious and acute diseases to chronic disease. This reduces the positive externalities of medical treatments as well as the extent of asymmetry of information between providers and patients. Also, the preferences of patients have shifted toward better quality health services with medical information. It is against this background that changes in the Japanese health care system are considered.

Japan's health system has some features in common with the Medicare program for the elderly in the United States, particularly in terms of how to reform the current welfarelike health scheme. The government of Japan made a series of health care reforms in the 1990s, including the recent 2003 health insurance reform. However, the favorable fiscal effects of the reforms, which raised the patient's share of medical costs, are quite limited, with the health budget falling into deficit again within five years. The major reform proposals include standardization of medical treatments, partial replacement of public health insurance with private health insurance, introduction of a partial managed care system, and introduction of for-profit hospitals to stimulate competition.

The first section of this paper explores recent demographic developments and outlines Japan's health system. The second section reviews the reforms of the 1990s and investigates the fiscal impacts of the 2003 health reform across different public insurers. The third section surveys the current major policy issues for health care reform. The final section concludes.

1.2   Outline of Japan's Health System and the Effects of Population Aging

1.2.1   Rapid Population Aging

Japan's official demographic projections are revised every five years, and the most recent 2002 population estimates support the more pessimistic scenario for the coming decades. Several factors contribute to pessimism regarding Japan's demographic trends. First, the total fertility ratio (TFR) has been revised downward repeatedly in the previous projections. The most recent medium projection (the most likely scenario) is that TFR will

---

1. The ratio of earnings of medical doctors to average employees was 2.5 in Japan compared with 5.4 in the United States in 1987, based on the OECD Health Data Base.

rise from 1.32 in 2001 and eventually stabilize at 1.4; this compares to a projected stable TFR of 1.6 in the 1997 estimates and 1.8 in the 1992 estimates. Contributing to these developments is the constant increase in the labor force participation of working-age women, resulting in increased opportunity costs of child rearing and decreased demand for children.[2] Thus, there is no concrete evidence that the fertility ratio will stabilize at the level officially projected in 2002. Unless there are major policy changes, the more pessimistic scenario (lower population estimates) is likely. In this scenario, TFR does not recover in the future and stabilizes at 1.1, the lowest level among OECD countries.

Second, average life expectancy at birth, which has continuously increased, is projected to rise from the current level of 77.7 years to 79.8 years for men, and from 84.6 years to 87.5 years for women in 2025. The recent increase is not due to a fall in infant mortality, but rather due to an extension in the life expectancy of the elderly. For example, males' life expectancy at age sixty-five is projected to increase from 17.5 years in 2000 to 18.9 years in 2025. Also, the gap between male and female life expectancy is projected to rise from 6.9 years in 2000 to 7.8 years in 2025. The factors behind the increases in longevity are still unclear but may be due to a mixture of nutrition, smoking behavior, and health service factors.

As a result, the rate at which Japan's population was aging was accelerating in the 1990s, far exceeding that of the United States (see figure 1.1). The accelerated rate of population aging, particularly the growth in the number of very elderly, is likely to impose increasing pressure on health costs.

1.2.2 Population Aging and Health Expenditures

The elderly account for nearly one-third of total health costs, but 90 percent of the annual increase in costs is attributable to the elderly, whose per capita costs were close to five times the average in 2000. This is mainly due to the fact that one-half and two-thirds of lifetime medical costs are spent for those aged seventy years and sixty years and above, respectively. It is natural that average medical costs increase with one's age and that the elderly generally have a higher risk of being hospitalized. The strong relationship between health expenditures and age is attributable to the following factors:

First, the elderly have longer hospital stays and, therefore, higher hospital costs. The average hospital length of stay in Japan is five times the aver-

---

2. The percentage of eighteen-year-olds who enrolled in college rose from 12.3 percent in 1980 to 33.8 percent in 2002. The percentage of female employees increased over the same period from 34.1 percent to 40.5 percent. This increases women's opportunity costs of raising children, particularly given the rigid labor market practices (e.g., long-term employment and seniority-based wages). A woman who leaves a firm to raise a child would find it difficult to be employed full time after the child-rearing period (Yashiro 1998).

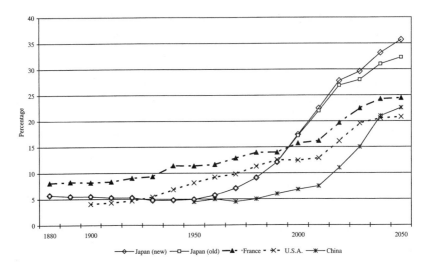

Fig. 1.1   International comparison of the elderly ratio (age sixty-five and above)

age in the United States. The number of hospital beds per capita in Japan is much higher than in other major OECD countries, which is related to the longer average length of stay (see figure 1.2). This partly reflects the fact that hospitals are used as nursing homes for the elderly, mainly due to the limited supply of other nursing care services for frail elderly and the fee-for-service reimbursement scheme. This misallocation of medical resources is a result of inconsistent policies, namely free access to certain health services but limited provision of nursing care services for frail elderly, resulting in the use of more costly services.

Second, end-of-life care is another factor in the relationship between age and medical costs. For example, hospital costs for those age seventy and over during the year before death account for 19.2 percent of total hospital costs for the elderly (Ogura, Fukawa, and Suzuki 1994). Another study shows that the health costs for the elderly controlling for end-of-life medical care costs are not different from those in other age groups (Suzuki and Suzuki 2002). This implies that the increase in medical costs with age may well be avoided if appropriate measures such as palliative care for the terminally ill are used in end-of-life care.

Third, the impact of population aging varies across health insurance plans. Unlike pension plans, employee health insurance plans are established at the firm level. Retiring workers who switch to the local authorities' insurance plan increase the burden on these plans. This raises the issue of how to construct a better risk-sharing mechanism across different insurance plans.

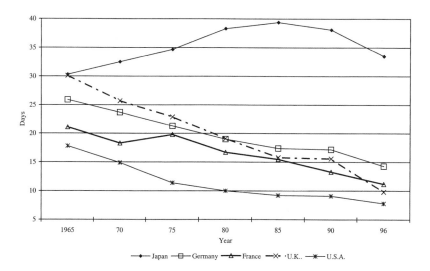

Fig. 1.2   Average duration of hospitalization
Source: OECD health data.

1.2.3   Health Insurance Schemes

The current health insurance plans have the following structure:

Coverage Rules

Japan's health insurance plans are entirely controlled by the government, including employer-provided plans and plans for individuals with low income and the elderly. Medical spending is shared by insurance (53 percent), government (32 percent), and out of pocket (15 percent). The coverage is identical across plans, including hospital services, physician expenses, laboratory tests, and outpatient prescription medications. Contributions to insurance are shared equally by employers and employees. The employee contribution is based on monthly earnings regardless of the individual's medical risk. The scheme has the effect of redistributing income from the poor to the rich, because contributions to health insurance are proportional to individual incomes, while benefits are not.[3]

Reimbursement System

Providers are paid on a fee-for-service basis, with fees for every medical treatment and drug determined by the government. The government con-

---

3. This is contrasted to the forced-savings of the earnings-related pension of which both contributions and benefits are related to the individual's wages.

trols health expenditures mainly through these fixed fees. A capitation system was partially introduced for hospital fees for the elderly with chronic diseases, though it still pays based on the day rather than the hospitalization. Diagnosis-related groups (DRGs) are now being used in some hospitals on an experimental basis, though the DRG system is difficult to use without standardization of medical treatments.

Access Rules

Access rules are the financial and nonfinancial barriers to receipt of health care. When out-of-pocket costs are low, patients consume medical care even when their symptoms are minor. Accordingly, many countries require patients to make copayments to prevent waste of medical service. The coinsurance rate in Japan is 30 percent, except for the elderly for whom it is 10 percent. This is relatively high by international standards, though there are no deductibles so that the insured are covered from the first dollar cost. Also, there is a stop-loss at 72,300 yen per month (40,200 yen for the elderly), and tax subsidies are granted with deductibles of 100,000 yen. On the other hand, free access is basically assured, that is, the insured need no physician's approval to enter a hospital.

Japan's health insurance schemes are complicated, reflecting their long-run historical development. Originally, public servants and employees in large firms (including their family members) were covered by employer-sponsored plans. A government policy of universal health care was then established, and employees in small firms and the self-employed began receiving health insurance from the Ministry of Health, Labor and Welfare and the local authorities, respectively.

The Society-Managed Health Insurance (SMHI) was established in 1922, consisting of individual company-based insurers. Their fiscal balances have been favorable for many years due to the growing number of young employees and generous employer contributions, reflecting high rates of economic growth. The Government-Managed Health Insurance (GMHI) was established for the employees in small companies that do not have their own plans. Third, the Citizens' Health Insurance (CHI), established in 1938, is regionally organized with cities and towns as insurers. The majority of members in these plans are self-employed and generally have lower incomes.

In Japan, health insurance schemes differ from public pensions in that most enrollees in SMHI and GMHI switch to CHI after retirement. As the result, the elderly share of enrollees is 25 percent in CHI compared to 3 percent in SMHI and 6 percent in GMHI. Thus, there are various mechanisms needed to keep contributions per household level across health insurance schemes, despite the differences in the elderly shares (see table 1.1).

First, there are subsidies from general government revenues. The largest subsidies are to CHI, accounting for half of the health costs of CHI en-

Table 1.1   Health insurance schemes in Japan, 2000

	Membership	Average age	Average household annual income (yen)	Contributions per household ([added by employers' contributions] 1,000 yen)	Medical expenses per individual (1,000 yen)	Subsidies from the government (billion yen)
Society-Managed Health Insurance (SMHI)	32 million (25.2%)	33.6	3.8 million	159 (364)	102	Fixed amount (26.2)
Government-Managed Health Insurance (GMHI)	37 million (29.3%)	36.9	2.5 million	152 (303)	123	13% of medical expenses (959.2)
Citizens' Health Insurance (CHI)	47 million (36.5%)	51.3	1.8 million	154	164	50% of medical expenses (3,057.7)
Mutual Aid Associations (MAAs)	10 million (7.9%)	n.a.	n.a.	n.a.	n.a.	n.a.
Others (sailors and minimum income assistance)	1.3 million (1.0%)	n.a.	n.a.	n.a.	n.a.	n.a.

Source: Ministry of Health and Welfare.
Note: n.a. = not available.

rollees. The rationale is that the majority of enrollees are self-employed, with relatively low incomes and without employers' contributions.

Second, there are income transfers among insurance plans. The Health System for the Elderly (HSE) was introduced in 1973 as a system for pooling the health costs for individuals age seventy and older across various health insurers. This system partly compensates for the adverse effects of the differences in elderly shares across insurers. Other insurers fund 70 percent of the costs of HSE, with contributions based on an estimate of what they would have paid in benefits if their elderly shares were the same as the national average. To cover the remaining revenues, 20 percent comes from the national government, and 10 percent comes from local governments.

Third, there is an additional income redistribution mechanism through the Retirees' Account in the CHI, which was introduced in 1984. It is designed to reduce the burden on the CHI, which still suffers from an increasing number of individuals age sixty to sixty-nine who switch from an employer-sponsored plan. Both SMHI and GMHI transfer funds to CHI in proportion to the former employees who joined the CHI (and are under age seventy).

With the increase in the elderly population in CHI, the transfers to CHI from SMHI and GMHI have increased and now equal 4.6 trillion yen for HSE and 1.1 trillion yen for the Retirees' Account in CHI. The redistribution scheme is a compromise between two contrasting ideas. One idea is to finance the HSE from the general government budget and make it entirely independent of other health insurance plans. Another idea is for employees to remain in their employer-sponsored plans after retirement, like a pension, so that the plans can negotiate the conflicting interests across generations. This would have an advantage over the current scheme in which SMHI and GMHI share revenue with HSE but take no part in governance.

1.2.4   Quality and Costs of Medical Services

Even accounting for the favorable demographic composition of the past and the high level of incomes and egalitarian distribution of incomes, it is still difficult to account for the relatively low health expenditures under the fee-for-service system in Japan. According to Ikegami and Campbell (1999), the comprehensive and mandatory fee schedule is a major factor in Japan's low health spending. Under this system, expensive procedures such as surgery and other capital-intensive treatments are often priced well below the U.S. level. Also, most surgeries are conducted in public-sector hospitals with rigid prices (though there are subsidies from the general budget to public-sector hospitals that are not counted as medical costs).[4] This con-

---

4. There are varieties of the public-sector hospitals managed by the local authorities as prefectures and cities, national universities, labor injury insurance, and so on.

Table 1.2   International comparison of indicators relating health care provision, 1995–1996

	Hospital beds per 1,000 population	Average duration of hospitalization days	Number of medical staff per patient	Number of doctors per 1,000 population	Number of nurses per 1,000 population
United States	3.37	6.5	5.5	2.59	8.04
Norway	3.29	6.3	4.35	2.79	13.92
Canada	3.62	7.5	2.8	2.13	8.92
Italy	5.13	8.4	3.15	5.37	5.47
France	4.46	5.8	1.52	2.93	5.89
Germany	6.74	11.5	1.88	3.35	9.0
Japan	10.16	29.2	1.15	1.84	7.38

Source: OECD Health Data.

trasts with the prices determined in the market for health service (except for Medicare and Medicaid) in the United States.

A key to understanding the relatively low medical costs in the past is the low intensity of services per patient. An international comparison of health services indicators show that Japan's medical staff per patient is quite low and is almost one-fifth the level in the United States (see table 1.2). However, this does not mean that the number of doctors and nurses is insufficient, given that the number of medical staff per capita is only slightly below most major OECD countries. The excessive number of hospital beds per capita, reflecting long hospital stays, is a major factor in the low intensity of hospital care with insufficient medical staff. Although the average number of days of hospitalization has been declining, the gap relative to other major countries has not narrowed. This is why the health insurance reform is closely related to the institutions for the nursing care of the elderly.

1.3   Reform of the Medical System in the 1990s and Its Effects

Medical expenditures as a share of national income in Japan rose from 5.9 percent in 1990 to 7.9 percent in 2000, despite the economic stagnation. With the decline in government tax revenues, financing health care becomes quite difficult. Hence, controlling the increase in government-managed medical expenditure has been a critical issue recently. The Japanese government has introduced various policies to control medical expenditures since the early 1990s. It is difficult to choose a desirable policy mix without having examined the effectiveness of these policies. This paper examines the economic effectiveness of various policies based on a literature review.

Two types of policies were introduced in the 1990s. One type focuses on patients' demand for services. An example of price policy on the demand side is an increase in patient copayments. Another policy is to limit free access to care. This includes the introduction of the family doctor as a gatekeeper and charging higher fees to patients without a gatekeeper's referral. The second type of policy focuses on suppliers, that is, medical institutions such as hospitals and clinics. Examples of supply-side policies include the introduction of a fixed reimbursement system instead of fee for service, limits on the number of hospital beds and physicians, and separation of long-term care from medical treatments.

1.3.1 What We Can Learn from Experiences of Other Countries

Many of the policies introduced by the Japanese government were similar to policies that had functioned effectively, to a certain degree, in other advanced countries. In the 1980s these other countries reconsidered their strict regulations and shifted to market-oriented policies based on economic incentives.

Quantitative analysis by the OECD points out that the policies implemented by the advanced countries had both effective and less-effective features. Examples of policies that have been effective in reducing medical expenses include the capitation system (in which doctors are paid per enrollee rather than per service), the refund system (in which patients pay the full cost of treatments up front and are partially reimbursed afterward), and the gatekeeper system. Policies that have little influence on medical expenditures include increases in copayment rates, strict budget ceilings, limits on the number of doctors, and the free-fee system.

The reason for the preceding contradictory analysis is that it reflects reverse causation, meaning that countries with a high level of medical expenditure tend to implement policies to control medical expenditures.

The experiences of other advanced countries are informative to some degree. Yet difficulties would arise if specific policies that worked effectively in other countries were applied directly to Japan.

1.3.2 Price Elasticity of Demand for Medical Care

In Japan, cost sharing decreased until the 1970s, but in the 1980s the government began increasing cost sharing. The price elasticity of demand for medical care was studied intensively by health economists in the 1990s. Cost sharing for the elderly in Japan has changed as follows: (a) Prior to 1973, the copayment rate was 30 percent for participants of the National Health Insurance and 50 percent for dependents of the Employees' Health Insurance. In 1973, the copayment rate shifted to 0 percent for both groups, (b) in 1983, free care (no copayment) was replaced by a cost-sharing system where inpatients paid a flat sum per hospital day, and outpatients paid a flat sum per month, (c) in 1997, the outpatient cost sharing arrangement was replaced with a per-visit copayment, and copayments were introduced for outpatient medicines, and (d) a 10 percent copayment was partially resumed in 2001 (outpatients choose either the 10 percent co-payment or a fixed sum per visit).

These policy changes led to research on their effects. Before medical care for the elderly people became free in 1973, per person medical expenditures among the elderly were twice as high as among the young. After the introduction of the free care system, this ratio increased to four times. This shows that the free care system stimulated the elderly to use more medical services. The price elasticity of demand for medical care, measured using aggregated time series data from 1955 through 1979, is over –0.3.

The increase in out-of-pocket payments in 1983 was so small that it did not effectively reduce demand. Some researchers argue that the fixed-price system had very little influence. Others argue that medical demand increased in spite of increasing out-of-pocket payments, mainly due to higher incomes.[5]

The copayment schedule differs between the Employees' Health Insurance and the National Health Insurance. The main reforms to the Employee Insurance have been (1) the coinsurance rate for dependents was reduced in 1973, from 50 percent to 30 percent, (2) the contribution rate for participants in the Employees' Health Insurance was increased in 1984 from 0 percent to 10 percent, (3) the contribution rate was increased again in 1997, from 10 percent to 20 percent, (4) additional copayments for outpatient prescription drugs were implemented for both types of insurance systems in 1997. There are few analyses that focus on the effects of the 1973 coinsurance decrease, except the analysis by Maeda (1978), which reports that medical expenses per person increased by around 12 percent.

These studies showed that the price elasticity of demand for medical care was very small, generally around –0.1. There are two remaining questions relating to future trends in medical expenditures. The first is the effects of the phasing in of the 10 percent copayment for the elderly, which, by 2002, had replaced the fixed-sum system. The second question relates to the effects of the stop-loss provision. The copayment rate of 10 percent or 30 percent is applied to up to a monthly stop-loss, and a copayment rate of 1 percent is applied beyond this limit. Although the copayment schedule has been changed considerably, out-of-pocket payments as a share of total national health expenditures has been almost constant over the last few decades. We suppose that the main reason for the stability is the low stop-

---

5. Ii and Ookusa (2002), using microlevel data, report price elasticities of medical expenditures for elderly outpatients and inpatients as –0.016 and –0.051, respectively. Sawano (2000) calculates the price elasticity outpatient visits in an elderly population (–0.125––0.085) and the price elasticity on the number of visits per case (–0.105––0.085) using semiaggregated data. Tokita et al. (2000) find that the price change in 1997 led to a decrease in the annual per capita medical expenses of those age seventy of around 500 yen, or 3.8 U.S. dollars. In particular, the demand for chronic disease care decreased remarkably. Average patient visits per month to doctors' offices fell by 0.33.

loss limit. But no study has been reported on the behavioral effects of the stop-loss provision.

1.3.3 Restriction of Free Access

One of the characteristics of the Japanese medical system is the guarantee of free access to medical institutions. However, the Japanese government does limit the extent of access, as long as patients' choices are not severely restricted. Increases in copayments, discussed previously, will, if they are large enough, restrict the access of low-income individuals. This section examines the referral system and the family doctor system. The purpose of the two systems is to prevent the waste of valuable medical resources from patients with minor symptoms using large hospitals.

Referral System for Large Hospitals

Ideally, patients receive medical care from their family doctors who admit them to large hospitals when necessary. After required treatments are received in the large hospital, the patients then return to their family doctors. In order to strengthen this linkage between family doctors and large hospitals, the government introduced a system in which patients must pay higher charges if they access care in large hospitals without a referral from their family doctor. In addition, patients are required to pay extra charges (beyond the basic charge) for their first consultation if they directly visit large hospitals with more than 200 beds.

The government also provides incentives for hospitals. Hospitals can receive an additional fee if more than 30 percent of their patients are referrals or if they decrease the number of outpatients. Further, the government introduced a reverse referral system, which encourages large hospitals to return patients to their family doctors.

No studies have been done on how the new system changed the behavior of patients and medical institutions. However, some researchers argue that the introduction of the referral system facilitates the effective use of resources in large hospitals. The reason is that referred patients tend to use medical resources more intensively than patients who directly accessed large hospitals. On the other hand, hospitals do not control the number of outpatients.

Family Doctor System

Family doctors provide primary care to local residents. They are expected to provide good access geographically, be available twenty-four hours a day, deal with all types of illness, and make referrals to specialists. Patients need referrals from their family doctors to get treatments at large hospitals without additional charges. A statement from a family doctor is necessary for judging applications for public long-term care. In these situations, the family doctor is intended to play the role of a gatekeeper who limits patients' access to high-level medical care and long-term care.

However, many patients do not have a family doctor. In addition, the gatekeeper function does not work effectively, as large hospitals tend to accept patients with referrals, regardless of which type of doctor referred the patient. Given this situation, the government has, since 1993, promoted the family doctor system through local governments with the cooperation of the Association of Doctors. However, it should be noted that patients and doctors still do not understand this system sufficiently. Because it is relatively new, the effects of the family doctor system have not been analyzed.

1.3.4   Partial Introduction of Inclusive Payment System

As discussed in the preceding, patients' out-of-pocket payments were increased. We expect this policy only to affect patients' decision regarding whether to visit a doctor. Because of information asymmetries, once a patient enters the medical care system, doctors have a great deal of discretion in the supply of medical services.

To control the increase in medical expenditures driven by doctors, the government in the 1980s decreased the prices paid for medical care through a series of revisions to the fee schedule—the price table for fee-for-service reimbursement to the doctors. Medical institutions, in order to maintain their revenues in the face of price decreases, increased the volume of medicines provided. This self-defense behavior by medical institutions has resulted in excessive use of medicines and medical examinations.

The government introduced an inclusive, or bundled, payment system in order to limit the excessive supply of medical services. In the inclusive payment system, a fixed price is set for a series of medical examinations. That is, one series of medical examinations is treated as one bundle. Accordingly, the inclusive payment system can limit the cost of medical services, unlike the fee-for-service system. At the same time, medical institutions have an incentive to reduce costs. Therefore, we expect a higher level of efficiency in the supply of medical services under the inclusive payment system. Nonetheless, there is a concern over whether medical institutions will continue to provide adequate services.

At first, the inclusive payment was applied only to a limited set of medical services. However, the use of inclusive payments gradually spread in the 1990s. Inclusive payments were implemented as follows: blood tests (biochemical examinations) in 1982; hospital care for the elderly with chronic diseases including nursing, examination, dosing, and injections in 1990; all-inclusive fee for outpatient care for the elderly with chronic diseases and pediatrics in 1996; and general examinations and treatments were included in the outpatient consultation fee in 2000.

Except for the bundling of blood tests, most of the inclusive payments introduced so far have failed to reduce medical costs, according to Kawai and Maruyama (2000) and Ikegami (2001). They point out that the main reason for the failure to control medical costs is that the inclusive payment was introduced as an alternative to fee-for-service payment. Under these circumstances, medical institutions can choose one of the two payment systems, which allows them to earn profits. Those institutions where the average fee for a patient had been low chose the relatively high inclusive payment, and the institutions that were treating very sick and costly patients remained in the fee-for-service system. As a result, the introduction of the inclusive payment actually increased medical costs. Another example of failure was the inclusive fee for outpatients of pediatrics. Since the fixed fee was set per day, the institution that chose the inclusive system increased the number of the days per patient.

1.3.5 Supply Controls

Regional differences in health expenditures have a strong relationship with the supply of medical providers, such as the number of beds and doctors per capita. The government, recognizing this, has sought to reduce the excess capacity in the medical system.

The government believes that having more hospital beds results in longer hospital stays, and, with this in mind, began to control the number of beds in 1985. This type of control denies the principle of free entrance into medical service markets. The government developed a detailed plan that specified the required number of hospital beds in several hundred areas. Doctors are prohibited from opening new hospitals or adding beds in areas where the number of existing beds is thought to exceed the originally planned number. As a result, we should not expect improvement in medical services because competition among hospitals was diminished due to the lack of new entrants in regions with excess beds.

The government also forecasted that, if the number of medical school graduates were frozen at the level of the early 1980s, there would be an excess supply of doctors in the future. The government asked medical schools to reduce the number of students in 1986 and requested a further 10 percent reduction in the number of students in 1994. However, only a 7.7 percent reduction was achieved by 1996.

If doctors are actually inducing demand for medical care in Japan, then supply control policies will help reduce excess medical expenditures by doctors. If a high density of doctors makes it easier for patients to access health services by reducing time costs, such as waiting time and transportation time, then limiting the number of doctors is not preferable. Nishimura (1987), using aggregated regional data, reports that the elasticity of elderly outpatient medical demand on the density of doctors was small, only 0.19. On the other hand, Suzuki (1998) using microdata, reports that the elasticity of the demand is not statistically different from zero and that the induced demand is not observed in the elderly outpatient medical market.

1.3.6   Limitations on the Scope of Health Services

Concentration on Acute Care

It is well known that average length of hospital stays in Japan is longer than any other advanced country. The main reason for this is that hospitals accept patients with chronic diseases who need long-term care. These patients require huge amounts of expensive health resources. In order to eliminate the wasteful use of these resources, the government has been trying to reduce the number of patients who stay in hospitals for long periods without receiving intense treatments. One approach has been to give hospitals an economic incentive by reducing the fee paid to a hospital for patients who stay longer than a certain period of time. Another approach is the introduction of public long-term care insurance. These measures are designed to divide patients into two groups, one in need of long-term care and another in need for acute medical care. The scope of health insurance is restricted to the latter group of patients.

Gradual Reduction Schedule of Hospital Fee

In the late 1980s, fees paid for extended hospital stays were reduced according to a stepwise schedule. The reductions were applied to consultation and nursing fees, which are major components of the fees that hospitals receive from public insurance. In order to make the fee cuts steeper, an inclusive payment was introduced in 1998 for elderly patients who stay in general hospitals for six months or longer.

In 2000, the hospital fee system was totally reformed and a new basic fee for hospitalization was established. The basic fee is set higher for hospitals where the average length of patients' stay is short. Those measures create strong incentives for hospitals to decrease the length of stays, though studies have not been done on the effects.

Shifting Long-Term Care to a New Insurance Scheme

To cope with the increasing number of elderly chronic patients, the government in the late 1980s designated certain hospitals, which did not meet a required level of health resources, as geriatric hospitals that provide inpatient care for the elderly. This policy was an exception to the laws governing the supply of medical facilities. In 1992, sanatorium beds were authorized by the medical law as one category of hospital beds for the exclusive use of elderly chronic patients. Furthermore, with the revision of the medical law in 2001, ordinary beds (formally known as *miscellaneous beds*) are now classified into two subgroups, one group for acute patients and the other for chronic patients.

In 2000, the government implemented a new system of public long-term care insurance. With the new insurance, patients can choose among a variety of hospitals and clinics as well as nursing homes and institutions for rehabilitation services. In order to meet the new demands for care, hospitals and clinics are rapidly recertifying their beds so that they qualify under the new long-term care insurance. As a result, we see a mixture of patients in the same hospital building, some financed by health insurance and others financed by long-term care insurance.

According to a government projection for fiscal 2000, 1,980 billion yen would be shifted from the old health insurance system to the new long-term care insurance. The Japanese Medical Association estimated that the actual amount shifted was 1,600 billion yen or 12.7 percent of the medical expenditures for the elderly, slightly smaller than the government had anticipated.

Separation of Pharmacy From Medical Care

Pharmacy services have been separated for the purpose of preventing hospitals from prescribing excess drugs under the fee-for-service payment system. It also benefits patients by prompting pharmacists to check the suitability of prescriptions as a second authority after doctors.

Consecutive price cuts for pharmaceuticals as well as the spread of inclusive payments made it less attractive for hospitals to have their own pharmacies. The less profitable the in-hospital pharmacy became, the more hospitals closed their pharmacies, and the separation gradually spread. However, only 30 percent of total prescriptions were sent to pharmacy from hospitals and clinics, mainly because the patients have not gained much advantage. Patients do not like to devote a lot of time to visit pharmacies after the consultation at hospitals. Patients dislike the additional cost of the "out-of hospital prescription fee" paid to doctors and the "compounding medicine fee" paid to pharmacists; these costs will raise health expenditures by 5.7 percent if the division of pharmacy is accomplished.

As has been shown, a variety of policies are implemented in order to control health expenditures by means of the efficient use of resources. The analyses on the policies have been accumulated steadily, though it does not reach a sufficient level. Another important policy to curb the health expenditure is to establish long-term nursing care insurance for the frail elderly for shifting the hospitalized elderly to nursing care services as discussed in the following section.

1.4   Long-Term Nursing Care Insurance for the Frail Elderly

1.4.1   Background

Public nursing care insurance was established in April 2000 as a major pillar of set measures designed to improve the system of long-term care for the frail elderly. In Japan, welfare has made up a relatively small share of total social security expenditures, compared with health insurance costs and public pension. For the elderly in 2000, welfare costs were only 9 percent as large as the public pensions and 34 percent as large as the health expenditures. This reflects the general acceptance that the family should play a major role in providing elderly care services. Nevertheless, inconsistent policies between health and welfare policies have resulted in an overuse of health resources. Until the year 2000, people needing care and their families have tended to make use of health insurance, which allows unlimited coverage of care costs with no gatekeepers. Public welfare, on the other hand, is limited and certain requirements must be met in advance. As the result, many people not actually in need of medical treatment have been hospitalized. This is mainly attributed to a limited supply of long-term care facilities and a lack of support for families taking care of the elderly. The insufficient supply of long-term care services compared with medical services results from the different sources of funds, that is, medical costs are based on insurance premiums directly linked to wages, while public welfare is based on general tax revenues with severe budget constraints.

In the new system of the public nursing care insurance, applicants for benefits will be assessed to determine the level of care they require. A ceiling will be put on the benefits to be covered by the insurance, and people needing care will be shifted from hospitals to care-providing institutions or their own homes (to receive care there). This would contribute not only to reducing medical costs but also to improving the living conditions of elderly needing long-term care by moving them out of the hospital setting.

1.4.2   Overview of Nursing Care Insurance

Long-term care for the elderly, which used to be financed from general revenues, is now funded by insurance premiums. This changes people's costs and benefits in various ways. It is expected that improved services will lighten the load on families, and reduced treatment costs should make it possible to reduce health insurance premiums. Also, stimulating competition among providers will make the provision of care services become more efficient. The introduction of nursing care insurance will also reduce the load on the state and local governments, which so far have borne the entire cost of nursing care from general revenue.

Nursing care insurance premiums will be withheld from the health insurance premiums of people forty years of age and over and from the public pensions paid to people sixty-five years of age and over. The average premium level is set at 2,900 yen per month per individual. In the case of people whose pension benefits are too low to allow such withholding, premiums will be collected directly from the individuals by municipal governments, taking into account their economic background. Only people over forty are required to pay into the system, on the grounds that young people are unlikely to require care before that age. This is a result of political compromise, but is not consistent with the rationale behind long-term care insurance, which is to lighten the care load on families. Also, exempting young people is inconsistent with the fact that they have to pay health insurance premiums even though they are at relatively low risk of falling ill.

Eligibility for nursing care insurance benefits is limited to individuals age sixty-five and over and those age forty and over who require care because of aging-related causes. The grounds for limiting the benefit on the basis of age is shaky. An alternative approach would be to provide care for anyone age twenty or over who requires it, regardless of cause. The fact that this sort of setup has not been adopted seems to reflect one of the flaws of the present segmented welfare system, which puts people with physical disabilities into a separate category of welfare.

Still, the nursing care insurance system does aim to provide services without regard to income level or other socioeconomic considerations and to determine the kind and level of services solely on the basis of need. It allows people to pay additional amounts out of their own pockets for services not covered by the insurance benefit; this is prohibited in the health insurance system, which is based on uniformity-driven egalitarianism. Also, it marks a major departure from the present public welfare system, the major aim of which is relief for the disadvantaged, not ordinary persons in the society. The nursing care insurance system, based on the premise that long-term care for the elderly should be considered an extension of daily life, aims to spread the costs through society. Unlike health insurance, though, the eligibility for the nursing care insurance has to be certified by a third-party gatekeeper.

1.4.3   Major Remaining Issues

A number of proposed improvements in nursing care payments (the equivalent of treatment payments in health insurance) are being studied. One is to set a ceiling on the level of benefits and make flat payments to the elderly individual based thereon (unlike health insurance, where payments are based on a detailed accounting of treatment provided or fee for service). Another is to allow regions and providers some leeway in lowering fees for care services. A third is to enable providers some leeway in adding extra fees, on the grounds that users will find it easier to gauge the quality of nursing care services than medical treatments. A fourth is to include payment for ancillary services, such as the cost of transporting people needing care and caregivers' travel time.

Nursing care payments, which vary with the seriousness of individuals' needs, differ substantially between private and public nursing care homes for the same level of seriousness. This is mainly because private nursing homes are treated as a sort of residence, and so-called hotel costs are not included in the benefits. Ideally, those in need of nursing care would be able to choose freely from diverse care settings.[6] The lack of equal footing between public and private nursing homes could be eliminated by treating the public care homes as homes that provide a combination of both public housing and care services at the same time.

1.5   Effects of the 2003 Health Reform

1.5.1   Major Components

The health reform implemented in 2003, which was designed to limit increases in medical expenditures, had the following major components:

First, the copayment rate was increased from 20 percent to 30 percent uniformly across health insurance schemes, though copayments for individuals seventy and over were kept at 10 percent, and copayments for children under three years old is set at 20 percent. Also, for the first time, an income criterion was introduced and the copayment rate for elderly individuals above the middle-class income level (6 million yen per year) is set at 20 percent, accounting for 11.3 percent of the total.[7]

Second, the insurance premium was raised with widening of the tax base from 8.5 percent of the monthly wages to 8.2 percent of annual wages including biannual bonuses (9.5 percent of monthly wages). The effect of widening of the tax base is important, as biannual bonuses account on average for nearly 14 percent of annual wages.[8]

Third, the HSE is to be applied gradually to those who are age seventy-five and above instead of the current age seventy and above, with the change phased in over five years. At the same time, the ratio of the subsidy from the general budget is to be raised from the current rate of 30 percent to 50 percent over the same phase-in period. The revision has a positive impact on the budget of the SMHI and GMHI by significantly reducing their transfer payments to the HSE. The effect on the CHI budget is uncertain, however, because the reduction of the transfer payments to the HSE is offset by the negative impact from an increasing number of the elderly moving from HSE.

Fourth, medical fees were reduced by 2.7 percent on average, of which the prices of drugs and doctor's fees are reduced by 1.3 percent, respectively. The fiscal impact is unclear because under the fee-for-service system

6. Paying benefits in the form of cash to the families of people needing care is basically not allowed. This is based on the argument that women in the Japanese family used to play the major caregiving role, and allowing cash payments may prevent improvements from the current situation.

7. The copayment rate for the elderly before the reform was also 10 percent, but the quite low ceiling on out-of-pocket payments was removed after the reform, which resulted in a de facto increase in the copayment rate.

8. This revision is necessary with growing number of part-time workers and specialists who do not have a typical division of monthly wages and biannual bonuses.

doctors could easily recover lost income by increasing the quantity of medical services provided. This is why the ceiling on medical expenses for the elderly was implemented in the first draft of the reform, though it was removed in the final stage. The original scheme consisted of setting a target growth of medical expenses based on the growth in GDP and elderly population, with the average fee in the following year automatically lowered to attain the target level.

1.5.2   Fiscal Impacts of the Proposed Medical Reform

Because the fiscal impacts of these reforms were not presented by the Ministry of Health, Labor and Welfare, we estimate the effects based on our own health insurance budget model. We use the revised version of Suzuki (2000), which reflects the recent institutional changes as well as an updating of the data. The major features of the model are the following:

First, the model consists of five blocks: the SMHI, the GMHI, the CHI, the Retirees' Account of the CHI, and the HSE. The data on health expenditures are based on five-year age groups[9] so that the changing age compositions in respective groups are reflected in their aggregated fiscal balance. In the first three blocks—SMHI, GMHI and CHI—total health expenditures are derived from the age composition of the population and the health expenses by respective age groups. Total expenditures in these groups are the sum of the health expenditures and the transfers to the Retirees' Account of the CHI and the HSE. The workers' contributions are calculated from the age composition and their wages, which are summed to the other revenues, leading to the total revenues. The fiscal balances in the three groups are shown by the difference between revenues and expenditures. The expenditures and revenues in the Retirees' Account of the CHI and the HSE are estimated by the population by age, and the transfers with the preceding three blocks.

Second, we use the population scenario from the Population and Social Security Institute to project the population in each age group based on the assumption of the fixed spending ratio across each group. The baseline for the national health expenditures is exactly the same as what was projected by the Ministry of Health, Labor and Welfare.[10] The effect of an increase in the ratio of the patients' payments on medical expenditures is measured based on the elasticity of demand of patients with respect to the price.

The major results are the following: First, the baseline case with no institutional changes indicates continuously worsening budget deficits through 2025. This is mainly due to the aging factor, while revenues from

9. The Mutual Aid Associations (MAAs) is not included as the data on age groups are not available.

10. This is consistent with the sum of the expenditures by health insurance schemes, excluding the MAAs due to unavailability of the data.

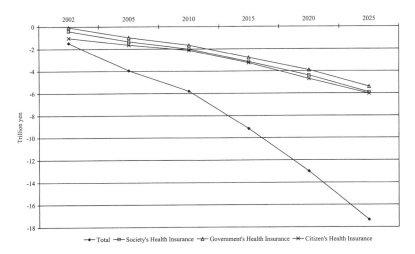

Fig. 1.3   Projections of health insurance budgets (baseline cases)

fixed premiums are not increasing at the same rate.[11] This trend—a widening gap between expenditures and revenues—is common to all health insurance schemes. The aggregate budget deficits are projected to grow from 1.4 trillion yen in 2002 to 16.9 trillion yen in 2025 (see figure 1.3).

Second, after the various reforms discussed previously are implemented, the aggregate health insurance budget will be improved, particularly in the coming few years. However, the budget deficit will begin widening again beyond that, and the aggregate deficit in 2025 would be close to 13 trillion yen, which is relatively lower than the baseline case but is still significant.

Comparing the individual elements of the reform, the largest effect comes from the increases in premiums and copayments in the immediate future, while the effect of reducing transfers to HIE grows over time (see figure 1.4). This is mainly because the major effect of the HIE reform comes from limiting the targeted elderly group from the current age of seventy to seventy-five and increasing the subsidies from the general revenue. This is simply a policy of shifting the burden between individual health insurance schemes and government and not an effective measure to constrain total health expenditures.

On the other hand, the relatively small effect from increasing patient copayments to 30 percent is not surprising. A higher copayment rate is usually assumed to stimulate cost consciousness toward the use of medical re-

---

11. This projection is consistent with the government projection based on the national health expenditures (30.7 trillion yen) in 2001. The basic assumption of the real economic growth is set to 2 percent in 2004 and beyond.

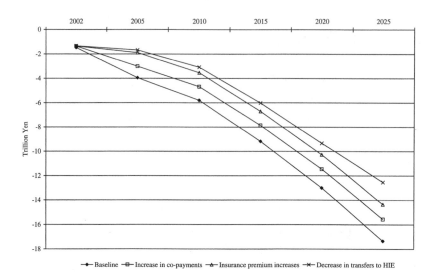

Fig. 1.4   Effects of the health insurance reforms (contributions of various reforms)

sources, and is, therefore, considered effective in curbing wasteful medical expenses (Newhouse and the Insurance Experiment Group [1993], Manning et al. [1987], Zweifel and Manning [2000]).[12] However, the effectiveness of copayments depends upon the content of medical services; the outpatient care may well be affected, but not hospital services for which there are fewer alternatives.[13] Also, the copayment ceiling, designed as a safety net to avoid excessive burdens on patients, lowers the effective copayment rate.[14] Compared with the current ceiling system, deductibles have an advantage in that the effective copayment rate drops as an individual's medical costs increase.

Third, the effects of the reform on health budgets are asymmetric between the health insurance for employees (SMHI and GMHI) and for the self-employed (CHI). In the former, the fiscal balance will be largely improved until 2010 but will fall again after that. This is mainly due to decreases in transfer payments to the HSE from raising the age criterion from the current level of seventy to seventy-five, as well as an increase in revenues

12. Zweifel and Manning (2000) offer the broadest and most detailed discussion of this theme. For a Japanese case, Tokita et al. (2002), Yoshida and Takagi (2002), and Battacharya et al. (1996) analyze it in detail.

13. This is consistent with the previous experience when the patient's share was raised from 10 percent to 20 percent in 1997. There was a one-time drop in medical expenses without any significant change in the trend growth.

14. Though the copayment ceiling safety net will be raised by 10 percent at the same time as the increase in copayments from 20 percent to 30 percent, patients can reach this ceiling more easily with the higher copayment ratio. Beyond the ceiling patients pay no more copayments, thereby lowering the effective copayment rate as a result.

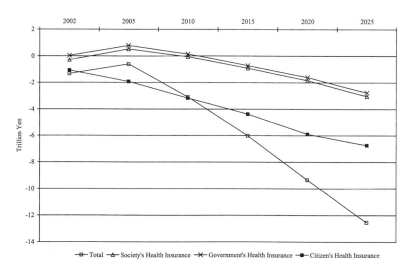

Fig. 1.5   Projection of health insurance budget (after the reform)

from expanding the tax base of the premium. In contrast, the reform would not contribute to the fiscal balance of the CHI, mainly because the positive effect from lowering of the transfer payments to HSE would be more than offset by the negative effect of the gradual increase in the number of enrollees age seventy to seventy-four who are newly covered by CHI under this reform (see figure 1.5).

1.5.3   Policy Implications

A major implication of the preceding analysis is that increasing the copayment rate and mechanisms for sharing revenue among health insurance providers are not sufficient to attain a sustainable fiscal balance in the long run. Further items being discussed as part of a reform agenda include the following:

The first item is the creation of an independent health insurance scheme for the elderly. This is included in the basic plan for health reform targets for 2008, released in March 2003 by the Ministry of Health, Labor and Welfare. This is based on a two-layer scheme for those who are age sixty-five to seventy-four and age seventy-five and above, which would correspond to the current Retirees' Account in the CHI and HSE, respectively. Though the details of the reform are not yet clear, the basic idea is to separate costly health care services for the elderly from those for the non-elderly and leave it to an independent health scheme that is financed by the tax revenue and contributions by other health plans.

Second, standardization of medical treatments has not been established, and medical costs vary widely across hospitals in Japan (Kawabuchi and

Sugihara 2003). This is mainly because the way medical doctors are trained is compartmentalized, and best-practices in most cases have not been established. Also, it is difficult to accumulate data on health costs for health insurance providers. A major factor behind this is the primitive method used to review bills for reimbursement. Hard-copy bills are printed in hospitals and sent to the government's intermediary clearing organizations to be checked and then sent again to insurance providers for additional checking. If medical bills were sent directly from hospitals to insurance providers over the Internet, health cost data would be more easily gathered at much lower cost. The administrative barriers preventing the use of information technology (IT) networks for processing health care bills are gradually being removed. This is a step toward collecting the data need to calculate average costs for standard medical treatments, which is necessary for a prospective payment system.

The third item is allowing for mixed financing between private and public health insurance. It is natural that the coverage of health insurance is limited, but what is particular to Japan is that patients are not allowed to pay extra costs for additional care for a series of medical treatments in hospitals in addition to the costs covered by the public health insurance. If a patient wishes to do so, he or she has to pay the whole costs including costs generally covered by insurance. There are only a few exceptions, such as amenities, selected high-tech medical treatments,[15] dental materials, reservations for outpatient services, and so on. This restriction makes it quite difficult for doctors to choose a variety of medical treatments that differ from a uniform formula under the current fee-for-service system. Introducing a mixed financing system with public and private insurance coverage for those hospitals that are evaluated as having a certain level of health service provision could provide several advantages: first, extra revenues from the private health insurance could provide resources for financing better quality health services; second, this could stimulate incentives for hospitals to improve health care services; third, it could substitute the expansion of public health expenditures with private health expenditures.

1.6 Conclusion

Japan's health care system, which has been successful in the postwar period, is now facing a series of structural problems arising mainly from the aging of the population. The combination of fee-for-service with free access to health services results in upward pressure on health expenditures, particularly given the increasing number of elderly. The government has

---

15. When a new high-tech medical treatment is first introduced, the costs for using it are not usually covered by public insurance. Instead, patients are subsidized for part of the cost by public insurance. If the technology becomes widely used, it is eventually fully covered by insurance.

tried to alleviate this pressure by introducing various policies in the 1990s, but they did not effectively solve the fundamental problems.

The establishment of the long-term nursing care insurance for the frail elderly in 2000 was intended to move the care for the frail elderly from costly hospitals to nursing care homes, but the effect has been marginal with free access to hospitals basically maintained. Another reform was raising the copayment rate and redistributing costs among various insurance providers, though the positive fiscal impacts of these reforms is projected to last only over the short run. In order to establish a health care system that is sustainable in a rapidly aging society, additional reforms may be needed to limit the expansion of the public health insurance by substituting partly with private health insurance. The 2003 health insurance reform is a first step toward a more comprehensive reform of the health care services sector.

References

Battacharya, J., W. B. Vogt, A. Yoshikawa, and T. Nakahara. 1996. The utilization of outpatient medical services in Japan. *Journal of Human Resources* 31 (2): 450–76.

Ii, M., and Y. Ookusa. 2002. *Economic analysis of demand for health care services* [in Japanese]. Tokyo: Nihon Keizai Shinbun sha.

Ikegami, N. 2001. Revision of remuneration for health services and inclusive payment [in Japanese]. 2001. *Journal of Health Insurance & Medical Practice* 56 (3): 3–7.

Ikegami, N., and J. C. Campbell. 1999. Health care reform in Japan: The virtues of muddling through. *Health Affairs* 18 (3): 56–75.

Kawabuchi, K., and S. Sugihara. 2003. Volume-output relationship in Japan: The case of PTCA for AMI Patients. Paper presented at NBER-JCER Conference. 10–11 May, Nikko, Japan.

Kawai, H., and S. Maruyama. 2000. An analysis of the effect of the inclusive payment system on costs and intensity of care [in Japanese]. *Japanese Journal of Health Economics and Policy* 7:37–64.

Maeda, N. 1978. Impacts of co-payment rate changes on health expenditures [in Japanese]. *Quarterly of Social Security Research* 14 (2).

Manning, W. G., J. P. Newhouse, N. Duan, et al. 1987. Health insurance and the demand for medical care: Evidence from a randomized experiment. *American Economic Review* 77 (3): 251–77.

Newhouse, J. P., and The Insurance Experiment Group. 1993. *Free for all? Lessons from the health insurance experiment.* Cambridge: Harvard University Press.

Nishimura, S. 1987. *Economic analysis of health care* [in Japanese]. Tokyo: Toyokeizai Shimpo Sha.

Okura, S., T. Fukawa, and R. Suzuki. 1994. *A Japan–U.S. comparative analysis on Medical care for the elderly in the last year of life* [in Japanese]. Tokyo: Foundation of Social Development for Senior Citizens.

Sawano, K. 2000. Co-payment, coinsurance rage and the elderly care in Japan [in Japanese]. *Journal of Health Care and Society* 10 (2): 115–37.

Suzuki, R. 1998. Allocation of health care resources and consumption of health care services [in Japanese]. In *Studies on health care expenditure by the elderly,* ed. A. Gunji, 50–60. Tokyo: Maruzen Planet.

Suzuki, W., and R. Suzuki. 2002. Is longevity a major cause for elderly health cost expansion [in Japanese]? *International Public Policy Study* 8 (2): 1–14.

Tokita, T., K. Hosoya, Y. Hayashi, and H. Kumamoto. 2002. Claim data analysis of medical fee revision [in Japanese]. *Economic Review* 53 (3): 226–35.

Tokita, T., T. Yamada, K. Yamamoto, N. Izumida, and H. Konno. 2000. A claim data analysis for Japanese medical demand and supply [in Japanese]. *The Economic Review* 1 (4): 289–300.

Yashiro, N. 1998. The economic factors for the declining birthrate. *Review of Population and Social Policy* (7): 129–39.

Yoshida, A., and S. Takagi. 2002. Effect of the reform of the social medical insurance system in Japan. *The Japanese Economic Review* 53 (4): 444–65.

Zweifel, P., and W. G. Manning. 2000. Moral hazard and consumer incentives in health care. In *Handbook of health economics,* ed. A. J. Culyer and J. P. Newhouse, 409–59. Amsterdam: Elsevier.

2

The U.S. Medical Care System
for the Elderly

David M. Cutler and David A. Wise

This paper examines the structure of the American medical care system, focusing primarily on the system of care for the elderly. Understanding the design of medical care systems is important for several reasons. First, we frequently want to know how to compare systems across countries. Is the American medical care system closer to the European model or the Japanese model? How different are the medical systems across continental European countries? To answer these questions, we need to characterize the systems themselves.

We are also interested in medical system structure because we want to relate structures to outcomes. Is the longer life expectancy in Japan than in the United States attributable to the Japanese medical system, or to other factors? Which country has the better medical care system? Understanding how medical systems work is the key to starting.

Medical care systems are multidimensional, and so our description must be as well. The basis for our analysis is the medical care triad, presented in figure 2.1.[1] There are three participants in the medical care system: pa-

David M. Cutler is the Otto Eckstein Professor of Applied Economics, Department of Economics and John F. Kennedy School of Government, and social sciences dean in the Faculty of Arts and Sciences, both at Harvard University, and a research associate of the National Bureau of Economic Research. David A. Wise is the John F. Stambaugh Professor of Political Economy at the John F. Kennedy School of Government, Harvard University, and director of the Program on Aging at the National Bureau of Economic Research.

We are grateful to the National Institutes of Health for research support through grants P01-AG05842 and P30-AG012810 and to participants at the NBER-JCER Conference on Health Care in the United States and Japan for comments.

1. Figure 2.1 is not new to us. The distinction between coverage, reimbursement, and access is common in the literature. See, for example, Reinhardt (2004), Evans (2002), and Chernichovsky (1995).

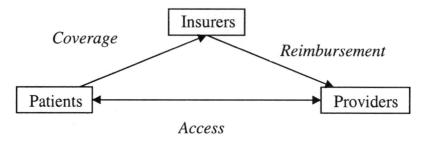

Fig. 2.1   The medical care triad

tients, providers, and insurers. Patients pay money to insurers (either directly or indirectly, as we discuss in the following) and pay for some care directly. Insurers reimburse providers for care and set rules under which the care can be provided. Providers diagnose and treat patients.

Corresponding to these three participants are three sets of interactions. The first is the *coverage rules*. This encompasses the mechanisms by which people get health insurance and who pays for that insurance. The second interaction is the *reimbursement system* between insurers and providers—how is payment determined and what rates are paid? Finally, there are the *access rules*—which providers are patients allowed to see and under what circumstances? In this paper, we describe the insurance, reimbursement, and access rules in the American medical care system. The paper can be compared with the work of Yashiro, Suzuki, and Suzuki (chap. 1 in this volume), who analyze the Japanese medical system in a similar framework. We present broad outlines of the system for everyone in the United States. Because the system is so heterogeneous, we focus particular attention on the system for the elderly. We note where research has explored a link between system provisions and outcomes, but we do not take the further step of relating system provisions to health outcomes in any systematic way.

We begin in section 2.1 by presenting a brief overview of medical systems in developed countries. We show the large differences in medical spending and health outcomes across countries that motivate our desire to make system comparisons. Section 2.2 discusses the methods through which Americans get insurance coverage and the flow of money. Section 2.3 highlights the reimbursement arrangements that providers operate under, and section 2.4 presents the access rules for patients and providers. We end with a brief conclusion.

2.1   The International Experience

The performance of medical care systems differs enormously across countries. To give a summary of this performance, we emphasize two dimensions most relevant for economic analysis: how much the system costs and how healthy people are, perhaps as a result of the medical system.[2]

To measure costs, we look at medical spending as a share of gross domestic product (GDP). Gross domestic product is a natural scalar by which to evaluate medical care; a richer country should spend more on medical care than a poorer country. In principle, a more accurate scalar would be the amount of medical spending that is expected, given the income elasticity of medical care. That elasticity is not known, however. In microdata, the elasticity of medical spending with respect to income is far below 1, generally about .2 (Newhouse 1993). This suggests that we should look at per capita spending more than spending relative to GDP. This comparison, however, presumes that prices are constant across countries at a point in time. In fact, medical prices rise with income (Baumol 1967). In macroregressions, the income elasticity is usually somewhat above 1 (Getzen 2000). But that is likely overstated, as it reflects demand as well as technology conditions. There is no obvious scalar, so we focus on the GDP comparison.

Figure 2.2 shows medical spending as a share of GDP in Organization for Economic Cooperation and Development (OECD) countries. The data are for 1998, the most recent year in which they are complete. The United States spends the most of any country on medical care, nearly 14 percent of GDP. The next highest country, Switzerland, spends only 11 percent of GDP on medical care. Among high income countries, the United Kingdom is a very low outlier, spending only 7 percent of GDP on medical care. The average in the OECD is about 8 percent.

To measure health, we use life expectancy at birth. Life expectancy is the most common summary of health in the literature. In using this indicator, we emphasize immediately that it is influenced by far more than medical care. Life expectancy is affected by lifestyle factors (smoking, diets), environmental conditions (air pollution), and other economic and social factors. Our purpose here is not to grade medical systems. Rather, we want to illustrate the range of variation in the data.

Life expectancy in OECD countries is shown in figure 2.3. Once again, there is wide variation. The mean across developed countries is seventy-seven years. The United States, although with a life expectancy of seventy-seven years (equal to the mean), ranks twenty-first of the thirty countries shown in the figure. Japan is the clear positive outlier, with life expectancy of eighty-one years.

Comparing figures 2.2 and 2.3 suggests little correlation between medical spending and life expectancy. Figure 2.4 shows this explicitly. The hor-

---

2. Other dimensions of performance include the degree to which the system treats people fairly and the extent to which it upholds normative values of right and wrong. We are less able to measure these dimensions quantitatively.

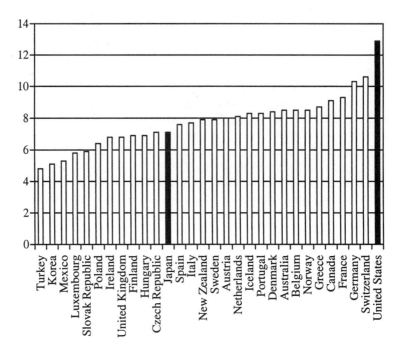

Fig. 2.2   Medical spending as a share of GDP
Source: OECD (2002).

izontal axis of figure 2.4 is medical spending as a share of GDP. The vertical axis is life expectancy. A regression line indicates a positive relation between the two, although this is driven primarily by the very low income countries (Turkey, Hungary, and the Slovak Republic). Among higher income countries, there is no relation between spending and health outcomes.

As we indicated in the preceding, we do not interpret this result as suggesting that the marginal value of medical care is low. That may be the case, but it is not proven by this comparison. Rather, the comparison illustrates the need to explore the issue further. What role do medical systems play in influencing these outcomes? Do system features relate to performance? The remaining sections of the paper start down this path.

2.2   Insurance Coverage in the United States

There is no single health care system in the United States. Rather, health insurance in the United States is provided through a mixture of public and private programs. The principal public plans are Medicare, which provides insurance for the elderly and some disabled nonelderly, and Medicaid, which provides insurance for poor women and children under sixty-five

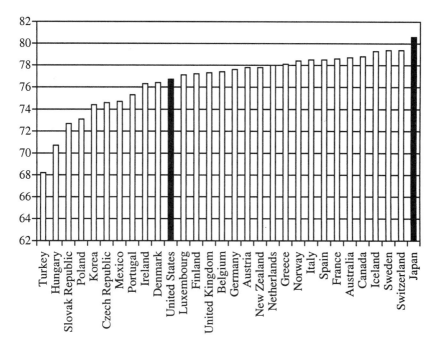

Fig. 2.3   Life expectancy at birth
Source: OECD (2002).

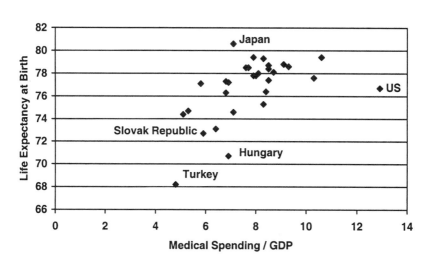

Fig. 2.4   Relation between medical spending and life expectancy
Source: OECD (2002).

(on a means-tested basis), the blind and disabled, and long-term care for persons age sixty-five and older. Employer-provided plans are the principle source of insurance for the nonelderly. We focus on the medical system for the elderly, but we begin by describing how insurance for the elderly fits into the total health care system.

Table 2.1 summarizes the sources of insurance coverage. We tabulate statistics separately for the nonelderly population (below age sixty-five) and the elderly. The source of care is presented in the left column of the table. Within each age group, we show the share of people with that source of insurance coverage and total spending for that age group accounted for by that source. Spending includes all medical services, with one exception: most long-term care spending is not accounted for in these data (most people in nursing homes are not in the spending sample). This reduces the share of spending for the elderly that is accounted for by Medicaid and out-of-pocket payments, but we do not have an easy way of adding that back in.

Public insurance covers 97 percent of the elderly population and about

Table 2.1   **Sources of health insurance and medical spending in the United States**

	Under age 65			Age 65 and over		
Source	Nature of coverage	% of population	% of payments	Nature of coverage	% of population	% of payments
Public insurance		16	17		97	65
Medicare	Disabled	2	4	Near universal	96	58
Medicaid	Poor women and children; Blind and disabled	11	10	Acute care for poor; Long-term care for poor	10	4
Private insurance		72	54		61	17
Employer	Workers and dependants	66		Employer retiree policies	34	
Individual	Family-purchased policies	6		Individually purchased supplemental plans	32	
Uninsured		16	21[a]		1	16[a]
Other		6[b]			2[b]	
Share of total		87	65 ($1,516)		13	35 ($5,662)
Total		100	100		100	100

Sources: Coverage data are from the Current Population Survey, March 2002. Spending data are from the Medical Expenditure Panel Study, 1997.

[a]Out-of-pocket spending

[b]Workers' compensation, other insurance (auto, etc.).

16 percent of the nonelderly population. Medicare is the dominant public program for the elderly, while Medicaid is more important for the nonelderly. The majority of the nonelderly, nearly three-quarters, are covered by private insurance. Most of this is provided through employment, but a significant share comes from individual purchase as well. The quality of this coverage varies by employer.

Sixteen percent of the nonelderly population is without health insurance, compared to less than 1 percent for the elderly. In total, 46 million Americans are uninsured. The uninsured are a heterogenous group. Some are young and perhaps feel that health insurance is not a pressing need, others are poor and don't buy insurance, many are unemployed or employed by small firms that don't provide insurance, still others have chronic diseases that prevent them from buying insurance. Some of the uninsured are eligible for Medicaid[3] but don't use the insurance. Many of the uninsured receive care through hospital emergency rooms. Much of this care is for serious illness or accidents, providing a sort of partial catastrophic insurance paid for by insured patients who pay more than the price of their care.

The share of medical spending paid for by various sources of insurance is shown in the next columns of table 2.1. In total, 35 percent of medical spending is for the elderly (the elderly make up about 13 percent of the population). At the time care is received, payment for the elderly comes from six sources—Medicare, Medicaid, privately purchased Medigap insurance, employer-provided retiree health insurance, out-of-pocket payments, and other miscellaneous sources. Medicare is the dominant payer, accounting for 58 percent of total spending. Including both Medicare and Medicaid payments, government programs pay for nearly two-thirds of the medical bills of the elderly. (The share would be somewhat lower if long-term care spending were included.) Private insurance and out-of-pocket payments account for the bulk of the remainder, in roughly equal proportions.

A large proportion of out-of-pocket payments are for outpatient prescription drugs. In addition, much long-term care spending is out of pocket, although these expenses are undercounted in this table.

In the nonelderly population, about 50 percent of medical payments are made by private insurers. Government payments account for 17 percent of spending, and out-of-pocket spending by individuals accounts for another 21 percent.

2.2.1   Who Pays for Insurance?

Inpatient insurance (Part A) under Medicare is paid for by the young through a 2.9 percent payroll tax—half of which is paid for by the employer and half by the employee. Outpatient care (Part B) under Medicare

---

3. About 40 percent of children who are uninsured are eligible for Medicaid, and additional children are eligible for coverage under the Children's Health Insurance Program (CHIP).

is financed through Supplementary Medical Insurance. Enrollee premiums are 25 percent of the cost of the insurance. The remainder comes out of general government revenues. In addition, Medicare beneficiaries can buy Medigap private insurance to cover the difference between Medicare payments and charges for care. About two-thirds of Medicare beneficiaries are covered by a private insurance policy in addition to Medicare—half are employer-provided retiree plans and half are purchased individually. As we discuss in the following, together these plans provide first-dollar coverage for a large portion of care, encouraging excessive use of services (Newhouse 1993).

Insurance premiums under employer-provided plans for the nonelderly are typically shared between the employer and the employee. On average, about 75 to 80 percent of premiums are paid for by the employer and the remainder by the employee. Unlike wages and salaries, compensation to employees in the form of health insurance is not taxed. Thus employees have a strong incentive to take compensation in the form of health insurance (Feldstein 1973). And employees have a strong incentive to encourage generous insurance plans with low out-of-pocket copayments, which are typically taxed. Thus, for the under sixty-five group as well, part of the system pushes toward first-dollar coverage with little constraint on expenditure at the time care is received.

The out-of-pocket bill facing individuals is the direct spending on medical care services plus the family cost of health insurance. These totals are not readily apparent in table 2.1, which records the payer at the time the service is used. To flow through these insurance payments to individuals, table 2.2 shows family spending on medical care. Among the elderly population, insurance payments are about $1,800 per family (largely for supplemental Medigap insurance coverage and the employee part of employer-sponsored retirement coverage), and direct costs are about the same magnitude. The amounts are similar in the nonelderly population, about $1,900 for direct payments and health insurance.

In addition to these payments, the nonelderly also pay indirectly for the

Table 2.2   **Family payments for medical care ($)**

Source	Under 65	Over 65
Direct	1,857	3,493
Insurance payments	884	1,775
Out-of-pocket	973	1,719
Employer	2,651	
Total	4,508	

Sources: Direct spending is from the Consumer Expenditure Survey, 2001. Employer payments are estimated assuming that three-quarters of insurance premiums are paid by employers.

employer's portion of employer-provided health insurance. Though the employer writes the check for insurance, economic research establishes quite clearly that the ultimate incidence of these payments is on workers (Summers 1989; Gruber 1994). A rough guess of these amounts is about $2,700 per family. Spending on health insurance and medical care is thus perhaps $4,500 in total for the nonelderly population.

The final set of payments are taxes to pay for public programs and the implicit income that retirees give up earlier in life to pay for employer-provided medical care when retired. The incidence of these payments by age is somewhat harder to assess. Previous taxes paid by the elderly for Medicare do not cover their current use, for example, and so some of that cost is paid for by the current young. The same is likely true with employer-provided supplemental insurance. Rather than deal with these generational incidence questions, however, we limit ourselves to payments targeted to immediate services use.

2.2.2 Gradations in Insurance Coverage

To this point, we have treated all private health insurance as identical. In practice, there are enormous differences in the types of insurance that people have. The services covered by Medicare differ from those covered by Medicaid and private insurance. Table 2.3 shows this comparison. Private insurance policies generally cover hospital care, physician services, outpatient tests, and prescription drugs. Long-term care is usually not covered, but those services are used infrequently by the nonelderly population.

Medicare is significantly less generous than the typical private insurance policy. Medicare covers hospital services, physician expenses, and laboratory tests. It does not cover outpatient prescription medications, however, and only very limited coverage for long-term care. Partly as a result of this, almost all elderly supplement Medicare in one form or another. As explained previously, some beneficiaries purchase private Medigap policies to cover cost sharing and occasionally prescription drugs. Other beneficiaries obtain supplemental insurance from a former employer. Still others enroll in Medicare Health Maintenance Organizations (HMOs) to obtain additional services, a topic we return to in the following. Finally, the poor

Table 2.3   **Typical coverage in insurance policies**

	Private	Medicare	Medicaid
Hospital	✓	✓	✓
Physician	✓	✓	✓
Laboratory	✓	✓	✓
Prescription medications	✓		✓
Long-term care		Modest	✓

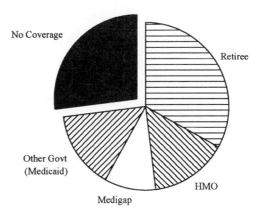

Fig. 2.5   Prescription drug coverage among the elderly
Note: Data are for 1998.

elderly have prescription drug and long-term care services paid for by Medicaid.

Figure 2.5 shows the share of elderly with insurance coverage for prescription drugs and the source of that coverage. Three-quarters of the elderly have prescription drug coverage. The bulk of such coverage is obtained through prior employment, with HMOs, private Medigap policies, and other public programs supplying the remainder.

Medicaid covers the range of acute and long-term care services. On paper, Medicaid is among the most generous insurance plans available. In practice, though, Medicaid payments are so tightly constrained that access to care for Medicaid beneficiaries is a significant concern. We do not focus greatly on the Medicaid program in the remainder of the paper.

The Medicaid experience raises the broader point that access is not just about covered services. The nature of the insurance policy differs in other ways as well. A major issue in the United States is whether the receipt of medical care is managed. Managed care is a form of vertical integration in medicine. Rather than dividing insurance from medical care provision, managed care integrates the two, having insurers become involved in what care is provided and how it is delivered. Private insurance has a range of different types of management. We provide more details in the following, but note here that the system is more complex than table 2.3 suggests.

There is some managed care in Medicare, but it is decidedly less important. About 90 percent of Medicare beneficiaries are in the traditional program, where the government determines the payment rates and access rules. The remaining 10 percent are in managed care plans, usually an HMO. Because of the dominance of the traditional Medicare program, we refer to Medicare as if it were just that policy.

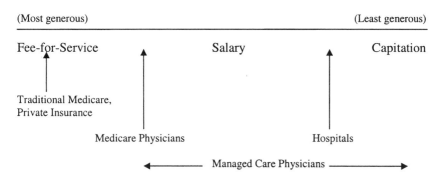

Fig. 2.6   Characterization of reimbursement systems

2.3   Reimbursing Providers

Given the many different ways that Americans obtain health insurance, it is not surprising that there is a wide range of reimbursement systems in use. Further, the reimbursement systems differ enormously in the incentives they provide.[4]

Perhaps the most critical feature of reimbursement systems is the degree to which payments are related to costs. Some reimbursement systems pay more when more care is provided, and others pay less. Consider a linear relation between payment for a service provided and the various costs of that service:

(1)   Payment $= a + b \cdot$ Practice Cost $+ c \cdot$ Time Cost,

where a, b, and c are parameters of the payment system. Practice costs include office expenses, nonphysician administrative personnel, malpractice insurance, and supplies. The time costs represent the opportunity costs of the physician devoting additional hours to care.

Historically, medical care in the United States was paid for on a *fee-for-service* basis. In this system, total reimbursement is equal to the cost of care provided (with some division between insurer and enrollee payments. In terms of equation (1), $a = 0$, $b = 1$, and $c = 1$. Fee-for-service insurance is shown at one end of the scale of payment generosity in figure 2.6.

There is a distinction between marginal and average cost that is important in understanding the incentives of fee-for-service systems. Medical care has very high fixed costs, but the marginal cost of additional production is often low. For example, it costs about $800 million to develop a new drug (DiMasi 2003), but the cost of producing additional pills once the

---

4. For a review of physician payment systems and the incentive they create, see McGuire (2000).

drug is developed is only pennies. Similarly, many of the costs for a physician are sunk costs—the opportunity cost of medical education most particularly. Other costs are fixed costs, depending only on the decision to practice medicine. Examples of these costs include malpractice insurance, office rent, and equipment overhead. True marginal cost is low.

Traditional fee-for-service payment systems paid on the basis of average costs. This reimburses physicians for sunk and fixed costs as well as marginal costs. In practice, this creates large profits for providing additional care because payment far exceeds costs at the margin. Thus, fee-for-service payment systems strongly encourage provision of medical care in almost all circumstances.

A somewhat less generous set of incentives is provided by a *salary system*. In many HMOs in the United States and in some European countries, physicians are paid a salary for providing care. The salary system corresponds to a payment rule where $a > 0$, $b = 1$, and $c = 0$. The physician earns a fixed amount of money and does not have to pay for any practice expenses but is not reimbursed more for additional time costs.

The salary system provides fewer incentives for care provision than does the fee-for-service system. In a salary system, additional care provided is not reimbursed at the margin, so there is no financial incentive to do more. In particular, because the doctor's time cost is not reimbursed at the margin, the doctor has an incentive to cut back on time inputs. A doctor on a salary earns the same amount if he shows up for a full day or half day of work (assuming his salary is not docked). Thus, doctors will attempt to arrive late and leave early and to substitute tests and devices for additional time.

The ability of physicians to do this varies by setting. In some countries, such as Italy, monitoring of physicians is poor, and doctors routinely violate the guidelines as to hours that must be worked (Cutler 2002a). In many HMOs, in contrast, monitoring is stronger, and physicians are not able to shirk.

The third type of payment system is *capitation*. In the extreme version of this system, physicians are paid a fixed amount and must pay for all care provided out of the capitation amount. In terms of equation (1), $a > 0$, $b = 0$, and $c = 0$. This type of system is most common with primary care physicians. If a patient of a doctor paid this way uses medications that the doctor prescribes or is admitted to the hospital, the costs of the medications or hospitalization are paid for out of the capitation amount.

There are a complex array of capitation systems used in practice. Some physicians are capitated for care used in the primary setting, medications, and nonemergency hospitalizations, but not for emergency hospitalizations. Others are capitated for all costs, but have reinsurance for very expensive patients. Still others have varying degrees of capitation depending on total spending in the practice as a whole.

Regardless of the specifics, capitated systems have the feature that physician earnings are negatively related to the amount of care provided. Doctors that do more earn less. Not surprisingly, the incentives of this system are the weakest (as shown in figure 2.6). A purely profit maximizing doctor paid a capitation rate would not see patients at all and would not provide any care. Of course, HMOs monitor physician behavior, and patients will find other doctors if no care is provided, meaning that future income will decline. Thus, the example is grossly exaggerated. But it shows the nature of the incentives.

In addition to varying across payers, reimbursement systems in the United States have changed over time. Figure 2.6 illustrates the evolution of these systems. Historically, both Medicare and private insurers reimbursed services on a fee-for-service basis. The reason for this was practical. When private insurers started to cover medical care, they did not know how to pay for care; medical care was separate from insurance. Doctors had list prices, however, and so insurers paid those prices. This ultimately turned into the fee-for-service system.

Over time, both Medicare and the private sector have moved away from fee-for-service payment. Medicare currently pays physicians on a fee schedule, based loosely on the estimated cost of services provided. In a number of detailed studies, the government attempted to determine the cost of different services and now reimburses physicians on that basis. The payment is still per service performed, but is somewhat less generous than it once was.

Bigger changes have occurred in the payment system for hospitals. Since the early 1980s, payment for Medicare patients admitted to hospitals has been under a partially capitated system termed the prospective payment system (PPS). When a Medicare patient is admitted to a hospital, the hospital reports the diagnosis the patient received and whether a surgical procedure was performed. These two attributes are used to classify patients into one of about 470 diagnosis related groups (DRGs). The payment received for the patient depends only on the DRG and hospital factors, such as the region of the country and whether the hospital is a teaching hospital, not the specific services provided (other than how the surgical or nonsurgical distinction affects DRG coding).

An example illustrates how this system works. Consider the treatment of patients with acute myocardial infarction, or heart attack (see Cutler and McClellan 1998). A patient with a heart attack will almost always be admitted to a hospital. Upon admission, the hospital will administer a number of medications, including aspirin, beta-blockers, and, potentially, thrombolytics. Under the old fee-for-service payment system, each of these medications would be reimbursed separately. In the DRG system, there is no additional payment for providing them.

Many patients with a heart attack receive cardiac catheterization, a diagnostic procedure that measures the extent of blood flow to the heart. Catheterization is a surgical procedure; hence patients receiving a catheterization will be in a different DRG than patients who do not receive catheterization. The exact cost of the catheterization is not a factor in payment; however, a hospital that takes longer for each catheterization will receive no more money than a hospital that takes less time.

Depending on the results of the catheterization, additional procedures may be performed. Bypass surgery is a procedure to reroute blood flow around the blocked area in the coronary arteries. Angioplasty is used to clear the original blockage and restore blood flow in the arteries. Each of these procedures moves the patient into a more highly reimbursed DRG. But the specifics of the services provided—the type of catheter, the number of recovery days in the hospital, and the follow-up tests—are not reimbursed separately.

In the DRG system, therefore, heart attack patients will be classified into one of four DRG groups: those medically managed only (without any surgical procedures), those who receive cardiac catheterization but not bypass surgery or angioplasty, those who receive bypass surgery, and those who receive angioplasty.[5] The incentives of this system are therefore relatively strong to perform surgery but weak to perform additional nonsurgical care in hospitals.

In the private sector, reimbursement is more variable. Some physicians are paid on a fee-for-service basis, although usually one where the payments are substantially less generous than they were formally. More common is for physicians to be paid on a salary basis or by full or partial capitation. Hospital payments are generally along the lines of Medicare, with a payment per admission (using the DRG system) or per day of care received (a per diem system). In the latter methodology, the payment does not vary with the services provided in each day. Thus, intensive care in the stay is discouraged, while marginal days of care are not so heavily penalized. For both hospitals and physicians, the rate of payment is generally lower in the private sector than in Medicare. As a result, the incentives for limited service provision are even stronger.

2.3.1   Evidence on Reimbursement Incentives

How much do these incentives matter? A large literature has examined the response of services provided to physician payment incentives (see Cutler and Zeckhauser [2000] for a summary). The issue is complicated because the incentives of patients may be different from those of physicians: doctors may have incentives to provide less care, but patients may want

5. There is a little variation in these groups between patients with complications and those who do not have complications, but this is based on diagnoses of the patient, not treatments provided.

more. The equilibrium in such a situation is unclear. Still, the literature shows unambiguously that reimbursement incentives do affect the amount of medical care provided.

The strongest evidence for this effect comes from work of Mark Mc-Clellan (1997), based on the experience of the Medicare program. McClellan looked at how surgical and nonsurgical hospital admissions changed after the PPS was implemented. Recall that surgery increases the DRG payment the hospital receives; thus, surgical admissions should rise after PPS. Nonsurgical admissions were predicted to fall, however, because the elimination of fee-for-service reimbursement made those admissions less generous.

Figure 2.7 shows admission rates for surgical and nonsurgical admissions before and after the implementation of PPS. The results strikingly confirm the theory. Admissions for nonsurgical patients fell substantially with the implementation of PPS; the decline was about 40 percent. Surgical admissions rose by nearly the same percent. The timing of this change is perfectly coincident with PPS.

Evidence from managed care in the private sector shows major reductions in hospitalization rates and lengths of hospital stay in response to those incentives (Glied 2000). Admission rates in managed care plans are well below rates in fee-for-service plans, and lengths of hospital stay are shorter as well. The total saving in hospital care is about 20 percent. Some of this difference is certainly due to reimbursement incentives, although direct regulations on use of care (described in the next section) are important, too.

Overall, the United States' medical care system has become substan-

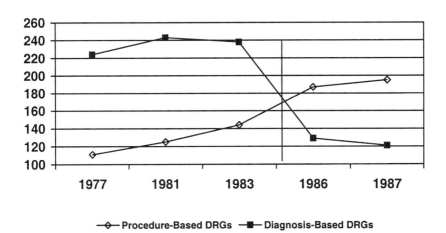

Fig. 2.7   Change in admissions after prospective payment
Source: McClellan (1997).

tially less generous in payment for care in the past two decades, and this has affected the care provided.

2.4 Access Rules

Access rules are among the most complex areas of medical care. There are myriad varieties of medical services that can be provided, with different rules for each. For example, patients may have different access to primary care, mental health specialists, and orthopedists. We synthesize the access rules in three parts. The set of services covered by insurance is the first element. Are prescription medications covered by the policy? We discussed variations in coverage previously. We focus here on two other parts of access: financial payments that individuals have to make when they use care (termed cost sharing) and nonfinancial barriers to the use of services.

2.4.1 Cost Sharing in Insurance

All insurance policies require patients to pay something when they access care. Cost sharing evolved as a way to limit moral hazard—excessive use of medical services only because they are insured. Since its beginnings, cost sharing has become much more elaborate.

Traditionally, private insurance policies had a varying schedule of patient payments. A typical private schedule is shown in figure 2.8. The deductible is the amount that a patient paid before insurance covered any care. A typical insurance policy had a deductible of about $500. After the deductible, costs were split between the insurer and the enrollee. The share of enrollee payments is termed the coinsurance rate; a standard coinsurance rate was 20 percent. Coinsurance would continue until the patient

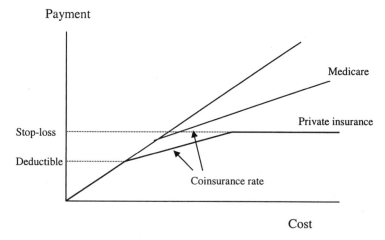

Fig. 2.8   Cost sharing in traditional insurance

reached a specified maximum, termed the *stop-loss*. Past this point, the insurer would pay all the costs of medical care. A common stop-loss was about $1,500.

The optimal insurance policy balances risk sharing against moral hazard. Making individuals pay more for medical care reduces the amount of moral hazard. But it also increases the financial risk that people are exposed to. In the optimal policy, these gains and losses are equal at the margin—a small increase in coinsurance rates leads to as much loss from increased risk as it brings in benefits from reduced moral hazard.

In practice, the tax system subsidized generous insurance and thus tilted policies toward being overly generous (Feldstein 1973). Employer payments for health insurance are not counted as income for tax purposes, while individual payments are. It was noted in the preceding that this provides incentives for people to have employer-based policies rather than individual policies. In addition, it encourages running as much money as possible through insurance rather than leaving costs to be paid for out-of-pocket, as insured services are paid for with pretax dollars rather than posttax dollars. This leads to a welfare loss—too little moral hazard and not enough risk sharing.

A substantial literature has examined the impact of this tax subsidy on overall medical spending and the losses to the economy. Martin Feldstein pioneered these calculations in the 1970s, and since then others have pursued this line of analysis (see, e.g., Enthoven 1993). Determining a final value for the impact of the tax subsidy on spending is complex, as the chain of causal events is long. The tax subsidy influences the structure of insurance policies, which in turn affects how much care people use and, thus, medical spending. A consensus estimate is that total medical spending is perhaps 5 to 10 percent higher as a result of the tax subsidy (Cutler 2002b).

The traditional Medicare program has the opposite problem. Cost sharing in the Medicare system is very high, particularly for catastrophic expenses. It was already noted that Medicare does not cover outpatient prescription medications, leading beneficiaries to face substantial risk. In addition, cost sharing for the set of covered services is high.

Table 2.4 shows the cost-sharing provisions in Medicare in detail, and figure 2.8 shows the schedule of payments for a typical enrollee.[6] Beneficiaries who use outpatient services have a deductible of $100 and a 20 percent coinsurance rate above that. The $100 deductible is not particularly large, but the coinsurance occurs without limit. This exposes Medicare beneficiaries to substantial risk—far more than in the private sector. Hospital cost sharing is also perverse. Medicare beneficiaries face a deductible equal to one day of hospital care, about $800 currently. This is very high by

---

6. We assume the person has one hospitalization during the year and no laboratory tests or mental health care utilization.

Table 2.4   Cost sharing in Medicare, 2002

Service	Beneficiary cost
Part A	
Inpatient hospital	*First stay in benefit period*
	$840 deductible for first stay
	$210 per day cost sharing for days 61–90
	Reserve days (60 lifetime)
	$420 per day cost sharing for lifetime reserve days
Skilled nursing facility	No cost sharing for first 20 days
	$105 per day cost sharing for days 21–100
	No coverage after 100 days
Hospice care	Nominal payment for drugs and respite care
Part B	
Overall deductible	$100 per year
Physician services	20 percent coinsurance rate
Outpatient hospital care	20 percent coinsurance rate based on median charge index
Ambulatory surgical	20 percent of Medicare-approved amount
Laboratory services	None
Outpatient mental health	50 percent coinsurance of Medicare-approved amount
Preventive services	20 percent coinsurance of approved amounts, waived for some services
Parts A and B	
Home health	None

Source: Hackbarth (2003).

private standards. After the deductible is paid, Medicare pays for the entire amount for the next sixty days of care. Beyond the sixty-day window, beneficiaries face increasing amounts of cost sharing for the next thirty days and then no further government reimbursement,[7] again exposing beneficiaries to large financial risk. By any calculation, the traditional Medicare program leaves people with far more financial risk than is optimal.

In response to this high degree of risk bearing, it is natural for Medicare beneficiaries to want more coverage than Medicare provides. For the low-income population, Medicaid provides this additional insurance, paying for the cost sharing required by the perverse Medicare reimbursement schedule.

The higher income population does not qualify for Medicaid but receives supplemental coverage in other ways. Some employers provide retiree health benefits that pay for the cost sharing required by Medicare. Others purchase individual insurance policies that supplement Medicare, termed *Medigap insurance.* Still others enroll in HMOs, which have lower cost sharing. All told, about three-quarters of the elderly have some supplemental insurance, through Medicaid or private supplements.

7. People do have sixty lifetime reserve days that they can use. Cost sharing in those days is half of the average daily cost.

Both employer and individual supplements provide first-dollar coverage—there is generally no cost sharing for hospital or physician services. The reason why first-dollar coverage is the norm is subtle. First-dollar coverage clearly leads to moral hazard. But a lot of the additional utilization is paid for by the traditional Medicare program, not the supplemental insurance. A beneficiary that goes to the doctor more as a result of having supplemental insurance pays for only 20 percent of the additional use in the insurance premium; the remaining 80 percent is covered by Medicare.

As a result, the cost of Medicare is much higher than it would be without supplemental insurance. Estimates suggest that people who have supplemental insurance cost Medicare about 20 percent more than they would without supplemental coverage (Christensen and Shinogle 1997). Of course, a better number to know is the additional spending beyond what Medicare would optimally spend if it were configured with the most appropriate degree of cost sharing. Because the optimal policy is more generous than the current policy, the savings from the optimal policy are lower. There are no estimates of these savings, however.

2.4.2   Nonfinancial Restrictions

All insurance plans impose some nonfinancial barriers to access medical care. People need physician approval before they can receive prescription medications or be admitted to a hospital, for example. But some plans have additional barriers to the use of care.

In the Medicare program, there are essentially no barriers to the use of care. Patients can see whatever doctor they want at whatever time they want. Referrals are not required, and no providers are out of bounds.[8] This led to an era of substantial increase in services provided. Recently, reimbursement has moved away from a pure fee-for-service basis into a more capitated basis, providing some incentives for doctors to do less. But the patient side is still very generous.

There are substantially more barriers to receipt of care in private insurance. The most important barriers are in managed care plans. Managed care was noted in passing earlier, but is particularly relevant at this point. We provide a taxonomy of managed care in table 2.5.

The most limited managed care arrangement is a managed indemnity insurance policy. It bundles a traditional indemnity policy with some *utilization review*—monitoring of providers to restrict the services that are performed and deny or reduce payment. For example, many insurance plans require that nonemergency hospital admissions be precertified. Utilization

---

8. This presents an interesting contrast with the extent of cost sharing, which was noted previously to be very high. If the traditional system were all that people had, there would be conflicts between people who want to spend less and doctors with incentives to do more. Because so many people have supplemental insurance, however, there is little restraint on care from the patient side.

Table 2.5   Key characteristics of insurance policies

Dimension	Indemnity insurance	Managed care		
		PPO	IPA/Network HMO	Group/Staff HMO
Qualified providers	Almost all	Almost all (network)	Network	Network
Choice of providers	Patient	Patient	Gatekeeper (in network)	Gatekeeper (in network)
Payment of providers	Fee-for-service	Discounted FFS	Capitation	Salary
Cost sharing	Moderate	Low in network; High out of network	Low in network; High out of network	Low in network; High/all out of network
Roles of insurer	Pay bills	Pay bills; Form network	Pay bills; Form network; Monitor utilization	Provide care
Limits on utilization	Demand-side	Supply side (price)	Supply side (price, quantity)	Supple side (price, quantity)

Source: Cutler and Zeckhauser (2000).

review can be conducted on an individual basis, as in tissue review committees or on a statistical basis, by monitoring a physician or hospital's overall utilization. As figure 2.9 shows, managed indemnity insurance, though nonexistent in 1980, claimed a 41 percent share of private insurance coverage by 1992. The share has fallen to 22 percent today.

Preferred provider organizations (PPOs), a second type of managed care, form a network of providers, including physicians, hospitals, pharmaceutical companies, and others, and control costs by securing discounts from them. The quid pro quo for the discounted fee is that insured participants are steered to in-network providers. Out-of-network providers may get reduced coverage on a limited basis (with higher cost sharing, for example) or may not be covered at all. In 1991, the typical PPO had an in-network coinsurance rate of 10 percent and an out-of-network coinsurance rate of 20 percent. PPOs usually impose preauthorization requirements as well, though they are rarely especially strict. As figure 2.9 shows, PPO enrollment, zero in 1980, now makes up about one-quarter of the privately insured population.

Full integration creates the strongest link between insurance and provision. In the United States, these merged entities are called HMOs. There are two major types of HMOs. Within a group or staff HMO—the most common form, with Kaiser being the best-known example—physicians are paid a salary and work exclusively for the HMO. The HMO may have

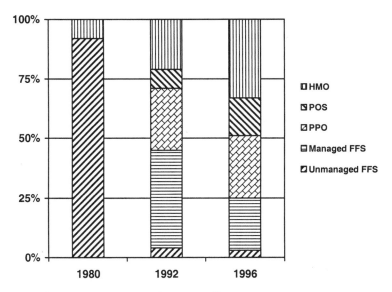

Fig. 2.9   Changes in private health plan enrollment

hospitals on contract or may operate its own hospital. Independent practice associations (IPAs), or network model HMOs, represent a more recent innovation in managed care.[9] These plans neither employ their own physicians nor run their own hospitals. Instead, they contract with providers in the community.

Health maintenance organizations employ a range of mechanisms to limit utilization. They reflect the traditional economic instruments of regulation, incentives, and selection of types. Health maintenance organizations frequently regulate physicians' practices, for example, limiting the referrals they can make or the tests they can order. In addition, there are financial incentives for physicians in HMOs to do less, as noted earlier. Moreover, HMOs monitor the services that physicians provide. They may reward parsimonious resource use directly with compensation, though more likely with perks or subsequent promotion. Extravagant users are kicked out of the network. Finally, because physicians differ substantially in their treatment philosophies, HMOs can select physicians whose natural inclination is toward conservative treatment.

In some HMOs, patients can go outside of the network and still receive some reimbursement. This is termed a point of service (POS) option. But reimbursement out-of-network is not as generous as reimbursement within. Use of nonnetwork services, for example, frequently requires a deductible followed by a 10 to 40 percent coinsurance payment.

9. Some IPAs are older, but that form gained popularity only recently.

The sweeping nature of insurer-provider interactions is indicated by figure 2.9 (see also Glied 2000). In 1980, over 90 percent of the privately insured population in the United States was covered by unmanaged indemnity insurance. By 1996, that share had shrunk to a mere 3 percent. Health maintenance organization enrollment of all forms (including POS enrollment) has increased from 8 percent of the population in 1980 (then predominantly group- or staff-model enrollment) to nearly half of the privately insured population today.

In exchange for tight access restrictions, most HMOs have very low patient cost sharing. A person might face a $10 copayment for seeing a network physician, compared to full price for the first dollar of care in some indemnity insurance plans.

2.4.3   The Impact of Nonfinancial Restrictions

Managed care clearly reduces utilization of some types of care. Managed care plans have a higher ratio of primary care physicians to specialists than do nonmanaged care plans (Glied 2000). In addition, nonnetwork providers are much less likely to be seen than are network providers. Perhaps most significantly, however, these requirements allow for substantially lower prices paid for medical care. Exact data on prices in different insurance arrangements is not known, but it is not uncommon to find discounts of 30 percent on physician and hospital care for insurance plans with tight networks. These price reductions are a major reason why managed care plans cost less than traditional indemnity insurance plans (Altman, Cutler, and Zeckhauser 2003).

Further, the evidence does not suggest large adverse effects of managed care on health outcomes. Some studies find that patients are worse off, some find that they are better off, and most find that they are about the same. Summary reviews of the literature suggest no outcome differences between managed care and traditional insurance policies (Miller and Luft 1997).

Even with this profile—cost savings and no adverse impact on health—managed care is not very popular. Utilization review is the aspect of medicine that physicians dislike the most. Doctors feel their professional integrity is challenged by these restrictions and have protested vehemently. Patients do not like managed care either, in large part because of the perception that managed care restricts the care they can receive. The widespread interest in a Patient's Bill of Rights is testament to this concern. As a result of physician and patient opposition, the extent of utilization review has changed over time. Where utilization review was common in the early 1990s, it is rarer now. Instead, managed care plans have substituted more financial incentives (such as capitation) to encourage physicians to provide less care.

2.4.4   Comparisons with Other Countries

The specific form of utilization review as we have described is most prevalent in the United States. But restrictions on utilization are widespread throughout the developed world. In most countries, utilization is restricted through overall limits on the availability of medical services. Canada, for example, imposes very tight controls on the number of hospitals that can acquire expensive new technologies. There is less technology than physicians would use by choice, so some rationing must occur. In practice, the rationing is done by physicians, who decide which patients most need access to the technologies.

The distinction between physician-driven rationing and insurer-driven rationing is fundamental in some ways but less important in others. Physicians are certainly happier with physician-driven rationing than with insurer-driven rationing, as they make the decisions in one case but have decisions imposed on them in the other. From the social perspective, however, both methods ration access to medical care. The empirical issue is whether that rationing works well and how much rationing is appropriate. International comparisons of medical care provided under different insurance arrangements should help to answer this question.

2.5   Conclusion

Because medical care systems are complex, they cannot be easily characterized. Still, some dimensions of organization are apparent. In this paper, we highlight three important domains of medical care: the rules about coverage, reimbursement between insurers and providers, and access to care.

While there is variability within the United States, we suggest the following simple summary. Coverage in the United States is spotty—quite good for the elderly, especially those with supplemental insurance, but not guaranteed for the nonelderly. Historically, reimbursement of providers was very generous, and access was open as well. Increasingly, though, the reimbursement and access routes are being restricted as insurers respond to moral hazard and the demand for cost containment.

The direction the medical system will go in the United States is not clear. Even in the past few years, reimbursement and access rules have changed, and coverage issues have dominated the public agenda. Changes along all three dimensions bear watching.

It is also important to extend this analysis to other countries. One of the central issues in all of health economics is determining which medical system is best. Only by characterizing existing systems and comparing outcomes across countries can we make progress in this effort.

References

Altman, Daniel, David Cutler, and Richard Zeckhauser. 2003. Patient mix, treatment intensity, and cost in competing health plans. *Journal of Health Economics* 22 (1): 23–45.

Baumol, William J. 1967. Macroeconomics of unbalanced growth: The anatomy of urban crises. *American Economic Review* 57 (3): 415–26.

Chernichovsky, Dov. 1995. Health system reforms in industrialized democracies: An emerging paradigm. *The Milbank Quarterly* 73 (3): 339–72.

Christensen, Sandra, and Judy Shinogle. 1997. Effects of supplemental coverage on use of services by Medicare enrollees. *Health Care Financing Review* 19 (1): 5–17.

Cutler, David. 2002a. Equality, efficiency, and market fundamentals: The dynamics of international medical care reform. *Journal of Economic Literature* 40 (3): 881–906.

———. 2002b. Public policy for health care. In *Handbook of public economics.* Vol. 4, ed. Alan Auerbach and Martin Feldstein, 2143–2243. Amsterdam: Elsevier.

Cutler, David, and Mark McClellan. 1998. What is technological change? In *Inquiries in the economics of aging,* ed. David Wise, 51–81. Chicago: University of Chicago Press.

Cutler, David, and Richard Zeckhauser. 2000. The anatomy of health insurance. In *Handbook of health economics.* Vol. IA, ed. Anthony Culyer and Joseph P. Newhouse, 563–643. Amsterdam: Elsevier.

DiMasi, Joseph A., Ronald W. Hansen, and Henry G. Grabowski. 2003. Cost of innovation in the pharmaceutical industry. *Journal of Health Economics* 22 (2): 151–85.

Enthoven, Alain C. 1993. The history and principles of managed competition. *Health Affairs* 12 (1): 24–48.

Evans, Robert G. 2002. Raising the money: Options, consequences, and objectives for financing health care in Canada. Commission on the Future of Health Care in Canada. Discussion Paper no. 27. Ottawa: Commission on the Future of Health Care in Canada.

Feldstein, Martin S. 1973. The welfare loss of excess health insurance. *Journal of Political Economy* 81 (2): 251–58.

Getzen, Thomas. 2000. Health care is an individual necessity and a national luxury: Applying multilevel decision models to the analysis of health care expenditures. *Journal of Health Economics* 19 (2): 259–70.

Glied, Sherry. 2000. Managed care. In *Handbook of health economics.* Vol. IA, ed. Anthony Culyer and Joseph P. Newhouse, 709–27. Amsterdam: Elsevier.

Gruber, Jonathan. 1994. The incidence of mandated maternity benefits. *American Economic Review* 84 (3): 622–41.

Hackbarth, Glenn M. 2003. Medicare cost-sharing and supplemental insurance. *Statement before the Subcommittee on Health, Committee on Ways and Means, U.S. House of Representatives.* 107th Cong., 2nd sess., May 1, 2003.

McClellan, Mark. 1997. Hospital reimbursement incentives: An empirical analysis. *Journal of Economic Management and Strategy* 6 (1): 91–128.

McGuire, Thomas. 2000. Physician agency. In *Handbook of health economics.* Vol. 1A, ed. Anthony Culyer and Joseph P. Newhouse. Amsterdam: Elsevier.

Miller, Robert H., and Harold S. Luft. 1997. Does managed care lead to better or worse quality of care? *Health Affairs* 16 (5): 7–25.

Newhouse, Joseph P. 1993. *Free for all: Lessons from the Rand Health Insurance Experiment.* Cambridge, MA: Harvard University Press.

Organization for Economic Cooperation and Development (OECD). 2002. *OECD health data.* CD-ROM.

Reinhardt, Uwe. 2004. The Swiss health system: Regulated competition without managed care. JAMA, 292 (10): 1227–31.

Summers, Lawrence. 1989. Some simple economics of mandated benefits. *American Economic Review* 79 (2): 177–83.

3

An International Look at the
Medical Care Financing Problem

David M. Cutler

Virtually all developed countries are worried about how to finance medical care. Medical costs are increasing more rapidly than tax revenues to pay for them, and populations are aging, each of which increases the burden on the public sector. In the United States, we speak of a *Medicare crisis* and a *Social Security crisis,* where the government will no longer be able to meet its health care bills. Other countries have an *aging crisis,* or an *old age insurance crisis.*

There is no doubt that medical care costs are certain to increase. But by how much? What is the magnitude of reform that is needed? Those are the questions I address in this paper.

To answer them, I develop a forecast model of medical spending in Organization for Economic Cooperation and Development (OECD) countries. The model uses as inputs current spending on medical care and the demographic mix of the population as it stands now and as it is expected to change. The model estimates the share of medical spending in gross domestic product (GDP) in the future. Because most countries pay for the bulk of medical services publicly, this forecast is closely related to the increase in the public-sector financing burden that can be expected.

The results yield several important conclusions. First, all OECD countries can expect an increase in the cost of medical care over time. On the basis of demographic change alone, the typical country can expect medical

David M. Cutler is the Otto Eckstein Professor of Applied Economics, Department of Economics and John F. Kennedy School of Government, and social sciences dean in the Faculty of Arts and Sciences, both at Harvard University, and a research associate of the National Bureau of Economic Research.

I am grateful to the National Institutes on Aging for research support, and to Seiritsu Ogura for comments on a previous draft.

care to increase by 2.2 percent of GDP in the next thirty years and by 3.6 percent of GDP in the next half century. Including continued technological innovation in medicine at the rate experienced in the past raises the projected increase in the next thirty years to 5.7 percent of GDP. Interestingly, the data suggest that the medical care problem is about equally split between the consequences of aging and the consequences of technological change in medical treatments.

The coming medical care burden differs substantially across countries. The countries that will be hardest hit by demographic change are Spain, Switzerland, the Czech Republic, Italy, and Greece. All of these countries have very low fertility rates and large projected increases in life expectancy. Demographic change will raise medical spending in these countries by 5 to 6 percent of GDP. Japan and the United States rank in the middle on this scale, ninth and twelfth, respectively, out of twenty-nine countries (expected increases of 4.4 and 3.7 percent). The least affected countries include Turkey, the United Kingdom, New Zealand, and Mexico, with an expected increase of 2 percent or less.

Accounting for technological change has a material impact on these rankings. Most importantly, it raises the financing burden in the United States. The United States spends more than other countries do on medical care and has the most technologically advanced medical system. Thus, if technology increases costs at the same rate everywhere, the United States will be particularly hard hit. Using historical growth rates of medical costs as a guide to the future, the projected increase in medical spending in the United States over the next thirty years is close to 10 percent. The increase in Japan will be over 6 percent of GDP.

These are sizeable estimates, although perhaps not cataclysmic. I show that affording such increases will require reductions in the growth of nonmedical consumption, but not absolute declines in the level of such spending.

This paper is structured as follows. Section 3.1 lays out the nature of the medical care problem and the structure of the simulation model. Section 3.2 describes the consequences of demographic change alone. Section 3.3 then adds in technological change in medical treatments. Section 3.4 discusses the implications for the affordability of medical care overall, and section 3.5 concludes.

3.1   Forecasting Medical Care Spending

The need to forecast medical spending is obvious. Medical care is 10 percent of GDP or more in most developed countries and is growing rapidly. Most of this medical care is paid for by the public sector (over 80 percent in most countries). Thus, public concern about rising costs is particularly high. But medical costs are a concern in the private sector as well. Increased medical spending involves painful adjustments as families shift their spending allocations among different goods and businesses pass on the costs of medical care to workers. None of this implies that medical spending increases are bad, but it indicates why we need to know what the medical burden will be.

Forecasting medical spending is simple in some ways and horribly complex in others. To understand the issues, I start with a truism: medical spending as a share of GDP is the division of per capita medical spending by per capita output. To forecast the share of GDP devoted to medical care, therefore, I forecast these two terms.

Start with medical spending. Per capita medical spending is the product of the number of people at each age times spending at that age, divided by the number of people in the country as a whole. Denoting age groups with the subscript a, this can be expressed as

$$(1) \qquad \text{Per capita medical spending} = \sum_a \text{Pop}_a \cdot \frac{\text{Spend}_a}{\text{Total Pop}}.$$

To forecast medical spending, therefore, we need projections of the population and spending at each age.

The United Nations publishes projections of population by age (United Nations Population Division 1998). The United Nations divides the population into people below age fifteen, people aged fifteen to sixty-four, and people over the age of sixty-five. I use these population projections at decadal intervals through 2050.

Forecasting spending in each age group is more difficult. Relative medical spending by age differs across countries, and the growth of overall spending differs across countries. Aging is more of a problem in countries where medical spending is more highly tilted to the aged and in countries where overall cost growth is more rapid. It is not clear what assumptions about spending growth are reasonable. For these simulations, I make relatively simple assumptions, based on data availability as much as economic theory.

The first assumption is about relative medical spending at each age. There is not a lot of data on relative medical spending by age in different countries, as the microdata that are needed for this analysis are not always available. For simplicity, I assume that the age distribution of medical spending is the same in all countries and is equal to the distribution in the United States. In the United States, the elderly spend 3 times what the adult population does on medical care, and the young spend 60 percent less than the adult population. As populations age, therefore, there will be a monotonic increase in spending.

Almost certainly, the elderly share in the United States is higher than in most other countries, as the technological intensity of the U.S. system is particularly brought to bear at older ages. If other countries keep spending for the elderly down in the future, this would blunt the impact of aging in those countries. Conversely, if spending on the elderly rises in other countries, to match the technological intensity of the United States, most other countries could face an even greater spending burden than my forecasts suggest.

I further assume that relative spending will remain the same at different ages in the future. In the United States, spending on the aged has increased more rapidly than spending on the nonaged, as technological change has tilted toward the elderly (Cutler and Meara 1998, 2001). In the absence of better information, however, there is little ability to forecast continued changes in this ratio.

The second assumption is about the impact of medical technology on costs. As the capabilities of medicine expand, what will happen to overall medical spending? It is clear that increases in the technical sophistication of medicine have been a fundamental factor in rising medical costs in the past, far surpassing the roles of increased income, more generous insurance, and an older population on medical costs (Newhouse 1992; Technical Review Panel on the Medicare Trustees' Reports 2000). The reason is clear—medical technology moved diseases from untreatable to treatable. For example, coronary bypass surgery replaced watchful waiting as a primary therapy for people with a heart attack in the 1980s and 1990s. Monitoring without intervention is cheap; bypass surgery is expensive. Hence, developing bypass surgery led to increased medical spending.

There is no indication that technological change is becoming less rapid. If anything, it is speeding up with the genomic revolution and advances in traditional therapies such as surgeries and diagnostic equipment (JAMA 2001). Thus, one might expect that medical spending will continue to increase.

But the translation between technological change and spending is more complex. Where lack of treatment was once the norm, today most conditions are treated in some fashion. As a result, in the future, new treatments will increasingly substitute for older ones. If the newer procedures are cheaper than the older procedures they replace, the use of new procedures may not lead to as rapid cost increase. To follow the heart attack example, angioplasty recently joined bypass surgery as a recognized therapy for heart attacks. Some angioplasties substitute for bypass surgery. Because angioplasty is cheaper than bypass surgery, the use of this technology saves money in some cases (Cutler and Huckman 2003).[1]

The ultimate impact of technological change on medical spending depends on the relative importance of these *treatment expansion* and *treatment substitution* effects. It will not necessarily be the case that medical

---

1. In total, though, angioplasty led to more spending, as it substituted for medical management in many people.

spending continues to rise as medicine becomes more technologically sophisticated.

Most forecasts suggest that technological change will increase to increase spending, however. A consensus estimate is that medical spending will increase 1 percent more rapidly than GDP in the next few decades (Medicare Technical Advisory Panel 2000). I use this estimate in my simulations.

Translating this estimate internationally requires additional assumptions. Medical spending is lower in other countries than in the United States. If medical costs increase 1 percent more rapidly than GDP everywhere, the dollar increase will be smaller abroad than in the United States. Thus, there will be a growing divergence between medical costs in different countries. Is this possible? In principle, yes. Even though medical technology has expanded in all countries over the past half century, the increase has been far larger in the United States than elsewhere, as figure 3.1 shows. The United States has thus become even more of an outlier than it was already. For lack of a better alternative, I assume this will continue in the future. One issue for future exploration is the implications of assuming some convergence in spending.

In addition to forecasting medical spending, we need to forecast per capita income. We can express per capita income using a formula similar to equation (1):

$$(2) \qquad \text{Per capita income} = \sum\nolimits_{a} \text{Workers}_{a} \cdot \frac{\text{Output}_{a}}{\text{Total Pop}}$$

A complete projection of equation (2) would forecast the number of workers at each age along with output of those workers. No projections that detailed are available. I thus make simpler assumptions. I assume that

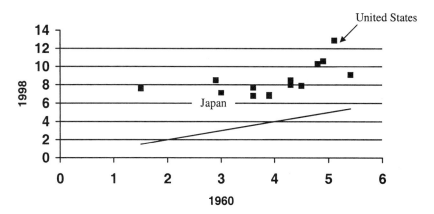

Fig. 3.1   Medical spending as a share of GDP
Source: OECD (2002).

labor force participation is confined to the fifteen- to sixty-four-year-old population and that labor force participation in that group remains constant. Further, I assume that output for all workers rises at the same rate. For these simulations, the rate of increase is immaterial; the key is the differential between health care cost growth and output growth. As discussed previously, I assume this differential is 1 percent.

Effectively, these assumptions mean that changes in output are driven entirely by changes in share of the population that is working age. As a first-pass simulation model, this does not seem unreasonable.

3.2   Demographics and Medical Spending

To understand the medical care problem, I start with some basic demographic information across countries. The share of the population that is elderly varies greatly across the developed world. Figure 3.2 shows this variation. Thirteen percent of the OECD as a whole is over the age of sixty-five. Italy has the largest elderly share, at 18 percent, with Greece, Sweden, Japan, and Spain also being very high. For all of the worries about aging in the United States, the United States population is not very elderly (by developed country standards); 12 percent of the U.S. population is over age sixty-five.

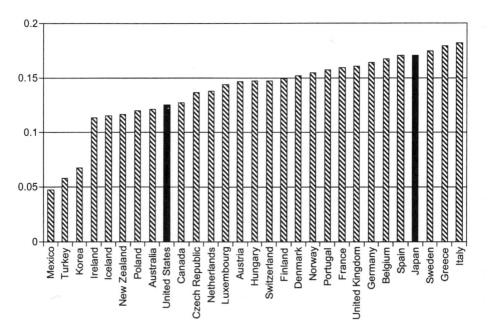

Fig. 3.2   Elderly share of the population, 2000
Source: United Nations Population Division (1998).

The major driver of aging is fertility. Most countries have fertility rates that are below replacement levels (about 2.1 births per woman). Italy, for example, has a birth rate of 1.2 babies per woman, and Japan is 1.4. Birth rates this low inevitably imply an aging population. Added to the low fertility rate are increases in longevity at older ages. In the United States, the average forty-five-year-old lives nearly five years longer now than in 1950. Finally, immigration rates are low in most OECD countries. Immigration from poor to rich countries does not change the world's share of elderly people, but it does change the share in any particular country. A country with low net immigration will be increasingly older.

The net impact of these demographic changes is a projection of substantial increases in the elderly population over time. Figure 3.3 shows the forecast increase in the elderly share between 2000 and 2050. The expected increase is large in all countries. The highest rates of increase are forecast in Spain, the Czech Republic, Korea, and Italy. These countries will see increases in the elderly population of over 15 percentage points if nothing else intervenes. The average OECD country will experience an increase of 11 percentage points, and even countries at the very low end (the United

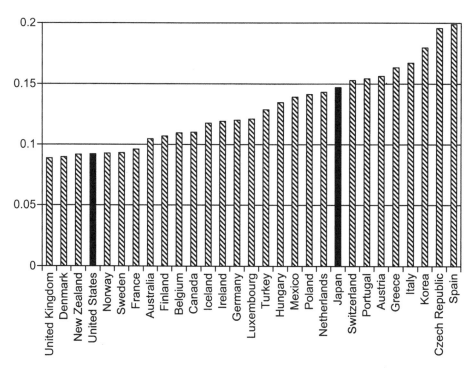

Fig. 3.3   Forecast change in elderly share of the population, 2000–2050
Source: United Nations Population Division (1998).

Kingdom and the United States, for example) will have increases of 9 percentage points.

One sunny side of aging is fewer children, and thus more workers among the nonelderly population (Cutler et al. 1990). This is not enough to overwhelm the effect of increased elderly shares on medical spending, however. To examine the effect of demographic changes on the medical system, I simulate spending assuming no change in per person medical care utilization in the next half century. While this is obviously unrealistic, it provides a benchmark to assess the importance of demographic changes.

The results of the simulation are shown in figure 3.4. Note the mean first. In the average OECD country, demographic change alone will increase medical spending as a share of GDP by 3.6 percentage points in the next half century. This is a large increase, but perhaps not insurmountable. Most of this increase is in the next thirty years, where the increase will average 2.2 percentage points. The retirement of the baby boom generation will lead the procession into an era of more rapidly rising medical costs.

The ranking of countries is similar in figure 3.4 as in figure 3.3, but the two are not exactly the same. The countries with the biggest increase are

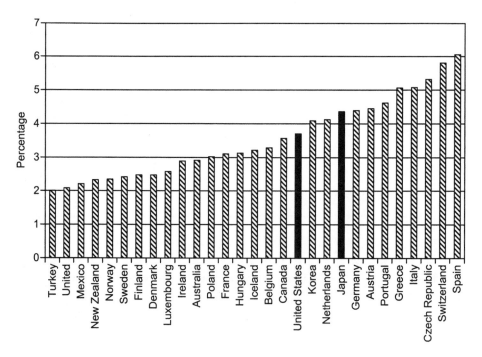

Fig. 3.4   Forecast change in medical care share of GDP, demographic change only, 2000–2050

Source: Author's calculations.

Spain, Switzerland, the Czech Republic, Italy, and Greece. All of these countries will have medical spending increases of over 5 percent of GDP, based on demographic change alone. The United States is higher ranked in figure 3.4 than in figure 3.3. Because medical spending in the United States is so high, the same amount of demographic change has a larger impact on per capita spending than it does elsewhere. The forecast increase in the United States is 3.7 percentage points. In Japan, the forecast increase is 4.4 percentage points.

At the bottom of the list are Turkey and the United Kingdom. The comparatively low rate of aging in the United Kingdom combined with a low level of medical spending blunts the impact of demographic change on medical costs. But even in the United Kingdom, demographic change will lead to a 2 percent increase in the share of medical care in GDP. It is clear that demographic change will present a financing hurdle for all developed countries.

3.3   Including Technological Change

A more complete simulation includes the effects of technological change as well as population aging. As noted previously, I assume that medical costs increase at all ages by 1 percent per year above the rate of per capita GDP growth. Forecast out forever, this is clearly unrealistic; it implies that medical care would ultimately account for all of GDP. Thus, some limit on the time period for forecasting is needed.

To illustrate the importance of technical change, I consider a more limited simulation of medical spending in the next thirty years, to 2030. A steady increase in costs over the next three decades is (perhaps) more realistic than assuming the same increase over the next fifty years.

Figure 3.5 shows the resulting estimates of the change in medical spending relative to GDP. Even in the next thirty years, the simulation implies large increases in medical spending. In the average OECD country, the increase in GDP share is 5.7 percentage points. That is greater than the 2.2 percentage points attributable to demographic change in this time period, although the additional part due to technical change (3.5 percentage points) is not much larger than the demographic component.

Most notable in figure 3.5 are the enormously high increases projected in Switzerland and the United States. Medical spending in each of those countries is projected to increase by over 9 percent, to levels of about 25 percent of GDP. The medical cost problem is more severe in these countries because medical spending in those countries is so high. Hence, continued increases in costs result in disproportionately large increases in the medical sector. In Japan, the increase in the medical care burden is between 6 and 7 percent.

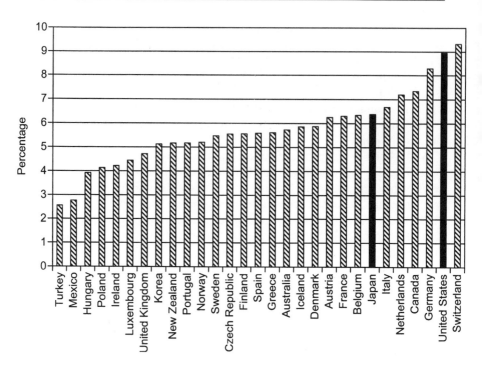

Fig. 3.5   Forecast change in medical care share of GDP, demographic and health cost changes, 2000–2030

Source: Author's calculations.

3.4   Is Such Spending Sustainable?

The increase in medical spending will have several implications for the economy. The first issue is whether such cost increases are good or harmful. Would society be harmed by spending so much on medical care?

Clearly, people can have different views about this. My belief is that increases in spending of this magnitude are affordable. Recall that economic growth is forecast to be relatively robust over the next half century. Hence, the size of the economic pie is expanding. The increase in medical care relative to GDP implies that the medical care slice of the pie is getting bigger. But the medical slice is not growing more rapidly than the pie itself. Even in these simulations, nonmedical consumption is still increasing over time.

Figure 3.6 shows this result analytically. I simulate nonmedical consumption assuming GDP increases by 2 percent annually and the differential between medical and nonmedical consumption is either 0 percent, 1 percent, or 2 percent annually. In ease case, nonmedical consumption rises from 2000 through 2050. The increase is significantly larger in the case of no excess medical care cost growth (nearly 70 percent larger), but consumption increases in all scenarios. Inherently, continued medical care

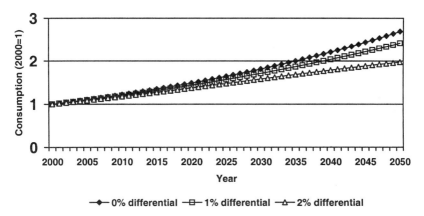

Fig. 3.6   Effect of increased medical costs on nonmedical consumption
Source: Author's calculations.

cost growth involves is less rapid increase in nonmedical consumption, but not an absolute decline. That does not seem implausible.

The statement that we *can* afford to spend more on medical care does not mean that we *should* do so. Most Americans could afford a large screen TV, but not everyone chooses to do so. Other goods and services are important as well. We thus need to evaluate whether money spent on medical care is worth the expense.

This question cannot be answered using the simulations here. These simulations show what we will pay for medical advance, but not what we will get for it. To examine what we will get in return, we need to value the health improvements that result from medicine.

I have done this in other work (Cutler 2003). My conclusion is that medical spending is almost certainly worth the cost. We spend more on medical care, but we get even more in return. As an example, consider treatment changes in cardiovascular disease. As noted previously, the average forty-five-year-old is expected to live another five years now compared to 1950. Other work that I have done suggests that about three years of this improvement comes from medical advance in the treatment of coronary heart disease. These advances are of several forms: intensive medical care that saves the lives of people having a heart attack or other acute incident (bypass surgery, angioplasty, thrombolytic drugs, beta-blockers, cardiac catheterization, and so on) and medications taken on a regular basis that prevent the incidence of acute events or lessen their long-term consequences (antihypertensive medications, cholesterol lowering drugs, and the like). Together with public health improvements such as reduced smoking and lower fat diets, these changes have led to significant increases in longevity.

Those three years of life came at a cost, however. I estimate that the average forty-five-year-old today will spend $30,000 more on cardiovascular disease over his remaining life than the equivalent person would have in 1950.

Hence, the tradeoff: $30,000 of spending for a three additional years of life. Is it worth it? Almost any sensible value for a year of life suggests that this is a good investment. A common metric in economics is that a year of life is worth about $100,000. In present value, therefore, the three years of additional life from medical advances in the treatment of cardiovascular disease is worth about $120,000 per person. This is four times the additional cost. The implication of this calculation is that medical spending is not bad. It is burdensome, to be sure, but not harmful overall.

3.5   Summary and Implications

The central issue in medical care is not whether we can afford to spend more on medicine or whether it is a good idea to do so, but how we should pay for it. There are three possible ways to pay for the coming medical care burden. The optimal tradeoff between them likely differs from country to country. To illustrate the issues involved, I focus on the possibilities in the United States.

The first option is to increase revenues from people currently alive to pay for medical care in the future. Money put aside now and saved until later can significantly reduce the burden of spending down the road. The increase in funds today can be either additional taxes, or (forced) private savings; economically, they are the same.

The preceding simulations give some guide as to what tax increase is necessary. If the government were to pay for all of the forecast increase, government spending in the United States would rise by about 9 percent of GDP in the coming three decades. If enacted immediately, a tax increase of a few percent of GDP would be needed to cover the deficit. Such a tax increase is large but not unheard of.

A second method is to wait until the future and then tax working generations to pay for the increased medical care burden that future elderly will incur. The simulations again show the size of the tax increase ultimately needed—9 percent of GDP. That is a hefty amount. The efficiency consequences of such a tax would be a major issue.

The third solution is to make people pay more for medical care when they use services, especially at older ages. Many elderly in the United States face no cost sharing when using services. While Medicare requires such costs, a large number of the elderly purchase supplemental insurance or have such insurance from a former employer to offset the required cost sharing (Cutler and Wise, chap. 2 in this volume). As a result, care at the time of use is generally costless, and like all free services is overused. Making people pay more at the time of use is a viable option, although one would need to account for the welfare loss from increased risk bearing along with the gains from reduced moral hazard. A system with appropriate cost sharing would cost less than the current one.

Evaluating these different options is beyond the scope of this paper. With the near certainty of increases in medical costs in the next few decades, however, governments will increasingly have to face the issue of paying for an older population that uses increasingly intensive, and expensive, medical services.

References

Cutler, David M. 2003. *Your money or your life.* New York: Oxford University Press.
Cutler, David M., and Robert Huckman. 2003. Technological development and medical productivity: The diffusion of angioplasty in New York State. *Journal of Health Economics* 22 (2): 187–217.
Cutler, David M., and Ellen Meara. 1998. The medical costs of the young and old: A forty-year perspective. In *Frontiers in the economics of aging,* ed. David Wise, 215–42. Chicago: University of Chicago Press.
———. 2001. The concentration of medical spending: An update. In *Themes in the economics of aging,* ed. David Wise, 217–34. Chicago: University of Chicago Press.
Cutler, David M., James Poterba, Louise Sheiner, and Lawrence Summers. 1990. An aging society: Opportunity or challenge? *Brookings Papers on Economic Activity,* Issue no. 1:1–56. Washington, DC: Brookings Institution.
Journal of the American Medical Association (JAMA). 2001. Thematic issue on "Forecasting Opportunities in Medical Research." 285 (5): 499–686.
Newhouse, Joseph. 1992. Medical care costs: How much welfare loss? *Journal of Economic Perspectives* 6 (3): 13–29.
Organization for Economic Cooperation and Development (OECD). *OECD health data, 2002.* Paris: OECD.
Technical Review Panel on the Medicare Trustees' Reports. 2000. *Review of assumptions and methods of the Medicare trustees' financial projections.* Washington, DC: Center for Medicare and Medicaid Services.
United Nations Population Division. 1998. *World population prospects.* New York: United Nations.

Removing the Instability and Inequity in the Japanese Health Insurance System

Seiritsu Ogura, Tamotsu Kadoda, and
Makoto Kawamura

4.1 Introduction

Japan's current public medical insurance can be compared to an unstable two-story building whose second floor is becoming heavier each day while its first floor is losing strength. There are three pillars in the first floor that support the weight of the whole building. The first of the three consists of insurance programs that cover the health care costs of employees and their dependents. These include health insurance managed by associations (HIMAs), most of which are firm-specific; health insurance managed by government (HIMG), which is the largest insurance program in Japan; and health insurance for government employees (HIGEs), organized separately for various national government agencies and for municipal government employees. These programs provide uniform medical insurance benefits but collect different premiums from their employees as fixed proportions of their wages or salaries. These premium rates are set individually for each program. Because they collect far more revenue than is necessary to pay for their own benefits, they provide the most important support for the health care costs of the elderly.

Seiritsu Ogura is a professor of economics at Hosei University and director general of the Hosei Institute on Aging. Tamotsu Kadoda is an assistant professor of economics at Daito Bunka University. Makoto Kawamura is a professor of economics at Hosei University.

This paper closely follows Chapter 1 of *Iryo Seido Kaikaku,* edited by Seiritsu Ogura and David Wise, published by Nihon Keizai Shimbun in 2002 by the same authors. The original title of Chapter 1 is "Reengineering Japanese Health Insurance System." The second part of the paper was rewritten to reflect the subsequent changes in the health insurance law for the elderly. We would like to express our appreciation for the Project on Intergenerational Equity (PIE) of the Economic Research Institute of Hitotsubashi University, the Toyota Foundation and the Ministry of Education and Science and Technology for a special grant to Hosei University for financial support. We thank Ms. Megumi Fukuda for her help in the translation.

The second pillar consists of the group of national health insurance programs (NHIs), consisting mainly of more than 3,200 municipal programs. They provide health insurance for self-employed workers, the retired, and others who are not covered by employees' programs. They are financially very weak, and their premium revenues amount to only 60 percent of the benefits for these people. They receive generous subsidies from the national and local governments and do not contribute at all to pay for the health care costs of the elderly.

The third pillar consists of all the subsidies from the national and municipal governments. Particularly important are those from the national government, which has been subsidizing half of the NHI's benefits and half of the elderly's health care charges levied on NHIs. The government also subsidizes 13 percent of the expense of the benefits for the HIMG and some of the elderly's health care charges.

The second floor of our building consists of the health care insurance for the elderly, which provides medical care benefits to those over age seventy for very little cost.[1] The insurance program for the elderly does not collect premiums on its own, and the benefits are paid by collecting charges from other primary public insurance programs. Thus, most of the health care costs of the elderly have been shifted to those in the first floor, most notably to the employee health insurance programs and the national government. Under the current system, 70 percent of the health care costs of the elderly (net of their small out-of-pocket costs) are charged to the insurance programs in the first floor, with each insurance program contributing an amount in proportion to the number of its insured individuals and the average health care cost of elderly in the system.[2] Of the remaining 30 percent, the national government contributes 20 percent, and the local governments contribute 10 percent. Moreover, as we have already mentioned, the national government provides very substantial subsidies to HIMG and NHIs to help them pay their contributions to the health insurance for the elderly.

This two-story structure has become very unstable, particularly in the last few years, for two reasons, one cyclical and the other structural. The first reason is the prolonged economic slump Japan has been experiencing for almost a decade now. It has had a large negative effect on the revenues of all the insurance programs in the first floor. The ones hit hardest by the slump are those of the employees; their wage rates and the size of the employment have shown little, if any, growth. The second reason is structural: there has been a rapid increase in the number of individuals who are reach-

1. To be exact, the scheme is for those seventy years of age and over and their families and those sixty-five years of age and over who are bedridden.
2. The actual computation of charges for individual insurance programs is slightly more complicated: it multiplies the amount by the ratio of the average health care cost of the elderly in the program to the national average figure.

ing age seventy and moving from the first floor to the second. With each person moving from the first floor to the second, a very large weight is added to the second floor. The government has tried to control the cost of health care for the elderly through various measures, but the effects seem to last for a relatively short period of time, and soon the medical costs of the elderly have started to increase again.

Given the current two-story system, the bulk of the increase in health care costs of the elderly has been absorbed by increases in employee insurance premiums and budget deficits. Furthermore, employees' out-of-pocket costs have been raised in steps, from 10 percent to 20 percent in 1997, and from 20 percent to 30 percent in 2003 for employees, and from 20 percent to 30 percent for their dependents. These changes have left employees on par with individuals covered by NHIs as far as the out-of-pocket costs are concerned, while making them pay almost twice as much on average in premiums. Similarly, the government has to deal with the swelling need for subsidies and the deepening of the budget deficit amidst a rapid decline in tax revenues.

In the next twenty-five years, Japan's population will age at a faster rate as the baby boomers move beyond age sixty-five. Under the current medical insurance system, the imbalance between benefits and costs will continue to grow over time. With this imbalance, moral hazard and waste will grow in the health care sector, and inequity will intensify the social conflict among generations. These developments may lead to a fundamental reform in Japan's health insurance system.

Our analyses in this paper address the two major weaknesses in our current health insurance system. The first is the insurance of the elderly, or the second floor of our insurance system. We will examine the consequences of the special treatment of the elderly, and we will assert it is difficult to continue to support them. The second weakness is the NHI system. We should remind everyone that the health insurance for the elderly was born out of the huge deficits of the NHI programs and the national government in 1984. Moreover, the national government has been subsidizing 50 percent of the expenses of the municipal NHI programs for over thirty years. This figure signifies that the NHI system has failed to function as an independent insurance system for the working generations. Thus, strengthening the financial base of the NHI as well as improving health insurance for the elderly may improve Japan's medical insurance system.

The remainder of this paper is constructed as follows. In section 4.2, we will show that the burden of medical expense is placed heavily on the employees and the government. In section 4.3, we will explain a set of procedures for simulating the benefits and burdens of medical services, with the household as a unit of analysis. In section 4.4, we will verify the validity of our simulation procedures by comparing the medical expenses and the number of patients derived from our baseline simulation with that of published statistics and discuss the results of the simulation. Last, section 4.5 will provide a conclusion and discuss the implications of our work.

4.2   Japan's Medical Care Financing

4.2.1   National Medical Expenditure and Payment Funds

We will first examine the medical expenditures and financial resources of each type of insurance system using the national medical expenditures of fiscal year 1996. For the fiscal year, national medical expenditures were 28.5 trillion yen, of which 1.3 trillion yen was paid directly by the government (as, for example, medical aid to low income families or by other agents). This leaves 27.2 trillion yen of medical expenditures covered by public health insurance. The breakdown of this figure is as follows: 14.5 trillion yen were paid as health insurance benefits for the nonelderly individuals, 9.3 trillion yen as the health insurance benefits for the elderly, and only 3.4 trillion yen were paid by individuals (including the elderly) as their out-of-pocket costs. The government and the health insurance system altogether spent approximately 25 trillion yen. Premiums collected by the insurance programs totaled 16 trillion yen, and subsidies from national and local government totaled 9.7 trillion yen.

We use those figures to calculate the average medical expenditure and insurance premiums per household. First, we divide the total medical expense by the number of households to obtain the average medical expenditure per household: 700,000 yen per year. As shown in table 4.1, the breakdown of the source of payment is as follows: 101,000 yen from the public funds, 516,000 yen from the insurance, and 83,000 yen from the household members themselves. The expense paid by the patients themselves refers to the amount actually paid at the medical institutions—this has an immediate effect on the household budget. The expense paid from public funds and from insurance do not directly strain the household budget but eventually affects it in the form of premiums and taxes. Thus, it is important to illustrate the ways in which the premiums and taxes burden the household.

Table 4.1 shows the results of such analysis. The numbers on the left column represent the amount spent on medical services per household. On the right are their estimated sources, categorized into three groups: premiums, taxes, and budget deficit. First, we obtain the amount of premiums paid per household by dividing the total sum of premiums by the number of households, which equals 392,000 yen.

Next, we estimated how much of the general fiscal revenue from various taxes and public bonds has been allotted to finance medical expenses. The tax revenue allotted is estimated to be 9.1 trillion yen—this figure is obtained by adding all the subsidies provided for the benefits of health insur-

Table 4.1   Sources and instruments of medical cost (NHCE) payments (in thousands of yen per household)

	Amount
Sources	
Health insurance programs	516
Government subsidies	101
Out-of-pocket costs	83
All sources	700
Financial instruments	
Insurance premiums	392
All taxes	147
Income tax	57
Corporate tax	40
Consumption tax	18
Other taxes	32
Fiscal deficit	77
Error	1
Out-of-pocket expenses	83
All instruments	700

ance and the charges for the health care for the elderly, paid from the general tax revenue. The estimated figure was computed by the following procedures:

1. The general account revenue from taxes for fiscal year 1996 reached 51.3 trillion yen, while revenue from public bonds was approximately 26 trillion yen. The revenue from taxes will be deemed to have been 49.5 trillion yen (the revenue from the gasoline excise tax, which would be allotted to finance road maintenance, has been subtracted), with the following breakdown: 19 trillion yen as income tax, 13.5 trillion yen as corporate tax, 6 trillion yen as consumption tax, and 8 trillion yen from other taxes.

2. Because the sum of general revenues from taxes and public bonds was 75.5 trillion yen, the public subsidies for health insurance programs amount to approximately 12 percent of these revenues.

3. We multiply this percentage by the revenues from each tax and public bond per household and obtain 57,000 yen as income tax, 40,000 yen as corporate tax, 18,000 yen as consumption tax, and 32,000 yen for other taxes, and 77,000 yen for public bonds. Per household, the subsidies to the health insurance programs were financed with 147,000 yen in taxes and 77,000 yen in bonds, respectively.

Thus, roughly speaking, the 700,000 yen health care costs per household are borne as follows: 392,000 yen as premiums, 147,000 yen as taxes, 77,000 yen as budget deficit and 83,000 yen as out-of-pocket costs. Or, in proportions, the health care cost is financed 56 percent by premiums, 21 percent by taxes, 11 percent by public bonds or budget deficit, and 12 percent from

Table 4.2   **Sources and instruments of medical cost (NHCE) payments (in thousands of yen per household)**

	Amount
Sources	
Health insurance programs	415
Government subsidies	82
Out-of-pocket costs	67
All sources	564
Financial instruments	
Insurance premium	316
All taxes	118
Income tax	46
Corporate tax	32
Consumption tax	14
Other taxes	25
Fiscal deficit	62
Error	1
Out-of-pocket expenses	67
All instruments	564

Notes: Figures exclude cost of dental care. Medical costs equal national medical expenditures minus the costs of dental care and pharmaceuticals dispensed to patients.

out-of-pocket expenses. It must be noted that each year a very significant proportion of health care costs, almost equal to the out-of-pocket costs, is financed with public bonds to be paid by future generations.

In this paper, we conduct various microsimulation[3] analyses of the benefits and burdens of health care costs, using *medical costs,* which equals national medical expenditures minus the costs of dental care and pharmaceuticals dispensed to patients. First, we calculate the expenditures and burdens of medical costs borne by each household as our reference case. According to the national medical expenditures for fiscal year 1996, medical costs accounted for 80 percent of national medical expenditures. Thus, the sources of payments for medical costs were calculated by multiplying this percentage (80 percent) by the numbers listed in table 4.1. As shown in table 4.2, the results are 564,000 yen for medical cost, and the same amount was paid by each household. The breakdown of the cost is as follows: 67,000 yen as out-of-pocket costs, 316,000 yen as premiums, and 118,000 yen as taxes. The tax burden can be further classified into income tax (46,000 yen), corporate tax (32,000 yen), and consumption tax (14,000 yen).

4.2.2   Concentration of Burden on Employees and the National Treasury to Finance the Insurance Scheme for the Elderly

The current insurance scheme for the elderly redistributes most of their medical costs to the government and employees. Take, as an example, the

---

3. For example, Harding (1996) is a collection paper of microsimulation.

Table 4.3   Changes in instruments in aged households by switching to Health Insurance for the Aged Health Insurance System in 1996 (in thousands of yen)

	NHI	HIMA and HIGE	HIMG	HIE	Changes
Insurance premiums	525	1,050	914	759	104
NHI	525	0	0	171	−197
HIMA and HIGE	0	1,050	0	341	236
HIMG	0	0	914	247	64
Government subsidies	525	0	137	666	271
National government subsidy	525	0	137	516	121
Other public subsidy	0	0	0	150	150
Out-of-pocket	450	450	450	75	−375
Total	1,500	1,500	1,500	1,500	0

Notes: HIMG = Health Insurance Managed by Government; HIMA and HIGE = Health Insurance Managed by Association and Health Insurance for Government Employees; NHI = National Health Insurance and other health insurances; HIE = Health Insurance for the Elderly.

hypothetical case of a couple, both sixty-nine years old, who receive a pension as their sole income. They are insured by their municipal national health insurance program and spend 1,500,000 yen in health care costs per year. The cost represents the average health care costs for an elderly couple (hospitalization and outpatient treatments) for fiscal 1995. The figures listed under the column "NHI" in table 4.3 show who bears the burden and by how much. The couple paid 450,000 yen, or 30 percent of the expense, as out-of-pocket payments to providers. The national health insurance and the government split the rest of the expense, worth 1,050,000 yen, each paying 525,000 yen.

Now we compare this with the following year when the couple turns seventy, making them eligible for the health insurance for the elderly. We assume that their medical costs remain at 1,500,000 yen per year. Note that there was not a single, fixed out-of-pocket rate for the elderly. But according to the national medical expenditure for the fiscal 1996, the average medical expense paid by the elderly themselves was around 5 percent, which is the ratio we have used in the table. As shown in the column labeled "HIE" in table 4.3, 30 percent of the cost will be paid by public funds (20 percent from national fund, 5 percent from prefectural fund, and 5 percent from municipal fund). This leaves 65 percent of the medical costs for the elderly couple, which will be charged to HIMA, HIMG, HIGE, and NHIs. Each insurance system contributes an amount equal to its proportion of the total number of participants (HIMA: 30 percent, HIMG and HIGE: 35 percent, and NHI: 35 percent). The HIMG and NHI receive subsidies from the national government for their contributions, equaling 16.4 percent and 50 percent, respectively.

The key factor that determines the changes in the burden of medical costs when the couple turns seventy is the type of insurance program they were enrolled in at age sixty-nine. Table 4.3 takes this into consideration and explores the cases in which the couple subscribes to NHI, HIMG, and HIMA and HIGE. We estimated the possibilities of the couple being subscribed to each insurance system at age sixty-nine as follows: 70 percent for the national health insurance, 20 percent for HIMG, and 10 percent for HIMA and HIGE. The figures in the last column illustrate the expected value of the changes. For every new couple becoming eligible for HIE

1. out-of-pocket costs are reduced by 375,000 yen;
2. the costs to NHI are reduced by 200,000 yen;
3. the costs to the public sector are increased by 270,000 yen; and
4. the costs to HIMA and HIGE will be increased by 240,000 yen, while

the costs to HIMA will be increased by 60,000 yen.

As mentioned in section 4.2.1, as a result of the revision to the Health Insurance Law, starting April 2003 the elderly are responsible for 10 percent of their medical expense. Our table 4.4 shows the results of this revision. If an elderly couple were responsible for 10 percent of their own medical expenses, for every new couple becoming eligible for the elderly benefits

1. the reduction in the out-of-pocket costs will be 300,000 yen;
2. the reduction in the national health insurance cost will be 210,000 yen;
3. the increase in the cost of the public sector will be 257,000 yen; and
4. the increase in the costs of HIMA and HIGE will be 210,000 yen and 43,000 yen, respectively.

These changes are not insignificant, given that an average of over 1.3 million people have reached the age of seventy each year during the last few

Table 4.4   Changes in payment sources for a new elderly health insurance system in 2002

Sources	NHI	HIMA and HIGE	HIMG	HIE	Changes
Out-of-pocket	450	450	450	150	−3,000
National government subsidy	525	0	137	502	1,070
Other public subsidy	0	0	0	150	1,500
NHI	525	0	0	158	−2,100
HIMA and HIGE	0	1,050	0	315	2,100
HIMG	0	0	914	226	430
Total	1,500	1,500	1,500	1,500	0

Note: See notes to table 4.3 for acronym explanations. The 2002 new health insurance law required 10 percent out-of-pocket costs, raising the copayment rate to 10 percent for the aged (more than sixty-five years).

years. Prior to the reforms implemented in April 2003, this translated into an annual increase of 195 billion yen in medical expenses for the employee health insurance and an annual increase of 178 billion yen for the public sector. On the other hand, the cost imposed on national health insurance decreased by 130 billion yen every year, and the individual payments decreased by over 195 billion yen every year. After April 2003, medical expenses for the employee health insurance will increase annually by 164 billion yen, and the public sector will have to bear an increase of 167 billion yen. The cost imposed on the national health insurance will decrease by 137 billion yen every year, and the individual payments will decrease by 195 billion yen every year. When people shift to the insurance scheme for the elderly, the burden shouldered by the employee health insurance and the public sector will decrease somewhat, and the decrease in individual payments will be kept small.

We must emphasize, moreover, that the shifts in financing burden are not temporary and will last for the rest of the elderly couple's life. If we assume that an individual reaching age seventy has ten more years to live on average, the current insurance system will shift a burden close to 4 trillion yen each year from the national health insurance and the elderly themselves to the employee health insurance and private sector. Even if the elderly were to pay 10 percent of their medical costs, it makes little difference. Given that the aging of the population will continue at least for another twenty years, the size of this transfer will easily double, amplifying the adverse effects on individuals' incentive to work and companies' incentive to hire.

There are grave problems in the current health insurance system. One is the fact that so much of the burden is shifted to the employee health insurance and the national treasury. Another is the fact that the percentage of individual payments drops dramatically after one turns age seventy. Generally speaking, Japanese health care professionals are very critical of any attempt to increase out-of-pocket costs. They are especially opposed to raising those of the elderly, fearing it would prevent poor elderly from receiving necessary medical services. The issue, however, is whether anyone who reaches age seventy should be exempt from paying out-of-pocket costs. Or why should we insist on making someone who is poor and very sick pay 30 percent of his or her medical costs because he or she is young? Younger individuals would also be discouraged from receiving needed medical care. The authors doubt that age alone is a clear guide for solving these issues. It has been shown that the increase in the number of elderly aged seventy years and older increases the burden on employees and the national treasury. In other words, the current insurance scheme may stymie the fair allotment of the burden between the elderly generations and the working generations. If we reform the insurance scheme, to what extent have we increased the fairness in the distribution of benefits and burdens of medical expenses per household? We used the following simulation to address this question.

4.3   Overview of the Microsimulation Model

In analyzing health care financing issues, it is not sufficient to have accurate information on total health care costs. A good framework for analyzing these issues should include information on the joint distributions of health care costs and such key socioeconomic indicators as age, income, and consumption. Ideally, such information should come directly from individual households in the real world, but because such a perfect household data set is not yet available for Japan, we have decided to construct our own microsimulation model of health care costs. This model consists of a large number of hypothetical households randomly created according to the known marginal distributions of key socioeconomic variables, together with a number of rules regarding their health care service demand functions. The model provides information on the changes in the costs and benefits of health as the parameters of the health care financing system are changed. Health care utilization by individual households can then be aggregated by household types.

First, we have to obtain data on the benefits and costs of medical services at individual household levels. For this purpose, the best public data set available for Japan is the *Comprehensive Survey of the Living Conditions of People on Health and Welfare* (Comprehensive Survey on Health and Welfare [CSHW]; Ministry of Health and Welfare 1997a). Extensive information has been collected in this survey regarding the socioeconomic characteristics of household members. The survey also gathers information on illnesses, symptoms, and treatments among household members. For our purposes, however, there are several serious shortcomings in this survey:

1. The survey respondents tend to underreport the use of medical resources.

2. The survey lacks annual medical expense data.

3. The aggregate totals for socioeconomic variables using the specified scales differ substantially from census data, system of national accounts (SNA) statistics, and social insurance statistics, as the surveyed households have not been randomly selected.

Details on how we addressed the preceding issues appear in the appendix.

Before moving on to the analyses of health care financing reforms, we will examine the quality of the information generated by our microsimulation model. We compare them to those of the national medical expenditures of 1996, using inpatient medical expenses, inpatient medical expenses by disease group, outpatient medical expenses, and total medical expenses.

4.3.1 Inpatient Medical Expenses

As shown in table 4.5, according to our simulation the inpatient expenses in fiscal year 1996 are 10.2 trillion yen. Actual total medical expenses for fiscal 1996 were estimated to be 9.9 trillion yen. Thus, the error is plus 3 percent, which can be considered reasonably accurate. Turning to total medical costs by age and disease for patients over the age of sixty-five, who account for almost half of the inpatient expense, our simulation yields 4.9 trillion yen, which is nearly the same as the figure in the national medical expenditure (5.0 trillion yen). However, some of the results of other groups show some inconsistencies; for example, our results for the patients between the ages of zero and fourteen, and the patients between the ages of forty-five and sixty-four are, respectively, 20 percent and 15 percent greater than the actual expenses.

Table 4.5 **Simulation estimates and estimates according to national health care expenditure (NHCE) for inpatient medical costs (in billions of yen)**

	Our simulation estimate	NHCE
Age		
0–14	513	433
15–44	1,433	1,518
45–64	3,342	2,924
65 and over	4,943	5,048
Disease		
Infectious and parasitic diseases	268	279
Neoplasms	1,706	1,533
Diseases of the blood and blood-forming organs	64	61
Endocrine, nutritional, and metabolic diseases	389	420
Mental disorders	880	1,074
Diseases of the nervous system	331	329
Diseases of the eye and adnexa	293	240
Diseases of the ear and mastoid process	36	33
Diseases of the circulatory system	2,664	2,431
Diseases of the respiratory system	481	492
Diseases of the digestive system	740	847
Diseases of the skin and subcutaneous tissue	46	55
Diseases of the musculoskeletal system and connective tissue	463	551
Diseases of the genitourinary system	410	404
Complications of pregnancy, childbirth, and puerperism	191	146
Congenital anomalies	138	56
Symptoms, signs, and ill-defined conditions	272	63
Injury and poisoning	858	847
Total (inpatient)	10,230	9,862

Source: Ministry of Health and Welfare (1998), *Estimates of National Medical Care Expenditure, 1996.*

4.3.2   Inpatient Medical Expenses by Disease Groups

In most disease groups, our simulated costs for inpatient care are reasonably accurate with moderate errors. For example, our estimate for circulatory diseases, the group that accounts for the largest share of spending, is 10 percent greater than the national medical expenditure figure. Our estimate for neoplasms is similarly overstated. Those two groups alone account for 40 percent of our national inpatient care costs. On the other hand, we substantially overestimate spending for the pregnancy group and for the eye disease group. Conversely, we have underestimated spending by 15 percent and 10 percent for the musculoskeletal and digestive diseases, respectively.

4.3.3   Outpatient Medical Expenses

Table 4.6 compares our simulation results for outpatient medical costs with the actual costs. According to our simulation, the total outpatient cost amounts to 12.0 trillion yen, which is almost equal to the actual value. Among the age classes, there is underestimation in the groups between the ages of zero and fourteen and between the ages of fifteen and forty-four, but there is an overestimation among those sixty-five years and older. While we do not find significant errors in most major diseases, note that we overestimate spending by 30 percent for musculoskeletal diseases and underestimate spending by 40 percent for urino-genital diseases.

4.3.4   Total Medical Expenses

Table 4.7 compares the actual total medical costs and our simulation results by age group. Actual medical costs equal 21.9 trillion yen, while our simulation figures total 22.2 trillion yen (only a 1 percent difference). By age group, the costs for those between zero and fourteen and those between fourteen and forty-four are underestimated, while the costs for those forty-five years old and older are overestimated. In percentage terms, the magnitude of the error is minus 10 percent for the younger generations, but note that their medical costs account for only 25 percent of the total. In contrast, for older patients, who consume around 75 percent of the total, the magnitude of the error is just a few percentage points. We conclude that our simulated spending is relatively accurate.

4.4   Simulation Results under Different Scenarios

In this section, we compare the simulation results for a number of scenarios designed to capture the effects (direction and the magnitude) of alternative policies. One alternative we consider is the combination of increased out-of-pocket costs and an additional consumption tax to finance all public health care costs. For the price elasticity of medical services, we consider only the demand side and set it at –0.3 for inpatient care and at

Table 4.6   Simulation estimates and estimates according to national health care
                   expenditure (NHCE) for outpatient medical costs (in billions of yen)

	Our simulation estimate	NHCE
Age		
Total	11,953	11,945
0–14	729	958
15–44	1,886	2,201
45–64	3,758	3,947
65 and over	5,581	4,840
Disease		
Infectious and parasitic diseases	413	374
Neoplasms	881	790
Diseases of the blood and blood-forming organs	41	77
Endocrine, nutritional, and metabolic diseases	980	945
Mental disorders	297	297
Diseases of the nervous system	265	194
Diseases of the eye and adnexa	515	565
Diseases of the ear and mastoid process	176	152
Diseases of the circulatory system	2,664	2,626
Diseases of the respiratory system	1,302	1,326
Diseases of the digestive system	1,149	1,199
Diseases of the skin and subcutaneous tissue	350	372
Diseases of the musculoskeletal system and connective tissue	1,544	1,211
Diseases of the genitourinary system	647	1,063
Complications of pregnancy, childbirth, and puerperium	30	58
Certain conditions originating in the perinatal period	1	5
Congenital anomalies	15	16
Symptoms, signs, and ill-defined conditions	153	115
Injury and poisoning	529	532
Medical expenditures for outpatients	11,953	11,916

Source: Ministry of Health and Welfare (1998), *Estimates of National Medical Care Expenditure, 1996.*

–0.15 for outpatient care (except in Scenario 5 as described in the following). For convenience, we assume zero income elasticity of demand for health care.

The details of the five scenarios are as follows:

Scenario 1: Maintain the current health insurance system (premiums and out-of-pocket costs) as of fiscal 1996.

Scenario 2: Maintain out-of-pocket costs as of fiscal year 1996, but impose 10 percent out-of-pocket costs for the elderly. The source of revenue will remain the same as of fiscal year 1996. The price elasticity of health care demand with respect to out-of-pocket costs will be set at –0.3 for inpatient care and –0.15 for outpatient care.

Table 4.7   Simulation estimates and estimates by national health care expenditure (NHCE) for medical costs (in billions of yen)

Age	Our simulation estimate	NHCE
Total	22,184	21,868
0–14	1,241	1,391
15–44	3,318	3,719
45–64	7,100	6,871
65 and over	10,523	9,888

Scenario 3: Maintain out-of-pocket costs as of fiscal 1996, but impose 10 percent out-of-pocket costs for the elderly. To pay for all the health care costs, an additional consumption tax set at 9 percent will be imposed. The price elasticity of health care demand with respect to out-of-pocket costs will be set at –0.3 for inpatient care and –0.15 for outpatient care.

Scenario 4: Out-of-pocket costs will be set at 20 percent for all patients, and an additional consumption tax set at 8 percent will be imposed. The price elasticity of health care demand with respect to out-of-pocket costs will be set at –0.3 for inpatient care and –0.15 for outpatient care.

Scenario 5: Out-of-pocket costs will be set at 20 percent for all patients, and an additional consumption tax set at 8 percent will be imposed. The elasticity will be set at –0.6 for inpatient care and –0.3 for outpatient care.

4.4.1   Characteristics and Results of Each Scenario

On one hand, we have Scenario 1, which was the status quo as of 1996, the year on which our microsimulation model is based. Scenario 2 is a simplified version of the new status quo since October 2002.[4] On the other, we have Scenarios 4 and 5 with uniform 20 percent out-of-pocket costs and an additional 8 percent consumption tax to finance health insurance benefits. Compared with the preferential out-of-pocket rates offered to the elderly and the weak financing mechanism in Scenarios 1 and 2, Scenario 4 offers an alternative that is both simple and stable. For this reason, we are particularly interested in finding out what changes would be involved in the transition to Scenario 4.[5]

The out-of-pocket costs in Scenarios 2 and 3 may be considered transitional steps between the 1996 system and a uniform rate of 20 percent. The

4. To be precise, since April 2003 an elderly couple with more than 1.24 million yen in taxable income or 6.37 million yen in pretax income is responsible for 20 percent of their health care costs.

5. We will emphasize the results of Scenario 4, but this should not be taken as support for the unification of all public medical insurances, a position strongly advocated by the Japan Medical Association. Our version of Scenario 4 is a system in which public insurance programs, sharing consumption-tax revenue with appropriate risk adjustments, compete to attract individuals by offering superior benefits. Unification of the out-of-pocket costs and the source of revenues would, we believe, be a first step to such a quasi-market mechanism.

rate was increased to 10 percent for the elderly in October 2002, but the rate for others remained the same at 20 percent. Moreover, because the out-of-pocket rates are the same in Scenario 2 and 3, the expected medical expenses for each household will be the same[6] and hence the differences between the two scenarios are solely on the revenue side.

The financing mechanism in Scenario 2 remains the same as in Scenario 1, so the difference between the two is due to the out-of-pocket rates for the elderly. A higher out-of-pocket rate in Scenario 2 will reduce the medical costs of the elderly, which will reduce the required contributions of each insurance program and lessen the burden on the government. This will reduce the financial burden for each household in Scenario 2. Scenario 3 is the same as Scenario 2, but with a consumption tax as the source of revenue.

In Scenarios 4 and 5, the out-of-pocket costs are set at 20 percent, and all health insurance benefits are funded by an additional consumption tax of 8 percent. In Scenario 5, however, individuals are assumed to be twice as responsive to the increased out-of-pocket costs as in Scenario 4, which will result in a fiscal surplus to be refunded to households. Setting the elasticity of inpatient care with respect to out-of-pocket costs at –0.3 means that as the cost increases by 1 percent, hospitalizations will decrease by 0.3 percent, resulting in a 0.3 percent decrease in inpatient medical costs. Setting the elasticity of outpatient care with respect to out-of-pocket cost at –0.15 means that as the rate increases by 1 percent, the outpatient visitation rate will decrease by 0.15 percent, resulting in a decrease in the number of outpatients and their medical costs.

4.4.2   Simulation Results

In this section, for each scenario we show total expenditures and expenditures aggregated by household age groups and by insurance programs. To calculate the total individual burden, we have to consider the government subsidy and the surplus or deficit of the medical insurance programs as well. All our simulations produced surpluses in every insurance program (see table 4.8),[7] and, hence, we estimated the household burden assuming that the surpluses would be returned to the households in equal amounts.

Household Payments by the Age of Householders

Our table 4.9 shows the mean costs of medical care consumed and the payments for medical care per household, by age group of the household head. To compare the scenarios, figure 4.1 shows mean payments as a fraction of mean medical costs by age group of the household head (100 per-

6. Recall that the income elasticity of demand for medical care is assumed to be zero.
7. In the case of Scenarios 2 through 5, there is a surplus ranging from 1.2 trillion to 2 trillion yen (table 4.8). In other words, financial resources are sufficient in each of our scenarios.

Table 4.8   **Medical costs and burden simulated by scenario and by age of head of household (in billions of yen)**

	15–39	40–64	65 and over	Total
A. Scenario 1				
Medical costs	2,144	11,109	8,917	22,170
Out-of-pocket costs	324	1,114	555	1,993
Burden of premium	2,567	7,885	1,752	12,204
Tax incidence and public subsidy	1,453	5,278	1,241	7,973
Sum of household burden	4,345	14,277	3,548	22,170
B. Scenario 2				
Medical costs	2,042	10,367	8,002	20,411
Out-of-pocket costs	344	1,371	895	2,610
Burden of premium	2,567	7,885	1,752	12,204
Tax incidence and public subsidy	1,097	3,587	913	5,597
Sum of household burden	4,008	12,842	3,560	20,411
C. Scenario 3				
Medical costs	2,042	10,367	8,02	20,411
Out-of-pocket costs	344	1,371	895	2,610
Burden of consumption tax (9%)	3,953	11,805	3,941	19,698
Health insurance surplus	−284	−1,351	−262	−1,897
Sum of household burden	4,012	11,825	4,573	20,411
D. Scenario 4				
Medical costs	1,993	10,354	8,304	20,651
Out-of-pocket costs	399	2,071	1,661	4,130
Burden of consumption tax (8%)	3,546	10,591	3,535	17,672
Health insurance surplus	−172	−820	−159	−1,151
Sum of household burden	3,772	11,842	5,037	20,651
E. Scenario 5				
Medical costs	1,934	10,112	7,923	19,968
Out-of-pocket costs	387	2,022	1,585	3,994
Burden of consumption tax (8%)	3,546	10,591	3,535	17,672
Health insurance surplus	−254	−1,208	−235	−1,697
Sum of household burden	3,679	11,405	4,85	19,968

cent would indicate that the household financial burden equals the cost of medical care consumed).

Under Scenario 1, or the 1996 system, the households headed by individuals age sixty-five or older bear only 39.8 percent of their medical costs on the average. In contrast, the households whose heads are in the prime of life and support their children (ages forty to sixty-four) bear about 128.5 percent of their medical costs on the average, and the households whose heads are between fifteen and thirty-nine bear over 200 percent of their medical costs.

Under Scenarios 4 and 5 (8 percent consumption tax, 20 percent individual payment rate), the households headed by individuals sixty-five and older will bear slightly over 60 percent of their mean medical costs. On the

Table 4.9   **The means for medical costs and burden simulated by scenario (per household) and by age of head of household (in thousands of yen)**

	15–39	40–64	65 and over	Total
A. Scenario 1				
Medical costs	185	465	741	487
Out-of-pocket costs	29	47	52	44
Burden of premium	233	330	165	268
Tax incidence and public subsidy	132	221	117	175
Sum of household burden	395	598	335	487
B. Scenario 2				
Medical costs	185	434	754	449
Out-of-pocket costs	31	57	84	57
Burden of premium	233	330	165	268
Tax incidence and public subsidy	100	150	86	123
Sum of household burden	364	538	336	449
C. Scenario 3				
Medical costs	185	434	754	449
Out-of-pocket costs	31	57	84	57
Burden of consumption tax (9%)	359	495	372	433
Health insurance surplus	−26	−57	−25	−42
Sum of household burden	364	495	431	449
D. Scenario 4				
Medical costs	181	434	783	454
Out-of-pocket costs	36	87	157	91
Burden of consumption tax (8%)	322	444	333	388
Health insurance surplus	−16	−34	−15	−25
Sum of household burden	343	496	475	454
E. Scenario 5				
Medical costs	176	424	747	439
Out-of-pocket costs	35	85	149	88
Burden of consumption tax (8%)	322	444	333	388
Health insurance surplus	−23	−51	−22	−37
Sum of household burden	334	478	461	439

other hand, the burden on households headed by individuals between forty and sixty-four will be reduced to less than 115 percent. Households with heads between the ages of fifteen and thirty-nine will bear around 190 percent of their medical costs, slightly lower than in Scenario 1. Under Scenario 3, the households with heads sixty-five or older will bear 57.2 percent of their costs, a little bit lower than Scenario 4, but considerably higher than the current rate.

Analysis of Individual Payment Per Household
by the Age of the Householder

We now examine the components of the total payments for medical care. Namely, in Scenarios 1 and 2, the payments consist of out-of-pocket costs,

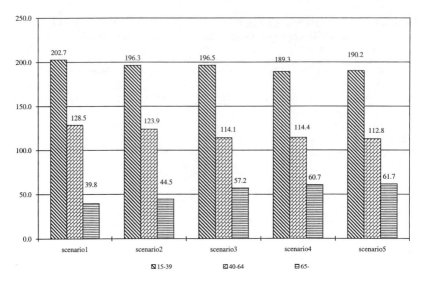

Fig. 4.1   The ratios of medical burden to cost per household by age class for household head (percentage)

insurance premiums and the imputed taxes, while in scenarios 3 through 5, the insurance premiums and imputed taxes and deficits are replaced by the consumption taxes. To facilitate comparison between these two groups of scenarios, the sum of all payments other than out-of-pocket costs (i.e., the premiums, imputed tax and surplus payments, and consumption tax)[8] will be referred to simply as "premiums and taxes."

Now we examine how the out-of-pocket costs and premiums and taxes shift as we move away from Scenario 1. Figure 4.2 illustrates two particularly interesting comparisons, namely Scenarios 3 and 4, relative to Scenario 1. The results are shown separately by age group of the household head.

If Scenario 4 is put into effect, the total payments of households headed by individuals age fifteen to thirty-nine and individuals forty to sixty-four, will decrease by 13 percent and 17 percent, respectively. Note that out-of-pocket costs contribute +1.7 percent and +6.7 percent, respectively, but premiums and taxes contribute –14.9 percent and –23.8 percent, respectively. We observe similar results for Scenario 3.

On the other hand, households headed by individuals sixty-five or older experience a 42 percent increase in total payments in Scenario 4. Specifically, out-of-pocket costs contribute +31 percent, and premiums and taxes contribute +11 percent. Thus, three-quarters of the change are due to the

---

8. The "deficit" and "surplus transfer" items refer to the average value of the deficit or the surplus, equally redistributed among the same age groups.

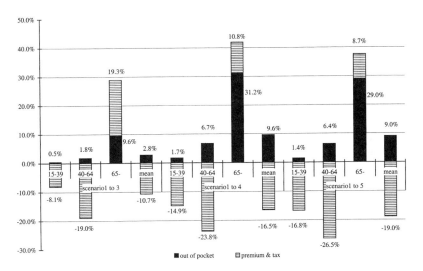

Fig. 4.2   Household medical burden changes by shifting Scenario 1 to other scenarios (by age class for household head)

increase in the out-of-pocket costs. In case of Scenario 3, the total payments will increase by 29 percent, with the out-of-pocket costs accounting for +10 percent, and premiums and taxes accounting for +19 percent. Because the out-of-pocket rate for Scenario 3 is only one-half of Scenario 4, the medical costs of the elderly will be larger, resulting in a higher consumption tax rate. Particularly for the elderly, if we lower the out-of-pocket costs, we should expect premiums and taxes to move in the opposite direction.

Comparing the Contributions across Insurance Types

Table 4.10 illustrates mean medical costs and financial burdens per household by type of insurance. We note that the insurance scheme for the elderly is not a primary medical insurance, but is more a reinsurance. As primary insurance programs in 1996, HIMA insured 940,000 elderly individuals, HIMG insured just over 2 million, and NHIs insured nearly 9 million.

Mean payments as a fraction of mean medical costs are shown in figure 4.3 for each type of insurance and for each scenario. Households insured by national health insurance programs only contribute around 60 percent of their total medical costs under the 1996 health insurance system. Households insured by HIMA and HIGE, on the other hand, contribute over 170 percent of their own medical costs. For households insured by HIMG, their contribution amounts to just under 115 percent of their medical costs. Scenario 2 is similar in these respects to Scenario 1.

In the case of Scenarios 3 through 5, in which consumption tax is used

Table 4.10   **The means for medical costs and burden simulated by scenario (per household and in thousands of yen)**

	NHI	HIMG	HIMA and HIGE	Mean
A. Scenario 1				
Medical costs	587	439	383	487
Out-of-pocket costs	53	38	35	44
Burden of premium	172	256	410	268
Tax incidence and public subsidy	126	210	219	175
Sum of household burden	351	504	665	487
B. Scenario 2				
Medical costs	534	412	356	449
Out-of-pocket costs	58	62	54	57
Burden of premium	172	256	410	268
Tax incidence and public subsidy	02	155	144	123
Sum of household burden	322	473	608	449
C. Scenario 3				
Medical costs	534	412	356	449
Out-of-pocket costs	58	62	54	57
Burden of consumption tax (9%)	396	438	481	433
Health insurance surplus	–27	–44	-60	–42
Sum of household burden	427	456	474	449
D. Scenario 4				
Medical costs	548	408	356	454
Out-of-pocket costs	110	82	71	91
Burden of consumption tax (8%)	356	393	431	388
Health insurance surplus	–16	–27	–37	–25
Sum of household burden	449	448	466	454
E. Scenario 5				
Medical costs	525	399	347	439
Out-of-pocket costs	105	80	69	88
Burden of consumption tax (8%)	356	393	431	388
Health insurance surplus	–24	–39	–54	–37
Sum of household burden	436	433	447	439

Note: See table 4.3 for acronym explanations.

to finance health insurance benefits, households with national health insurance contribute around 80 percent, households with HIMA or HIGE contribute around 130 percent, and households with HIMG contribute around 110 percent. Clearly, even when the consumption tax is used to finance the medical insurance benefits, the total contribution varies widely across different types of insurances. Because the average health care costs of the elderly are several times of those of the rest of the population, and because they contribute substantially less than their full costs, the insurance programs with larger-than-average percentages of the elderly, such as NHIs, will have contribution-to-cost ratios of less than 1. These ratios, however, will move in the same direction as the contribution-to-cost ratio

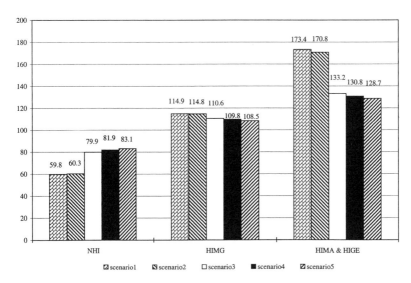

Fig. 4.3   The ratios of medical burden to cost per household by branch of health insurance (percentage)

of the elderly: for example, a consumption tax raises the contribution-to-cost ratio of the elderly and NHIs as well.

4.4.3   Implications for Different Types of Insurance and Age Groups

Table 4.11 shows mean contributions as a fraction of mean medical costs, by type of insurance and age group of the head of household, for each scenario. For a given age group, the fractions under Scenarios 3 through 5 are far less dispersed than under Scenario 1. This implies that these systems are more horizontally equitable than the 1996 system. Comparing the contribution-to-cost ratios within the given insurance types (i.e., vertically), or across different insurance types (i.e., diagonally), we observe that the ratios narrow considerably under any of these three scenarios. This implies that these systems are far more equitable between the generations than the 1996 system.

Now we examine how the total contribution-to-cost ratio changes for households whose heads are between the ages of fifteen and thirty-nine under each scenario. It should be noted that even under the 1996 system, the younger households with NHIs contribute 125.0 percent of their total costs. Although this figure is lower than those of HIMG households (191.0 percent) or of HIMA or HIGE households (252.7 percent), the ratios of other age-groups in NHIs are below 100 percent. In Scenario 2, the figures are similar to those in Scenario 1.

If all the health insurance benefits are financed by a consumption tax, as in Scenario 4, younger households in NHIs contribute 197.6 percent,

Table 4.11   The means for ratios of medical burden to cost simulated by scenario (per household) and by age and branch of insurance for the head of household

Age	NHI	HIMG	HIMA and HIGE	Mean
		A. Scenario 1		
15–39	125.0	191.0	252.7	202.7
40–64	90.9	119.7	173.7	128.5
65 and over	37.3	52.8	48.7	39.8
Mean	59.8	114.9	173.4	100.0
		B. Scenario 2		
15–39	116.3	182.5	249.1	196.3
40–64	82.9	119.0	171.1	123.9
65 and over	42.1	56.1	52.3	44.5
Mean	60.3	114.8	170.8	100.0
		C. Scenario 3		
15–39	201.3	188.0	199.5	196.5
40–64	102.6	110.1	129.2	114.1
65 and over	56.7	59.6	58.6	57.2
Mean	79.9	110.6	133.2	100.0
		D. Scenario 4		
15–39	197.6	181.9	189.7	189.3
40–64	104.9	109.8	127.6	114.4
65 and over	60.3	62.4	61.6	60.7
Mean	81.9	109.8	130.8	100.0
		E. Scenario 5		
15–39	200.2	187.4	186.9	190.2
40–64	105.2	107.2	124.8	112.8
65 and over	61.6	61.5	62.2	61.7
Mean	83.1	108.5	128.7	100.0

Note: See table 4.3 for acronym explanations.

households in HIMG contribute 181.9 percent, and households in HIMA or HIGE contribute 189.7 percent of their own health care costs. In other words, households with NHIs contribute greater proportions than households with employee health insurance, primarily due to their lower medical costs. Similar results were obtained in Scenarios 3 and 5.

For households with heads age forty to sixty-four, in Scenario 1 the contribution-to-cost ratios are as follows: 90.9 percent for those in NHIs, 119.7 percent for those in HIMG, and 173.7 percent for those in HIMA or HIGE. If all the insurance benefits are financed by consumption tax, as in the case of Scenario 4, the contribution-to-cost ratios are 104.9 percent for households in NHIs, 109.8 percent for HIMG households, and 127.6 percent for HIMA or HIGE households. Thus, by switching to a consumption tax, the ratio increases for NHI and HIMG households and drops for HIMA/HIGE households, bringing the ratios to converge around 110 percent. In other words, a switch to a consumption tax is a reform that brings the burdens of households who are raising families more or less in line with their medical costs.

Last, in the 1996 system, for households with heads age sixty-five or older, the contribution-to-cost ratios show substantial variations; they are 37.3 percent for national health insurance, 52.8 percent for HIMG, and 48.7 percent for HIMA or HIGE, respectively. The low ratio for NHIs reflects the preferential treatments in out-of-pocket costs, premium assessment, and income tax. The higher rates for HIMG and HIMA or HIGE probably reflect the insurance premium payments by the heads who are still employed by firms.

It must be noted that by switching to a consumption tax to finance health insurance benefits, the contributions of this older age group will be increased for all types of insurance. For example, in Scenario 4 such households would be responsible for around 61 percent of their medical costs, regardless of insurance type. The disincentive for the working elderly can be solved by switching to a consumption tax. The fact that the elderly would be responsible for 60 percent of their costs needs to be scrutinized more closely, but there are clear advantages to the use of a consumption tax to finance benefits.

4.4.4   Income Distribution and Contribution-to-Medical-Costs Ratios

Table 4.12 is the average figures of medical costs and total contributions of households by quartiles of household income. The bottom figures in each scenario stand for the contribution-to-medical-costs ratios. In our baseline Scenario 1, the bottom income quartile households pay 54.2 percent of their health care costs, while the top income quartile households pay 131.8 percent. In each of our scenarios, we observe a positive relationship between the household income and contribution-to-medical-costs ratios, and, in each of our scenarios, the top income quartile pays more than 100 percent. However, as we move from Scenario 3 to 5, the bottom quartile's contribution-to-medical-costs ratios increase from 71.6 percent to 82.1 percent. Particularly in Scenarios 4 and 5, there is a tendency for the contribution-to-medical-costs ratios to move toward 1, regardless of income quartiles, which reflects the fact that, proportionally speaking, consumption tax tends to take more bite out of the income of the poorer households.

Nevertheless, it is clear that the rich are paying more than they consume under the present system and under any reform plan. Technically, this result is a trivial one because our simulation started from our (estimated) household demand functions for medical services with zero income elasticity. We should note, however, more recent studies by other authors more or less confirmed that income elasticity for medical services is either very small or even negative. This result seems to contradict the widely held belief that health care services are luxury goods. An economically sensible

Table 4.12   The means of medical burden to cost simulated by scenario (per household) and by percentile for household income (in thousands of yen)

	Below 25th percentile	25th through 50th percentile	50th through 75th percentile	75th percentile and above	Total
A. Scenario 1					
Medical costs	449	468	460	570	487
Out-of-pocket costs	32	44	48	52	44
Burden of premium	71	190	320	494	268
Tax incidence and public subsidy	141	167	188	205	175
Sum of household burden	243	400	556	751	487
Contribution to medical costs	54.20	85.49	120.79	131.80	100.00
B. Scenario 2					
Medical costs	408	430	428	528	448
Out-of-pocket costs	40	57	62	71	57
Burden of premium	144	237	305	388	268
Tax incidence and public subsidy	101	118	132	140	123
Sum of household burden	286	412	498	600	448
Contribution to medical costs	70.08	95.67	116.55	113.59	100.00
C. Scenario 3					
Medical costs	408	430	428	528	448
Out-of-pocket costs	46	53	59	72	57
Burden of consumption tax (9%)	278	390	466	599	433
Health insurance surplus	−32	−39	−45	−51	−42
Sum of household burden	292	404	480	619	448
Contribution to medical costs	71.68	93.91	112.19	117.28	100.00
D. Scenario 4					
Medical costs	419	436	429	531	454
Out-of-pocket costs	79	84	88	112	91
Burden of consumption tax (9%)	249	350	418	537	388
Health insurance surplus	−19	−23	−27	−31	−25
Sum of household burden	309	410	479	618	454
Contribution to medical costs	73.78	94.04	111.67	116.47	100.00
E. Scenario 5					
Medical costs	401	421	416	516	439
Out-of-pocket costs	59	85	94	114	88
Burden of consumption tax (9%)	299	363	411	482	388
Health insurance surplus	−28	−35	−40	−46	−37
Sum of household burden	329	413	464	549	439
Contribution to medical costs	82.10	98.01	111.44	106.54	100.00

answer to this apparent contradiction is that under the Japanese public health insurance schemes, by and large, medical services are rationed goods, whose quantities or qualities consumers have relatively little to say.

There are some clear exceptions; first, some categories of illnesses are not covered by public health insurance, e.g., pregnancies, car accidents, or injuries incurred in fights. They constitute only a few percentage points of the national medical services market. Second, there is potentially a very large market for services not approved by public health insurance programs, including many high-tech medical services or unapproved drugs. Up to now, providers have been obligated to separate the medical services covered by the public health insurance and the medical services not covered by the public health insurance, and mixed billing have been strictly prohibited.

4.5 Conclusion

In this paper, we showed that in the 1996 health insurance system an imbalance of the benefits and burden of medical services was created across generations and that the imbalance was growing rapidly due to the aging of the population. The working generations are forced to bear an increasingly large load while their benefits are reduced. The view that the current medical insurance system is not sustainable in the long run is spreading very fast and eroding the credibility of the government, which has been stressing the system's equality. The Health Insurance Reform in April of 2003, which retained most of the privileges of the elderly, seems to have been another stopgap measure that failed to restore public confidence.

In order to defuse an approaching crisis, we consider a system that is simple, fair, and self-sustaining at the same time. We have constructed a microsimulation model as a tool for judging the properties of a given health insurance system. This simulation model consists of a large number of individual households that collectively represent the economic and health statistics of our economy. We conducted several simulations to explore policy alternatives and analyzed the resulting incidence of medical costs and benefits.

The purpose of this simulation was to find a scenario in which an employee in his or her working prime (i.e., a household head age forty to sixty-four), who may be supporting children, would have a financial burden appropriate to the benefits he or she receives.

One scenario that would satisfy these two conditions is Scenario 3, which relies on a consumption tax as the sole financial tool to pay for insurance benefits, raises to 10 percent the out-of-pocket costs for the elderly, and maintains the current out-of-pocket costs for other consumers. Another is Scenario 4, which uses the consumption tax as the sole financial tool to pay for the insurance benefits and raises everyone's out-of-pocket costs to 20 percent. These scenarios call for 8 percent (Scenario 3) or 9 percent (Scenario 4) consumption tax rates.

These two scenarios would make the elderly responsible for far more than the 40 percent they are paying for now, but not for more than 60 percent (Scenario 4). In Scenarios 3 and 4, the contribution-to-costs ratios are far less dispersed across different types of insurance for a given age group, compared to the current system (Scenario 1 or 2). In terms of horizontal equity, the overall allocation of health insurance costs and benefits are far better in Scenarios 3 and 4. The current system consists of very different premiums, subsidies, and reinsurances. By replacing it with the consumption tax to finance health insurance benefits, it is also possible to reduce the huge disparity in the contribution-to-costs ratios across different age groups and improve the vertical equity of the medical insurance system.

Last, we would like to address the limitations of our analysis. First of all, the microsimulation model is a static model. It would have been better if we could have explicitly incorporated health capital as a determinant of medical costs and income. We also do not take savings into consideration. If we introduced savings into our model, it would be possible to examine the effects of increasing the burden on the elderly that would result from changes in the medical insurance system (changes in out-of-pocket costs of the patients, the use of consumption tax, etc.) on household assets. We also did not consider population dynamics in our model, fixing the population structure to year 1995. Thus, our simulation results depend on the given year's population structure. On the other hand, we did take into account the annual budget deficit of the national government as one component of household financial burden, but not the enormous stock of public bonds. We should also remind our readers that we have assumed zero income elasticity in the demand for medical services in our model. It is not difficult to incorporate this element, but we decided against doing so to simplify comparisons across scenarios.

Appendix

Calibration of our Microsimulation Model

Creation of Standard Households and the Fixing of Scaling Factor

First, we created 100,000 probabilistic virtual households based on the CSHW data on the distribution of household and individual attributes. These virtual households will hereafter be called *standard households.* The standard households are categorized in the same manner as the census using the age of householder, sex, marital status, the number of members, and so on. Next, we fixed the weights for the standard households so that the number of each type of household in each prefecture would conform to the number in the most recent census. We then adjusted the weights so that the aggregate employment income, consumption expenditure, and social insurance premiums of all the households would be reasonably close to the SNA statistics. Finally, we adjusted to the weights again so that the distribution of employment income from the survey would be reasonably close to the known distribution of household monthly compensation.

Estimating The Number of Patients

Next, we constructed a stochastic model that can be used to reproduce the medical utilization patterns recorded in the Patient Survey 1996 (Ministry of Health and Welfare 1997b). We use the Patient Survey 1996—rather than the CSHW—because it is the most extensive and most accurate survey on the utilization of medical institutions by individual patients. The utilization information provided in the CSHW is plagued by serious downward bias. Thus, we assigned various illnesses to members of the standard households randomly, using the statistics on major illnesses in sex and age groups of Patient Survey 1996. The place of treatment, nature of treatment, and the length of the treatment time are determined accordingly.

Estimating the Number of Outpatients

We calculated the probability that a patient would come for his or her first visit and for follow-up visits for each illness based on sex and age from the Patient Survey 1996 (Ministry of Health and Welfare 1997b). We then generated a random number every other day starting from January 1, and calculated the probability of a sick person going for a checkup. Once the date for the first checkup is fixed, the date for the follow-up visit and the span of the treatment is determined by a stochastic process.[9] By repeating this process every day for one year,[10] we were able to determine whether a member of a simulated household would visit a particular medical institution for a checkup and determine the beginning and end date of treatment in addition to the frequency of the treatment.[11]

Estimating the Number of Inpatients

The simulation of hospital care was conducted in the following manner. From the Patient Survey 1996 we estimated the daily probability of a new patient being admitted to a hospital or clinics based on sex and age group. For the number of days hospitalized, we estimated a single Weibull survival function, using the same survey and sex, age-group, and disease dummies

---

9. The number of first outpatient visits and return visits for each sex and age group was calculated from the Patient Survey 1996 (Ministry of Health and Welfare 1997b). We also extracted total population data for sex and age groups from the national census of 1995. For a given sex and age group, the probability of an outpatient visit is the sum of the first-visit probability and the return-visit probability.

10. 240 days will be regarded as one year.

11. Some simulated individuals never visit a hospital in a given year.

(table 4.5). We used the estimated distribution function in our stochastic decision making.

The date of hospitalization for each household member was determined in the same way as the date of outpatient checkup. We drew a random number every other day starting from January 1 for each member of a household and determined if he or she is to be hospitalized on that day, given his or her age group. Once admitted, we draw another random number to determine if he or she is discharged on that day, based on the estimated Weibull distribution. By continuing this process until December 31, we were able to determine when each household member was in or out of the hospital.

The Distribution of Medical Costs Based on the Survey of Medical Care Activities in Public Health Insurance (SMCA)

Because there are no medical costs data in our Patient Survey 1996 we have to gather medical cost information from the Survey of Medical Care Activities in Public Health Insurance (SMCA; Ministry of Health and Welfare 1997c).[12] While the latter survey provides information on disease groups, type of hospitals, and the patient's sex and age, it does not provide any information on his or her household characteristics. Here we assume that the medical cost per day is a random variable that follows the empirical distribution of SMCA medical costs for a given patient and hospital attributes in the SMCA. In order to improve the concordance between the simulation results and aggregated medical costs, small adjustments were made to the empirical SMCA distributions to remove the bias in its samples.[13] A random number was generated for every practicing day, and the medical expenditure for each household member was obtained.

Repeating the process for all members of the standard households, we obtained the number of inpatient and outpatient visits and the total costs of outpatient care and of inpatient care for the year, as well as the annual insurance premium borne by households.

References

Harding, Ann, ed. 1996. *Microsimulation and public policy.* Amsterdam: North-Holland.

12. This survey is also known as the Survey of Socialized Medicine; we use the official English name and acronym (SMCA).
13. From SMCA, for each combination of sex, age group, disease, and type of medical institution, we first calculated the 5 percent, 15 percent, 30 percent, 50 percent, 70 percent, 85 percent, 91 percent, 93 percent, 95 percent, 97 percent, and 99 percent values of medical costs. The partitions for calculating these cost figures are set at the following percentiles: 10th, 20th, 40th, 60th, 80th, 90th, 92nd, 94th, 96th and 98th. We then reduced these medical costs uniformly by nearly 10 percent.

Ministry of Health and Welfare. 1997a. *Comprehensive survey of living conditions of the people on health and welfare for 1995* [in Japanese]. Tokyo: Health and Welfare Statistics Association.

———. 1997b. *Patient survey 1996* [in Japanese]. Health and Welfare Statistics Association.

———. 1997c. *Report of survey of medical care activities in public health insurance, 1995* [in Japanese]. Health and Welfare Statistics Association.

———. 1998. *Estimates of national medical care expenditure, 1996* [in Japanese]. Tokyo: Health and Welfare Statistics Association.

Statistics Bureau. 1997. *1995 population census of Japan* [in Japanese]. Japan Statistical Association.

5

The Volume-Outcome Relationship in Japan
The Case of Percutaneous Transluminal Coronary Angioplasty (PTCA) Volume on Mortality of Acute Myocardial Infarction (AMI) Patients

Koichi Kawabuchi and Shigeru Sugihara

5.1 Introduction

Everyone agrees that high quality health care is a very important policy objective, but there are disagreements on how to measure quality. A popular quality measure is the volume of procedures performed by a hospital or physician. The presumption is that as the number of procedures increases, the quality will improve due to, for example, the learning-by-doing (or "practice makes perfect") effect. We refer to an inverse relationship between volume and adverse medical outcomes such as mortality as the *volume effect*. Many studies have examined whether volume affects outcomes, and a consensus seems to have emerged that a volume effect does exist.

Against this background, the American College of Cardiology/American Heart Association (ACC/AHA 2001) recommends that a physician should perform more than 75 percutaneous transluminal coronary angioplasty (PTCA) procedures per year and a hospital should perform at least 200 PTCA procedures per year, and ideally more than 400, to ensure the quality of PTCA procedures.[1] In Japan, the Ministry of Health, Labor and Welfare adopts differential reimbursement policy for PTCA procedures based on hospital PTCA volume, with no adjustment for risk factors.

Koichi Kawabuchi is a professor of health economics at the Tokyo Medical and Dental University. Shigeru Sugihara is a professor at the Osaka School of International Public Policy, Osaka University.

The views expressed in this paper are those of authors and not those of institutions to which the authors belong. We are grateful to David Cutler, Jonathan Skinner, and Chapin White for helpful comments and to Isao Igarashi for skillful editorial work. Remaining errors are ours.

1. In addition, the ACC/AHA recommends that a low-volume physician with fewer than 75 procedures should work only in a high-volume hospital with more than 600 procedures because of direct correlation between both hospital and physician volume and outcomes.

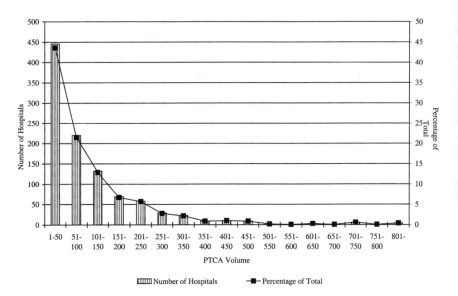

Fig. 5.1   Number of PTCA procedures per hospital

Specifically, if a hospital performs fewer than 100 PTCA procedures per year, its reimbursement rate is reduced by 30 percent.

In Japan, hospitals perform limited numbers of PTCA procedures each year. Figure 5.1 shows the distribution of hospitals according to their PTCA volume in 1997.[2] Nearly half of the hospitals performed fewer than 50 PTCA procedures, and only 15 percent of the hospitals performed more than 200 PTCA procedures per year. Hospitals with more than 400 PTCA procedures are quite rare.[3]

It is sometimes suggested that by increasing PTCA volume per hospital, the quality of health care can be improved. However, empirical studies of the volume effect in Japan are scarce. The reimbursement policy of the Ministry of Health, Labor and Welfare is, therefore, not strongly evidence based. Even in the U.S. context, evidence for the volume effect is, arguably, still mixed. At the least, there is great uncertainty about the nature of the volume effect (how does volume relate to outcomes?), and little is known about the channels through which a volume effect might operate.

This paper examines the empirical relevance of a hypothesized volume effect in Japan in the case of PTCA performed on acute myocardial infarc-

2. This figure is taken from Takeshita (2000).
3. Even in the United States, PTCA volume per hospital or physician is low. Jollis et al. (1997) document that the median annual PTCA procedures on Medicare patients are 98 for hospitals and 13 for physicians. They note that median annual PTCA volumes for all patients including non-Medicare patients are 196 to 294 for hospitals and 26 to 39 for physicians considering that Medicare patients consist of one-third to one-half of total patients.

tion (AMI) patients. We also investigate the nature and channels of the volume effect. The results have implications for reimbursement policy as well as competition policy. If there is a strong volume effect, policies should favor the concentration of PTCA procedures in a small number of hospitals or physicians. If this is not the case, policies favoring concentration of PTCA procedures may be inappropriate.

5.2 Literature Review

A comprehensive review of the volume effect was conducted by Halm, Lee, and Chassin (2000), covering a wide range of diseases and operations. The overall conclusion supports the existence of a volume effect in most diseases and operations including PTCA, coronary artery bypass graft (CABG), and treatment of AMI patients.

However, we suspect that the evidence on the volume effect is still mixed for PTCA. In fact, Halm, Lee, and Chassin (2000) report that, of the seven articles that examined hospital PTCA volume, only three found an inverse relationship between volume and mortality and that, of the four studies that analyzed physician volume, only one found a significant association between volume and mortality and one found a trend toward such a relationship.[4] Empirical studies on the existence of a PTCA volume effect in Japan are not easy to find.[5] Tsuchibashi et al. (2003) find no significant relationship between hospital volume and in-hospital death or CABG.

Even when a volume effect is reported, its statistical significance and empirical relevance need to be scrutinized carefully. For example, one of the most reliable studies identified by Halm, Lee, and Chassin (2000) is Hannan et al. (1997). This study classified hospitals into five categories according to their PTCA volume. They compared risk-adjusted–in-hospital mortality rates across these categories and concluded that patients undergoing PTCA in hospitals with annual PTCA volume less than 600 experienced significantly higher risk-adjusted mortality rates and risk-adjusted–same-stay CABG rates.[6] However, the statistical significance of these differences is not certain because the confidence intervals for the estimated mortality rates are very wide and often overlap. In the same spirit, Ellis et

---

4. The inverse relationship is found more often for emergency CABG. All seven articles that examined hospital volume and three out of four articles that examined physician volume found that low volume are associated with higher rates of emergency CABG. Very recently, an increasing number of studies are being published that demonstrate a volume effect at the hospital level as well as the physician level.

5. A series of papers by Fujita et al. (2000); Fujita and Hasegawa (1999, 2000); Fujita, Hasegawa, and Hasegawa (2001); and Hasegawa, Hasegawa, and Fujita (2000) find support for a volume effect in the context of operations on cancer patients, cardiovascular operations, and treatment of AMI patients.

6. Hannan et al. (1997) also examined physician volume effects on mortality and emergency CABG and found analogous results.

al. (1996, 1997) purport to find an inverse relationship between PTCA volume and adverse outcomes, but they caution that the magnitude of the relationship is not estimated exactly.

Further, in Hannan et al. (1997), the differences in mortality rates across categories are very small. For example, risk-adjusted mortality rates are 1.12 percent for hospitals with fewer than 400 PTCA procedures, around 0.80 percent for hospitals with 400 to 999 PTCA procedures, and 0.95 percent for hospitals with more than 1,000 PTCA procedures.[7] Arguably, these differences may be statistically significant, but clinically insignificant.

Many of the studies focus on short-term outcomes such as in-hospital mortality and death within thirty days after PTCA. However, Doucet et al. (2002) and Kimmel et al. (2002) show that a relationship between PTCA volume and outcomes may exist for short-term outcomes but not for longer-term outcomes.

And there is great uncertainty about the nature of volume effect. First, the volume effect does not look like a simple linear relationship. In Hannan et al. (1997), mortality and emergency CABG rates are highest among hospitals with low volumes, and they are lower among hospitals with intermediate volumes. However, hospitals with the highest volumes have higher mortality rates than hospitals with intermediate volumes (although they still have lower mortality rates than hospitals with the lowest volume). Also, Ellis et al. (1997), Ho (2000) and Thiemann et al. (1999) found an inverse exponential relationship between PTCA volume and adverse outcomes using the logarithm of PTCA volume as an independent variable in either logistic regression or a Cox proportional hazard model. However, Vakili, Kaplan, and Brown (2001) concludes that there is no significant departure from linearity for the hospital and physician volume-outcome relationship. The question remains whether the volume effect is nonlinear and, if so, why. Policies based on a simple "the more, the better" principle may not be appropriate.

Second, as mentioned in the preceding, the systematic review by Halm, Lee, and Chassin (2000) indicates that hospital volume and physician volume may have different effects on outcomes. In the same vein, Vakili, Kaplan, and Brown (2001) find that physician volume has an effect on in-hospital mortality rate but that hospital volume does not. Complicating the picture further, McGrath et al. (2000) show that hospital volume has a significant effect on mortality but an insignificant effect on emergency CABG, while physician volume does not have a significant effect on mortality but does have a significant effect on emergency CABG.[8] Further, Mc-

7. These mortality rates are for all patients who underwent PTCA, including AMI and non-AMI.
8. See also Jollis et al. (1997).

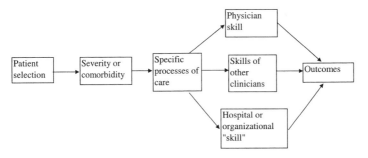

Fig. 5.2   Conceptual framework proposed by Halm, Lee, and Chassin (2000)—How could volume affect quality?

Grath et al. (2000) and Vakili, Kaplan, and Brown (2001) find significant interaction or spillover effects between hospital volume and physician volume. Recently, Birkmeyer et al. (2003) examined the relative importance of hospital and physician volumes in eight cardiovascular procedures or cancer operations and concluded that for many procedures, the observed association between hospital volume and operative mortality is largely mediated by physician volume. The exact relationship between hospital and physician volume deserves further scrutiny.

Fundamentally, it is not obvious why volume should affect outcomes. To date, the literature has presented the "practice makes perfect" hypothesis and the selective referral hypothesis. The former asserts that as physicians perform more PTCA procedures, they become more skillful.[9] This hypothesis implies causality from PTCA volume to outcomes at the level of the individual physician. The latter hypothesis states that physicians or hospitals with better outcomes tend to receive more referrals. According to this hypothesis, the volume effect is not causal and occurs at both the hospital level and the physician level. Admittedly, these hypotheses are rather patchy and do not cover all the aspects of volume effect.

An overall conceptual framework for understanding the volume effect is proposed by Halm, Lee, and Chassin (2000). This framework identifies various channels through which a volume effect could operate, including improved physician skills per se, spillover effects from the skills of other physicians, and organizational skill. Figure 5.2 is a schematic representation of these channels.

We begin with patient selection. The relationship between volume and patient selection may result from selective referral patterns mentioned previously, or patients of high-volume hospitals or physicians may be more appropriate candidates for PTCA than patients of low-volume providers. In

---

9. Ellis et al. (1997) report that, even though a PTCA volume effect is present, it is not attributable to the physician's years of experience.

relation to this analysis, note that patients suffering AMI usually have little time to select hospitals or physicians.

The severity of patients' illness and the presence of comorbid conditions also affect outcomes. If high-volume hospitals or physicians treat patients who are systematically healthier than their low-volume counterparts, they would tend to have better outcomes. Hence, risk adjustment is essential.

Halm, Lee, and Chassin (2000) note that volume cannot directly produce better outcomes. If volume is related to outcome, that association must be due to differences in the components of care or in the skills with which patients are treated. In the case of AMI patients, components of care might include PTCA, CABG, thrombolytic therapy, aspirin, beta-blockers, angiotensin converting enzyme (ACE) inhibitors, and so on. Provision of different components of care by high-volume hospitals will result in outcomes that differ from low-volume hospitals.

Then, Halm, Lee, and Chassin (2000) distinguish three kinds of skills, namely, physician skill, skills of other clinicians, and hospital or organizational skill. Physician experience (volume) may be a proxy measure of a certain skill level that results in superior performance. Further, the volume or experience of other physicians, the staff team performing PTCA, and the hospital as a whole may be important. We will examine these skills in more detail in the following.

A summary of the current state of research on the volume effect shows that the evidence is still mixed as to whether the volume effect exists; which volume effect is important, hospital or physician; what kind of effects they are; and the direct channel through individual physician's skills, spillover effects from other physicians, or organizational skills of the hospital as a whole.

Investigation into these questions is especially urgent in Japan because no reliable measures of the quality of care are published beyond the number of procedures or operations, a measure that is not only very popular but also adopted by the Japanese government as a criterion for determination of reimbursement. This paper will contribute to our knowledge about the existence, the nature, and the channels of the volume effect and will pave the way to evidence-based policy making in health care.

5.3   Research Strategy

Our research strategy in this paper is as follows. We restrict our analysis to AMI patients who underwent PTCA.[10] This, we believe, minimizes the potential for bias due to patient selection and different combinations of treatments. As explained later, we also adjust for risk of mortality based on

---

10. Canto et al. (2000) and Thieman et al. (1999) also examine volume effect on AMI patients.

individuals' severity of illness and comorbidities, as measured by International Classification of Diseases (ICD) codes.

Our main focus is the nature of the volume effect and the channels through which it operates. The first question about the nature of the volume effect is whether it operates at the hospital level or physician level. A direct channel for the volume effect would be through individual physicians' skills. However, the volume effect may also operate at the hospital level if there are interactions among physicians or spillover effects from other physicians or overall hospital skills. Therefore, we will analyze the volume effect at the hospital level as well as the physician level.[11]

The second question about the nature of the volume effect is whether the volume effect is linear or nonlinear. A "practice makes perfect" effect does not necessarily imply a linear relationship between volume and outcomes. The marginal effects of volume may be decreasing, that is, may exhibit decreasing returns to scale. And the volume effect could be negative after a certain point due to, for example, congestion effects. Physicians and hospitals have limited capacity due to constraints on time, physical strength, mental acuity (especially concentration), operating space, equipment, staff, and so on. Hence, very high volumes could result in worse outcomes.

As for the channels through which PTCA volume affects outcomes, we will examine externalities or spillover effects among physicians and from team staff or the hospital as a whole. We can imagine the existence of organizational skills or teamwork effects because physicians do not treat patients alone. Physicians may benefit from good team work, suggestions from experienced mentors, and peer pressures from other physicians. Furthermore, high-volume hospitals may have superior equipment and systems that support complex treatments, or they may have the advantage of ample staff and physicians to provide high quality care. In particular, hospitals may adopt continuous quality improvement (CQI), which consists of the repetitive cycle of process and outcomes measurement, design and implementation of interventions to improve the process of care, and remeasurement to determine the effect on quality of care (Ferguson et al. 2003). Halm, Lee, and Chassin (2000) note that the more complex the treatment process, the more likely it is that physician or surgeon skill will be only one of many important components of the full complement of effective care. One advantage of our data set is that it permits the identification of individual physicians, although the identification is not perfect. By using hospital volume in conjunction with physician volume, we can distinguish between the effects of physician volume per se and overall hospital effects and the spillover effect from other physicians.

As we will see later, a physician in a high-volume hospital does not nec-

---

11. The unit of analysis is patients. Hospital or physician volume is common to patients who underwent PTCA at the same hospitals or by the same physicians.

essarily perform a large number of PTCA procedures. If we were to judge hospital quality by hospital volume, either organizational skills or spillover effects would have to exist so that even a low-volume physician would have better outcomes if he or she works at a high-volume hospital.[12]

An important question is whether volume might simply be a proxy for other effects specific to a hospital or physician. In the case of AMI, Thiemann et al. (1999) report that adjustment for differences in process of care such as use of aspirin, thrombolytic agents, beta-blockers, and ACE inhibitors account for a good part of the survival benefits attributed to high-volume hospitals. Canto et al. (2000) also point out that the lower mortality rates at high-volume hospitals may be due in part to the earlier administration of primary angioplasty after hospitalization.[13] These results suggest that the reported volume effects only represent unobserved effects specific to hospitals or physicians.[14] We are currently investigating this type of factor specific to hospitals or physicians (see Kawabuchi and Sugihara 2003a,b,c).

5.4 Data and Models

The data used in this paper were collected by Kawabuchi in collaboration with the Japan Medical Association. He conducted three waves of surveys of hospitals gathering data on patients' disease diagnoses (ICD-9 or ICD-10), the main operations or procedures patients underwent, and hospital characteristics such as teaching status and the number of beds.

In this paper, we use data from the second and third waves, conducted in 2000 and 2001, respectively.[15] In each wave, thirty-six hospitals participated, of which thirty hospitals took part in both waves. Of the forty-two hospitals in total, sixteen are public (established by the central govern-

12. Another interesting question about the channels through which the volume effect operates is whether experience on AMI patients per se may be important, rather than experience on PTCA. If the volume effect represents the direct effect of physicians' PTCA techniques, then experience on PTCA is essential. However, if it represents overall management of the disease, experience in handling AMI patients may be valuable. Canto et al. (2000) report that even after controlling for the number of patients with myocardial infarction, hospital PTCA volume is inversely related to mortality. Another interesting question is whether the volume of related operations such as CABG is relevant. Percutaneous transluminal coronary angioplasty and CABG are performed by different categories of physicians, but those physicians face the same problems in treating AMI patients and share common knowledge, skills and equipments.

13. Canto et al. (2000) note, however, that there were no important differences in the use of antiplatelet agents, beta-blockers, or heparin among quartiles of hospitals classified by volume.

14. In the case of hip fracture patients in Quebec, Hamilton and Ho (1998) find a volume effect when hospital-specific effects are not included, but when he controls for hospital-specific effects, the volume effect vanishes.

15. The data in the first wave are less reliable due to coding errors, so we exclude it from the analysis.

ment, prefectures, or municipals), and the rest are private. The distribution of hospitals according to the number of beds is as follows: six hospitals have fewer than 200 beds, twelve have 200 to 299, sixteen have 400 to 599, three have 600 to 799, three have 800 to 999, and two have more than 1,000 beds. The total number of patients of all diagnoses is 482,000, of which 3,220 are AMI patients. The number of AMI patients who underwent PTCA is 906.

Diseases and operations or procedures are identified by ICD-9 or ICD-10 codes. Acute myocardial infarction patients are defined by having an ICD-10 code of I21. Percutaneous transluminal coronary angioplasty is identified by ICD-9-CM codes of 3601, 3602, 3605, and 3606, and CABG is identified by ICD-9-CM codes of 3610, 3611, 3612, 3613, 3614, and 3615. In the following we discuss other ICD codes for comorbidities, which we use for risk adjustment.

The main limitations of our data set include the small number of PTCAs per hospital or physician and limited risk adjustment because we obtain information on severity of illness only from ICD-9-CM codes. Hence, as a sensitivity analysis, we report in the appendix supplemental results using the data collected by the Japanese Society of Interventional Cardiology (JSIC). The JSIC data set contains detailed clinical indicators and a large number of PTCA procedures per hospital. Details are described in the appendix.[16]

We focus on the volume effect among AMI patients who underwent PTCA. Focusing on AMI patients has the benefit of reducing referral bias because AMI patients usually have little time or opportunity to select hospitals or physicians, in contrast with elective PTCA.

We use the annual number of PTCA procedures as the volume variable, which is a flow concept.[17] It may be more appropriate to measure volume based on the stock of experience, such as the cumulative number of PTCA procedures performed by a hospital or physician. Due to the limitation of our data set, however, we measure volumes for only up to two years. We leave the question of stock measures of volume for future research. As an outcome we adopt the hazard rate, $h(t)$, which is the instantaneous probability of death at a point in time, conditional on the patient having survived up to that point. This is defined as

$$h(t) = \lim_{\Delta t \to 0} \frac{p(t \leq T < t + \Delta t \mid t \leq T)}{\Delta t},$$

where $p(\cdot)$ denotes a conditional probability and T is a random variable that represents the time of the occurrence of the event (death). By inte-

---

16. See also Chino, Nakanishi, and Isshiki (2000) and Chino et al. (2001).

17. We use the number of PTCA procedures performed on all patients, not just AMI patients because PTCA is essentially the same skill when it is performed on AMI patients as when it is performed on patients with other diseases.

grating this hazard function with respect to time, T, one can infer a patient's probability of death and, hence, the probability of survival.[18]

Conventional practice is to compare in-hospital mortality rates among hospitals with different volumes after adjusting for severity of illness of individual patients. This approach has at least two drawbacks, however. One is that the in-hospital mortality rate contains information only on whether a patient died in the hospital or was discharged alive, neglecting information on whether the patient died soon after PTCA or survived for some time. Our assumption is that a patient who survived for thirty days but then died, for example, was closer to recovery than a patient who died on the first day. This distinction is in line with Doucet et al. (2002) and Kimmel, Sauer, and Brensinger (2002) who show that longer-term outcomes differ from short-term outcomes, implying that the time dimension is important in the evaluation of the quality of health care. The other drawback to the conventional approach is that the first-stage–risk-adjustment regression omits PTCA volume.[19] If PTCA volume truly affects outcomes, the regression without volume variables will result in biased estimates. Therefore, we estimate hazard functions using volume variables as well as other risk factors as independent variables and directly test the hypothesis that the coefficients on the volume variables are significantly different than zero or the associated hazard ratios are significantly different than one.[20]

On the other hand, our estimates may be biased because flow volume is endogenously determined. If, for example, a hospital or physician that is very good at performing PTCA due to reasons other than the volume effect tends to perform a large number of PTCA, as is implied by the selective referral hypothesis, this will result in correlation between the volume variable and the error term in the regression of mortality rates on PTCA volume. To resolve this difficulty, one may explicitly specify the simultaneous determination of volume and quality. Or one may estimate hospital- or physician-specific effects on mortality first and relate such specific effects to volume. We are now investigating this line of research in Kawabuchi and Sugihara (2003a,b,c).

Because the dates of PTCA procedures are unknown in our data set, we cannot specify how long patients survived after they underwent PTCA procedures. Hence, we analyzed survival time after the beginning of hospitalization, not after PTCA. This treatment can be justified on the ground that the timing of performing PTCA is chosen as part of the process of care

18. A survival function, $S(t) \equiv \text{prob}(T > t)$, is related to the hazard function by the following formula: $\int_0^t h(u)du = -\log S(t)$.

19. If a volume variable is included in the regression, the risk-adjusted mortality rate will be independent of volume.

20. This kind of regression approach to the volume effect is adopted by Ellis et al. (1997), Ho (2000), and Thiemann et al. (1999).

so that it is appropriate to measure survival time from the time physicians accept patients and become responsible for them, not from the time they decide to perform PTCA.

Because analysis of the volume effect using the hazard rate is rare,[21] we repeated the analysis using more conventional logistic regression as a sensitivity analysis. We obtained almost identical results, some of which are reported in the context of emergency CABG as an alternative indicator of quality.

We employ three functional forms: linear, log-linear, and quadratic. These cover a wide variety of nonlinearity and have very different policy implications. In the log-linear model, the hazard ratio declines indefinitely as volume increases if the coefficient on the log-linear term is negative. On the other hand, in the quadratic model, the hazard ratio declines up to a certain volume, but increases after that. How much concentration of PTCA procedures is desirable differs between these two models.

In the literature, emergency CABG is often used as an alternative indicator of the quality of health care, as the fact that a patient needs CABG after a failed PTCA clearly represents a bad outcome. It is often found that the volume effect exists for emergency CABG even when no evidence is found for a volume effect on mortality.[22]

Therefore, we conducted multinominal logit analysis using CABG as the dependent variable. However, our data set has two limitations. One is that we cannot distinguish CABG after failed PTCA from other CABG. Hence, we treat CABG in the same hospitalization as emergency CABG. This choice is common in the literature but may be problematic. The second limitation is that only ten patients underwent CABG in the same hospitalization as PTCA. Due to these limitations, we may be unable to obtain reliable estimates. Therefore, in the appendix we conduct a sensitivity analysis using the JSIC data set, which contains more-accurate information on emergency CABG.

We adjust for mortality risk using age, age squared, sex, comorbidities, and the number of occlusions (single- or multivessel disease). We include the following comorbidities (ICD-10 codes in parentheses): diabetes mellitus (E10 to E14), hypometabolism of lipoprotein (E78), hypertension (I10), angina pectoris (I20), chronic ischemic heart disease (I25), heart failure (I47), paroxysmal tachycardia (I48), ventricular fibrillation and flutter

---

21. As far as we know, Thiemann et al. (1999) is the only study which explicitly presents results of estimating Cox proportional hazard models with hospital volume as an independent variable.

22. For example, Halm, Lee, and Chassin (2000) report that, of seven articles that examined hospital volume, only three found an inverse relationship between volume and mortality, but all seven found that lower volume was associated with higher rates of emergency CABG as well as the combined endpoint of inpatient death or emergency CABG.

(I49), other arrhythmia (I50), shock (R57), and transplant or graft (Z95). The ICD-10 code for multivessel angioplasty (multiple occlusions) is 3605.

We use a parametric hazard model, in which the survival time is distributed as the Weibull distribution.[23] That is, let t_{ij} be failure time of the jth patient treated by the ith hospital. In the proportional hazard model, $\lambda_{ij}(t_{ij}) = \lambda_0(t_{ij})\exp(\mathbf{X}_{ij}\beta)$, where $\mathbf{X}_{ij}$ is a matrix of explanatory variables. We specify the baseline hazard as $\lambda_0(t_{ij}) = rt_{ij}^{r-1}$. Then, the survival time follows the Weibull distribution with two parameters, r and μ_{ij}: $f(t_{ij}, \mathbf{X}_{ij}) = r\mu_{ij}t_{ij}^{r-1}\exp(-\mu_{ij}t_{ij}^r)$, where $\mu_{ij} \equiv \exp(\mathbf{X}_{ij}\beta)$.

It is often pointed out that patients are heterogeneous. Even after controlling for severity of illness, some patients are likely to recover, while others are not. This may be due to unobservable patient characteristics or due to the patient's situation, such as distance to the nearest suitable hospital.

To allow for this kind of patient heterogeneity, we incorporate frailty into our model as an unobservable multiplicative effect, α_{ij}.[24] Let $\lambda_{ij}(t_{ij})$ be the usual hazard function. Incorporating frailty, the hazard function becomes $\lambda_{ij}(t_{ij} \mid \alpha_{ij}) = \alpha_{ij}\lambda_{ij}(t_{ij})$. If the realized value of α_{ij} is greater than (less than) 1, then the jth patient treated at the ith hospital tends to fail at a faster (slower) rate. To achieve identification, it is assumed that α_{ij} is a random variable with mean zero and variance θ and that the frailty density function, $g(\alpha)$, is distributed as Gamma$(1/\theta, \theta)$.[25]

Most patients survive their hospital stay and are discharged alive. For these patients we only know that they survived up to the discharge date, which means that our data are right censored. If we ignore censoring by, for example, including only the patients who died or by regarding time to discharge as time to failure, we are certain to obtain incorrect estimates of the survival probabilities. Let T_j be a possibly censored failure time for the jth patient and C_j be the censoring time. Then, the observed time is $Y_j = \min(T_j, C_j)$. If Y_j is not censored, the contribution of the jth observation to the likelihood function is the density function, $f(Y_j)$, for T evaluated at Y_j. If Y_j is censored, we only know that T_j is greater than Y_j, so that the contribution to the likelihood function is the probability that $T_j > C_j$, that is, prob$(T_j > Y_j)$, which is a survival function, $S(Y_j)$. Hence, the joint likelihood function over all observations, $j = 1, 2, \ldots, n$, is $L = \Pi_{j:Y_j \text{ uncensored}}^n$

---

23. The following exposition of the model and estimation methods is fairly standard. See, for example, Harrell (2001) and Klein and Moeschberger (1997).

24. The frailty here is specified at individual-patient level. This treatment is different than the shared frailty models usually encountered in survival analysis. The modeling here is similar to that of stochastic frontier analysis (see Kumbhakar and Lovell 2000).

25. That is, $g(\alpha) = (\alpha^{1/\theta-1})(e^{\alpha/\theta})/\Gamma\,(1/\theta)\theta^{1/\theta}$. Then, the survival function, $S_0(t)$, of a frailty model is related to the survival function, $S(t)$, of a nonfrailty model as $S_0(t) = \{1 - \theta \ln[S(t)]\} - 1/\theta$. If $\theta = 1$, the frailty model is just a usual model without frailty (take the log of both sides). Therefore, we can test the relevance of frailty by checking whether $\theta = 1$. Empirically, we cannot reject the hypothesis that $\theta = 1$ in our sample. We use the frailty model, however, in light of the often expressed concern with patient heterogeneity.

$f(Y_j) \times \Pi_{j:Y_j\text{censored}}^n S(Y_j)$. Taking the logarithm and maximizing L gives estimates of the parameters of $S(t)$.[26]

If hospitals or physicians have different skills, then patients who are treated by different hospitals or physicians will tend to have different outcomes. On the other hand, patients who are treated by the same hospitals or physicians will tend to have similar outcomes. For example, if a hospital or physician is very skillful, patients who are treated by that hospital or physician will have higher probability of recovery relative to the average. Patients who are treated by an unskilled hospital or physician will have higher probability of death relative to the average.

Therefore, in regression analysis, the residuals among patients who are treated by the same hospital or physician are likely to be correlated. Hence, in calculating our standard errors, patients are assumed to be clustered by hospital or physician.[27] Conventional standard errors assume there is no correlation of random errors among patients.

5.5   Overview of the Data

Of 3,220 AMI patients, 906 patients underwent PTCA, and 51 patients died, resulting in a mortality rate of 5.6 percent. There were twenty-three hospitals that performed PTCA, with an average of 96.6 PTCAs per year.[28] This ranges from a minimum of 1 to a maximum of 312. The number of PTCA procedures per hospital in our sample is generally small, but this is not atypical for Japanese hospitals. As we saw in figure 5.1, a vast majority of Japanese hospitals perform very few PTCA procedures. We should be careful in interpreting the results of the analysis because the small number of procedures could potentially mask volume effects. However, in the appendix, we performed a sensitivity analysis with a data set that contains hospitals with much higher volumes. The results of this sensitivity analysis are consistent with the results in the text.

We identified forty-nine physicians who performed more than 5 PTCA procedures on AMI patients in our sample. In our analysis of physician volume, we exclude patients of physicians who performed fewer than 5

26. Here, we are assuming that censoring is uninformative in the sense that censoring occurs independently of the risk of death. This assumption implies that the contribution of the censoring to the likelihood function simply multiplies L and that the censoring distribution contains little information on the survival distribution. Although this is not necessarily true in our sample, we adopt this assumption for the sake of estimation. Incorporating dependence between the censoring time and the risk of death is left for future research.

27. This relates to the concept of shared frailty in the survival literature (see Hougaard [2000], Kalbfleisch and Prentice [2002] and Klein and Moeschberger [1997]). In this analysis we do not incorporate shared frailty into the hazard functions because of technical limitations. We leave this for future research.

28. Nine hospitals performed PTCA in both the second and third waves. In this calculation, we calculated the number of PTCA procedures per hospital on an annual basis for hospitals with survey periods less than twelve months.

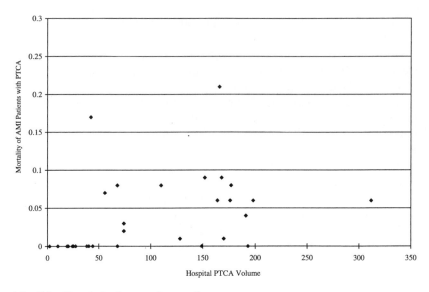

Fig. 5.3   Hospital volume and mortality

PTCA procedures on AMI patients in the data set because these physicians are likely to have extreme outcomes (0 percent or 100 percent mortality, for example) by sheer chance. The average number of PTCAs per physician is 29.5 per year.[29] The maximum number of PTCAs is 144. The average mortality rate is 6.0 percent. The number of observations is 571 when we exclude patients treated by physicians with fewer than 5 PTCA procedures on AMI patients.

Figure 5.3 is a scatter diagram of hospital-level PTCA volume and mortality rates for AMI patients. No clear relationship is apparent. Although this figure shows raw data without risk adjustment, this casts some doubts on the existence of the volume effect at the hospital level.

Figure 5.4 is an analogous scatter diagram for physicians. For physicians with very low volume, mortality rates tend to be high, while for the physicians with higher volume, mortality rates tend to be low. And the relationship seems to be nonlinear, convex to the origin.

Figure 5.5 plots physician PTCA volume against hospital PTCA volume. This figure clearly shows that even within the same hospital, physician volume differs substantially. Physicians in a high-volume hospital do not necessarily have high volume. If there are spillover effects or hospital organizational skills, physicians with low PTCA volume in high-volume

29. Three physicians performed more than five PTCA procedures on AMI patients in both the second and third waves. As with hospitals, we calculated the number of PTCA procedures per physician on an annual basis for physicians with a survey period of less than twelve months.

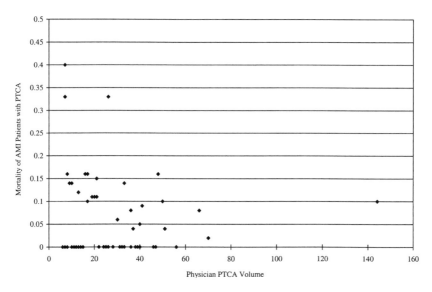

Fig. 5.4   Physician volume and mortality

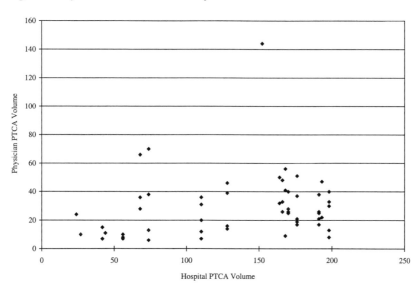

Fig. 5.5   Hospital volume and physician volume

hospitals would tend to have better outcomes. Without such external effects, however, low-volume physicians should have inferior outcomes even if they are at high-volume hospitals. If this is the case, then we should not expect aggregate outcomes at high-volume hospitals to be better than those at low-volume hospitals.

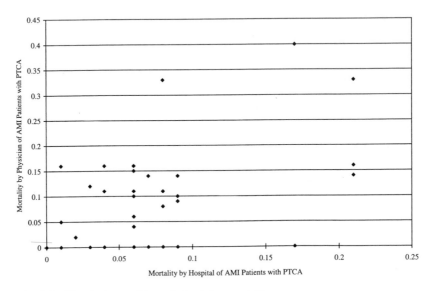

Fig. 5.6   Hospital mortality and physician mortality

Figure 5.6 plots physician-level mortality rates against hospital-level mortality rates. We can see a modest but positive relationship between the two. This might be surprising given the fact mentioned previously that physicians in a high-volume hospital do not necessarily have high PTCA volume. One possibility is that hospital volume has a significant influence on physicians' outcomes. The other possibility is that unobserved common factors affect hospital- and physician-level mortality rates while physician-level mortality is independent of hospital volume.

5.6   Survival Analysis I: Hospital Volume Effect

We estimate hazard functions using three functional forms. One is a linear model in which simply the number of PTCA procedures of each hospital enters as an independent variable. The second is a log-linear model in which the logarithm of PTCA volume enters as an independent variable. The third is a quadratic model in which PTCA volume and squared PTCA volume enter as independent variables.

The results are shown in table 5.1, where we report the hazard ratio for each variable, its standard error, and the p-value for the hypothesis that the hazard ratio is 1. If the hazard ratio of a variable is larger than 1, it means that the variable significantly raises the mortality rate.

We first examine the results of the linear model. Percutaneous transluminal coronary angioplasty volume is not statistically significant at

Table 5.1 Hospital volume effect

Independent variables	Linear model			Log-linear model			Quadratic model		
	Hazard ratio	Standard error	p-value	Hazard ratio	Standard error	p-value	Hazard ratio	Standard error	p-value
Volume variables									
PTCA volume	1.001	0.003	0.752	1.050	0.324	0.874	1.004	0.009	0.653
PTCA volume squared							1.000	0.000	0.652
Demographic characteristics									
Age	0.947	0.104	0.620	0.946	0.102	0.610	0.949	0.103	0.628
Age squared	1.001	0.001	0.385	1.001	0.001	0.372	1.001	0.001	0.387
Sex	1.612	0.634	0.225	1.604	0.620	0.222	1.621	0.639	0.220
Risk adjustment									
Diabetes mellitus	0.904	0.264	0.729	0.906	0.263	0.734	0.897	0.260	0.709
Hypometabolism of lipoprotein	0.337	0.259	0.156	0.336	0.257	0.154	0.335	0.258	0.155
Hypertension	0.365	0.111	0.001	0.364	0.112	0.001	0.364	0.111	0.001
Angina pectoris	0.485	0.266	0.188	0.486	0.269	0.192	0.491	0.274	0.202
Chronic ischemic heart disease	1.113	0.448	0.791	1.113	0.441	0.787	1.095	0.426	0.816
Heart failure	1.139	0.441	0.736	1.129	0.437	0.755	1.125	0.444	0.766
Paroxysmal tachycardia	0.448	0.485	0.458	0.451	0.486	0.459	0.443	0.476	0.449
Ventricular fibrillation/flutter	1.330	1.303	0.771	1.333	1.308	0.770	1.337	1.307	0.766
Other arrhythmia	1.296	0.417	0.420	1.301	0.416	0.410	1.298	0.423	0.423
Shock	2.082	1.411	0.279	2.105	1.427	0.272	2.083	1.415	0.280
Transplant/graft	1.116	0.680	0.858	1.108	0.703	0.871	1.128	0.682	0.842
Multiple occlusions	3.955	0.896	0.000	3.966	0.942	0.000	3.813	0.954	0.000
Number of observations	906			906			906		
Log likelihood	−232.999			−233.031			−232.930		

conventional significance levels. Among risk factors, multiple occlusions significantly raises the hazard ratio.

The overall results are similar in the log-linear and quadratic models. In the log-linear model, the logarithm of PTCA volume is not statistically significant, and neither is the squared PTCA volume in the quadratic model.

We find no evidence that hospital volume has a significant influence on the hazard ratio in either the linear or nonlinear case.[30] In other words, we do not find either a learning-by-doing effect or a congestion effect at the hospital level. This result is in sharp contrast with the common belief that the more PTCAs a hospital performs, the better the hospital becomes in the provision of PTCA. This could be due to the fact that physicians in a high-volume hospital are not necessarily high-volume physicians. Even when the volume effect is operative at the physician level, it may not be translated into a volume effect at the level of the hospital as a whole if there are no spillover effects from other physicians or organizational skills. If this is the case, it is not appropriate to judge the quality of care of a hospital based on the hospital's PTCA volume.

5.7 Survival Analysis II: Physician Volume Effect

Next, we examine the effects of physician volume on mortality. From the outset, caution is in order. In our data set, the identification of physicians is uncertain because a physician code does not necessarily identify the physician who performed PTCA, but may instead identify the physician who was responsible for the overall management of the patient.

As with hospital volume, we estimate hazard functions using three functional forms: linear, log-linear, and quadratic. For each functional form, we also examine additional effects of organizational skill and spillover effects from other physicians by including hospital PTCA volume and the volumes of other physicians at the same hospital.

Table 5.2 reports the results when only physician volume is used as an independent variable. We show the coefficients and standard errors for the volume variables in parentheses in addition to the hazard ratio, its standard error, and p-values for the hypothesis that the hazard ratio is 1. In the linear model, physician volume is not statistically significant. Among risk factors, shock and multiple occlusions significantly raise the hazard ratio.

In the log-linear model, the logarithm of physician volume significantly affects the mortality rate. The parameter estimates for the other variables are similar to those from the linear model. We can infer from the estimates how much the hazard ratio decreases as physician volume increases. The

30. To check the sensitivity of the results to small numbers of PTCA per hospital, we repeated the analysis excluding patients who were treated at hospitals with fewer than five PTCA procedures on AMI patients recorded in the data set. The results (not shown) were quite similar.

Table 5.2   Physician volume effect

	Linear model			Log-linear model			Quadratic model		
Independent variables	Hazard ratio[a]	Standard error[b]	p-value	Hazard ratio[a]	Standard error[b]	p-value	Hazard ratio[a]	Standard error[b]	p-value
Volume variables									
PTCA volume	0.99369 (−0.00633)	0.00521 (0.00524)	0.227	0.65616 (−0.42135)	0.12410 (0.18913)	0.026	0.96807 (−0.03245)	0.01529 (0.01579)	0.040
PTCA volume squared							1.00019 (0.00019)	0.00009 (0.00009)	0.047
Demographic characteristics									
Age	1.052	0.186	0.772	1.047	0.172	0.780	1.035	0.168	0.830
Age squared	1.000	0.001	0.963	1.000	0.001	0.983	1.000	0.001	0.967
Sex	3.259	1.277	0.003	3.191	1.187	0.002	3.035	1.191	0.005
Risk adjustment									
Diabetes mellitus	0.846	0.500	0.778	0.865	0.496	0.800	0.827	0.472	0.739
Hypometabolism of lipoprotein	0.220	0.239	0.164	0.229	0.253	0.183	0.227	0.248	0.175
Hypertension	0.467	0.281	0.206	0.470	0.283	0.210	0.455	0.277	0.196
Angina pectoris	0.393	0.278	0.187	0.392	0.265	0.166	0.394	0.262	0.161
Chronic ischemic heart diseases	1.908	0.803	0.125	2.053	0.882	0.094	2.071	0.898	0.093
Heart failure	0.811	0.701	0.809	0.944	0.799	0.945	0.99	0.839	0.989
Paroxysmal tachycardia	0.363	0.440	0.404	0.334	0.406	0.367	0.325	0.395	0.355
Ventricular fibrillation/flutter	2.092	1.961	0.431	2.223	1.990	0.372	2.134	1.850	0.382
Other arrhythmia	1.072	0.419	0.859	1.078	0.398	0.840	1.108	0.410	0.782
Shock	7.508	6.742	0.025	6.351	5.147	0.023	5.985	4.928	0.030
Transplant/graft	2.522	1.976	0.238	2.529	1.902	0.218	2.422	1.832	0.242
Multiple occlusions	6.464	1.838	0.000	7.058	2.200	0.000	5.952	1.602	0.000
Number of observations	571			571			571		
Log likelihood	−155.317			−154.343			−154.175		

[a]Coefficients in parentheses.
[b]Standard errors of coefficients in parentheses.

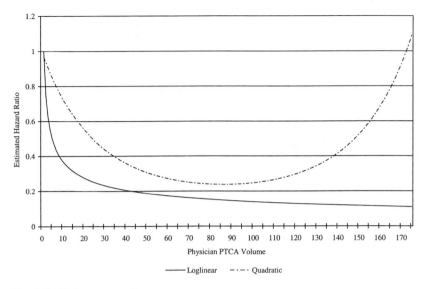

Fig. 5.7   Volume-mortality curve

solid line in figure 5.7 shows this relationship. By assumption, the log-linear model implies that the hazard ratio decreases indefinitely, asymptotically converging to zero. In the very low-volume region, the decrease in the hazard ratio is dramatic. However, the rate of decrease decelerates quickly. Around sixty or seventy PTCA procedures, the decrease becomes quite moderate. Note, however, that the standard error of the estimate on the logarithm of physician volume is so large that the 95 percent confidence interval for the hazard ratio is very wide, ranging from 0.45 to 0.95, with a point estimate of 0.66.

In the quadratic model of physician volume, both the quadratic term and the linear term are statistically significant. The coefficients in parentheses indicate that the lowest hazard ratio is attained at around 85 PTCA procedures. Up to that point, the hazard ratio decreases as physician volume increases, but after that point the hazard ratio increases as physician volume increases. The dotted line in figure 5.7 depicts the relationship between the estimated hazard ratio and PTCA volume in the quadratic model. Again, the initial reduction in hazard ratio is impressive. At the lowest point, the hazard ratio is slightly over 0.2. However, after around 85 PTCA procedures, the hazard ratio increases rapidly. Of course, we should be cautious in extrapolating hazard ratios because we have only one physician with more than 100 PTCA procedures. However, the nonlinearity found in our regression results makes us skeptical of the simple "the more, the better" principle.

We find that performing more PTCA procedures produces learning-by-doing effects at first but congestion effects later.[31] This result seems reasonable because physicians have limited capacity so that with too many PTCA procedures, they may be too busy to perform well. This also implies that an incentive to increase volume over certain levels may have adverse effects.

Although we find significant physician volume effects, it is important to note that risk factors such as shock and multiple occlusions significantly raise the hazard ratio. In the log-linear and quadratic models, the existence of shock or multiple occlusions raises the hazard ratio by a factor of about 6 to 7. These estimates may appear to be extreme, but it is certainly true that risk factors have large effects on mortality. When we analyze the JSIC data with different and more detailed risk adjustment in the appendix, we also find strong effects from risk factors such as the existence of occlusion in the left main trunk, the number of occlusions, and an AMI severity index. The AMI severity index takes the value 1 if any of the following are observed and zero otherwise: sustained ventricular tachycardia/ventricular fibrillation (VT/VF), shock, heart failure, insertion of a pacemaker, or cardiopulmonary resuscitation. This result reinforces the fact that risk adjustment is essential for the evaluation of the quality of health care. Even with significant volume effects, judging the quality of health care only by volume is inadequate.

We then examine the question of whether organizational skills related to overall hospital volume are important. To do this, we include the number of PTCA procedures performed at each hospital in the regression. In this case, hospital volume represents the effects of hospital volume after controlling for physician-specific effects. If hospital volumes are significant in addition to physician volumes, it provides evidence for effects of organizational skills and spillover effects from other physicians. Three functional forms are again employed, linear, log-linear, and quadratic.

Table 5.3 shows the results. In the linear model, hospital volume is not statistically significant, and physician volume is also insignificant. In the log-linear model, hospital volume is not statistically significant, while physician volume is significant. In the quadratic model, both physician and hospital volumes are strongly significant. However, the effect of hospital volume is difficult to interpret. The estimated coefficients imply that the hazard ratio increases as hospital volume increases up to a little more than ninety PTCA procedures and decreases after that.

Overall, hospital volume does not seem to be an additional contributing factor to the higher quality of health care. The fact that we find a

31. As a sensitivity analysis, we analyzed in-hospital mortality as the dependent variable in a logistic regression treating the observations as a panel data with random effects. We obtained similar results, including the volume at which the lowest mortality is attained. See also the first equation of the multinominal model in table 5.4 below in the context of emergency CABG as an alternative indicator of quality of health care.

Table 5.3   Physician volume effect with hospital volume

Independent variables	Linear model			Log-linear model			Quadratic model		
	Hazard ratio[a]	Standard error[b]	p-value	Hazard ratio[a]	Standard error[b]	p-value	Hazard ratio[a]	Standard error[b]	p-value
Volume variables									
Physician PTCA volume	0.99388 (−0.00613)	0.00491 (0.00494)	0.215	0.65216 (−0.42747)	0.14086 (0.21599)	0.048	0.96289 (−0.03781)	0.01477 (0.01534)	0.014
Physician PTCA volume squared							1.00020 (0.00020)	0.00009 (0.00009)	0.033
Hospital PTCA volume	0.99734 (−0.00266)	0.00336 (0.00337)	0.429	1.02584 (0.02551)	0.38686 (0.37712)	0.946	1.05265 (0.05131)	0.02688 (0.02553)	0.044
Hospital PTCA volume squared							0.99979 (−0.00021)	0.00010 (0.00010)	0.035
Demographic characteristics									
Age	1.047	0.182	0.793	1.048	0.170	0.773	1.103	0.196	0.580
Age squared	1.000	0.001	0.993	1.000	0.001	0.977	1.000	0.001	0.751
Sex	3.094	1.314	0.008	3.209	1.331	0.005	3.203	1.337	0.005
Risk adjustment									
Diabetes mellitus	0.895	0.531	0.851	0.861	0.498	0.796	0.941	0.562	0.919
Hypometabolism of lipoprotein	0.221	0.238	0.162	0.229	0.254	0.184	0.221	0.249	0.180
Hypertension	0.469	0.278	0.198	0.470	0.286	0.215	0.434	0.264	0.170
Angina pectoris	0.375	0.266	0.167	0.394	0.267	0.169	0.412	0.281	0.194
Chronic ischemic heart disease	2.090	0.859	0.073	2.037	0.858	0.091	2.192	0.846	0.042
Heart failure	0.805	0.694	0.801	0.944	0.799	0.946	0.716	0.623	0.701
Paroxysmal tachycardia	0.374	0.451	0.414	0.333	0.404	0.365	0.362	0.462	0.426
Ventricular fibrillation/flutter	2.421	2.328	0.358	2.199	2.023	0.392	3.256	3.029	0.204
Other arrhythmia	1.085	0.410	0.829	1.077	0.400	0.841	1.248	0.459	0.546
Shock	9.016	8.177	0.015	6.242	5.314	0.031	11.276	10.355	0.008
Transplant/graft	2.323	1.857	0.291	2.545	1.923	0.216	2.154	1.709	0.333
Multiple occlusions	7.018	2.323	0.000	7.021	2.400	0.000	5.296	1.795	0.000
Number of observations	571			571			571		
Log likelihood	−155.070			−154.341			−152.120		

[a]Coefficients in parentheses.

[b]Standard errors of coefficients in parentheses.

significant volume effect only at the physician level, not at the hospital level, can be interpreted in two ways. One interpretation is that the volume effect operates only through a direct channel, namely physicians' PTCA techniques and that spillover effects and effects of organizational skill are weak. Another interpretation is that organizational skills resulting from teamwork, good management, and so on are not related to hospital volume. Even a hospital with a small number of PTCA procedures could provide an excellent medical team and good management and, in particular, could adopt CQI, which stresses that outcomes of health care are direct results of the properties of the system of care (Berwick 1996), although the evidence for the effectiveness of CQI is rather mixed (Shortell, Bennett, and Byck 1998). To disentangle these possibilities will be an important agenda for future research.

5.8   Alternative Outcome Indicator: Emergency CABG

In this section, we analyze another indicator of the quality of health care. There are several candidates, including readmission rates and emergency CABG. Our data set includes information on single hospitalizations, so readmission could not feasibly be measured.

Therefore, we focus on emergency CABG after failed PTCA. However, due to the limitations of our data set, we define *emergency CABG* as all CABGs occurring in the same hospitalization as a PTCA. Though this definition is not ideal, many other studies define emergency CABG in the same way. This analytic strategy is justified on the assumption that if a patient's medical condition requires CABG at the beginning of the hospitalization, the patient would not be subjected to a PTCA. We must be careful in interpreting the results, however, because what we define as *emergency CABG* likely includes some CABGs performed prior to PTCA and some nonemergency CABGs after PTCA.

We estimate multinominal logit models for patients who underwent PTCA, in which the dependent variable can take the following three values: discharged alive without CABG, died in hospital without CABG, and received emergency CABG (whether discharged alive or died in hospital). Conventional studies compare emergency CABG rates among hospitals or physicians independently of whether patients are discharged alive or died in hospital. In that case, there are only two outcomes, received emergency CABG and did not. In reality, however, there are three outcomes after PTCA: discharged alive without CABG, died in hospital without CABG, and received emergency CABG. Therefore, we simultaneously model outcomes of PTCA using multinominal logit models. Of course, our approach is still incomplete in that multinominal logit model assumes independence of irrelevant alternatives (IIA). This assumption is almost certainly violated in this case. But we do have enough information to conduct multinominal probit analysis, which does not require the IIA assumption. We leave for future research the question of robustness of the IIA assumption.

We analyze the effects of hospital volume as well as physician volume using, as usual, three functional forms: linear, log-linear, and quadratic. Table 5.4 reports the results, in which two equations are being estimated simultaneously. One is the equation on the probability of death, denoted "Died." The other is the equation on the probability of CABG in the same hospitalization, denoted "CABG." Only the parameter estimates for the PTCA volume variable are reported.

The left half of the table shows the hospital volume effects. In both the death equation and the CABG equation, the effect of hospital volume is

Table 5.4   Emergency CABG as an alternative indicator of quality of care

	Hospital volume			Physician volume		
Independent variables	Hazard ratio[a]	Standard error[b]	p-value	Hazard ratio[a]	Standard error[b]	p-value
Died						
PTCA volume	1.00242	0.00324	0.456	0.99405	0.00619	0.338
	(0.00241)	(0.00324)		(−0.00597)	(0.00623)	
CABG						
PTCA volume	1.00213	0.00600	0.723	1.00434	0.02294	0.850
	(0.00212)	(0.00598)		(0.00433)	(0.02284)	
Number of observations	906			571		
Log likelihood	−205.842			−114.183		
Died						
PTCA volume	1.35706	0.52742	0.432	0.63929	0.14454	0.048
	(0.30532)	(0.38865)		(−0.44739)	(0.22609)	
CABG						
PTCA volume	0.86768	0.69850	0.860	1.48060	1.77685	0.744
	(−0.14193)	(0.80502)		(0.39245)	(1.20009)	
Number of observations	906			571		
Log likelihood	−205.842			−113.135		
Died						
PTCA volume	1.00423	0.01030	0.681	0.96348	0.01682	0.033
	(0.00422)	(0.01026)		(−0.03720)	(0.01746)	
PTCA volume squared	0.99999	0.00003	0.809	1.00023	0.00011	0.026
	(−0.00001)	(0.00003)		(0.00023)	(0.00011)	
CABG						
PTCA volume	1.00728	0.02481	0.769	1.07816	0.11898	0.495
	(0.00725)	(0.02463)		(0.07525)	(0.11035)	
PTCA volume squared	0.99998	0.00008	0.804	0.99946	0.00061	0.376
	(−0.00002)	(0.00008)		(−0.00054)	(0.00061)	
Number of observations	906			571		
Log likelihood	−2205.778			−112.358		

[a]Coefficients in parentheses.
[b]Standard errors of coefficients in parentheses.

not statistically significant in either the linear model (upper panel), the log-linear model (middle panel), or the quadratic model (lower panel).

The right half of the table examines the physician volume effect. In the linear model, physician volume is not statistically significant in either the first equation on the probability of death or in the second equation on the probability of CABG. In the log-linear and quadratic models, physician volume is statistically significant in the death equation. These results are consistent with the earlier survival analysis using a parametric hazard function. In the second equation on the probability of CABG, physician volume is not statistically significant in either the log-linear or quadratic models.

In sum, the probability of death results presented here confirm the earlier results from the survival analysis using parametric hazard function. We do not, however, find evidence for an effect of hospital or physician volume on emergency CABG. This could be due to imprecise identification of emergency CABG, however. When we do the same exercise in appendix using the JSIC data set, which has more accurate identification of emergency CABG, we find a significant effect of hospital volume on emergency CABG in the quadratic model, although the results are not consistent across specifications.

5.9   Conclusion

This paper has examined the empirical relevance of the volume effect in Japan and investigated the nature and channels of volume effect. The main conclusions are as follows:

1. *The volume effect operates not at the hospital level but at the physician level.* This seems plausible because in a hospital different physicians have different volumes, so we should not expect an aggregate volume effect to exist for a hospital as a whole. This finding is robust even when we utilize a data set with detailed risk adjustment and larger PTCA volume per hospital (shown in the appendix). This result implies that policies focused on the hospital as a whole are not appropriate.

2. *The volume effect is nonlinear.* We find significant volume effects for physicians, but the relationship is not linear. The principle of "the more, the better" applies only up to a certain volume. If the quadratic model holds, volumes above a certain level result in worse outcomes, or, as an old sage in China said, "too much is as bad as too little." We suspect that this is due to congestion effects resulting from the fact that physicians themselves have a limited capacity to perform PTCA. The result implies that incentives to increase volume over certain levels may have adverse effects.

However, the log-linear model seems to be equally plausible. We cannot determine which model is more appropriate because very few physicians performed sufficiently large numbers of PTCA procedures. Note, however, that even if the log-linear model holds, in which mortality rate decreases indefinitely, the benefit of higher volume is exhausted rather quickly. In terms of competition policy, nonlinearity of the volume effect implies that, from a medical point of view, a highly concentrated market is not required.

3. *Risk adjustment is essential for the evaluation of the quality of health care.* Although we find significant physician volume effects, it is important to notice that risk factors such as shock and multiple occlusions greatly increase the hazard ratio. Even with significant volume effects, judging the quality of health care by volume alone is inadequate.

4. *We observe virtually no spillover effects nor organizational skill.* We find no evidence for spillover effects or organizational skills as represented by hospital volumes, which may imply that physicians learn by themselves. This does not necessarily mean, however, that there is no role for peer groups, teamwork, mentors, and so on. Presumably, it simply means that these effects are independent of volume.

5. *More intensive as well as extensive data collection is needed.* Although we believe that the data set we used is one of the best currently available, it has limitations. Possible improvements include a much larger sample size, more-detailed clinical indicators, information on the timing of treatments, more-accurate outcome measures, precise physician identification, proper measures of volume and emergency CABG, and so on.

6. *Future research should focus on the question of whether volume effects simply reflect other factors specific to hospitals or physicians.* These factors include the style of care, adequate staffing and good teamwork, sufficient equipment, the role of the hospital in the health care system (designated emergency hospitals, teaching status, etc.) and internal as well as external governance mechanisms (not-for-profit or incorporated status, the extent to which appointments of physicians are controlled by the professors in the university departments from which physicians are graduated, whether the head of the hospital is dictatorial or not, etc.). We are measuring hospital and physician-specific effects and making a first step in this direction in Kawabuchi and Sugihara (2003a,b,c).

Appendix

Sensitivity Analysis Using the JSIC Data Set

Our sensitivity analysis focuses on three aspects of our methodology. The first is concerned with our strategy of limiting the analysis to include only AMI patients receiving PTCA. The second is the sensitivity of our results to the limited risk adjustment and the small number of PTCA procedures per hospital. The third is the incomplete identification of emergency CABG in the analysis of emergency CABG as an alternative indicator of the quality of health care services.

As for the first aspect, we could have included in our analysis non-AMI patients who underwent PTCA. In the main text we showed that the number of PTCAs per hospital has no effects on the outcomes of AMI patients. One may wonder, therefore, whether we obtain different results if we analyze the volume effect on all patients, including non-AMI patients.

For the second aspect, our data set contains limited information on risk factors, obtained from ICD codes so that insufficient risk adjustment may be responsible for our results. Furthermore, hospitals in our data set perform very few PTCA procedures per year. In the literature, a volume effect is often found among the highest-volume hospitals, although even in the United States typical hospitals perform only a limited number of PTCA procedures.

As for the third aspect, we regard CABG in the same hospitalization as emergency CABG and find no evidence for an effect of volume on CABG. However, this result may be due to the limitation of our data set, namely that we cannot distinguish between emergency CABG post-PTCA, CABG before PTCA, or nonemergency CABG.

For these sensitivity analyses, we use a data set collected by the JSIC, which includes both AMI and non-AMI patients who underwent PTCA. However, the volume variable only captures the number of PTCA procedures performed at the hospital level. We cannot determine the number of PTCA procedures by each physician.

The main advantage of using this data set is that it contains detailed clinical indicators such as which vessels were occluded, the number of occlusions, and a severity index (which reflects sustained VT/VF, shock, heart failure, etc.). Furthermore, this data set has the merit of identifying emergency CABG explicitly. We have information on whether a patient underwent CABG operation after PTCA during the same hospitalization. In addition, the hospitals in the sample performed large numbers of PTCA procedures per year.

Of thirty-eight hospitals that participated in the survey, thirty-four hospitals performed PTCA on patients with AMI, unstable angina, or other diseases. The average number of PTCAs per hospital is 261, with the maximum of 750 and the minimum of 40. There were 2,011 patients who underwent PTCA procedures in the data set, of whom 640 were AMI patients, and 1,370 were non-AMI patients. Mortality rates in the sample are 6.2 percent for AMI patients and 0.5 percent for non-AMI patients. See Chino, Nakanishi, and Isshiki (2000) and Chino et al. (2001) for more detail.

Risk factors included in the regression are age, age squared, sex, the vessel where occlusions occurred (right coronary artery, left coronary artery, circumflex artery, left main trunk), the number of vessels occluded, and the AMI severity index. The severity index takes the value 1 if any of the following occurred and zero otherwise: sustained VT/VF, shock, heart failure, insertion of a pacemaker, or cardiopulmonary resuscitation. We experimented with including other risk factors such as diabetes mellitus, comorbidities, and Type C lesion but found these generally to be insignificant so that we drop them in view of the limited number of observations.

We exclude variables specifying the type of procedure, such as intra-aortic balloon pumping (IABP) and primary PTCA. This is because the procedures are endogenously determined in the process of care so that the inclusion of procedural variables could result in biased estimates.[32] If we were to include this type of variable, we would have to take into consideration explicitly the simultaneity of procedures and outcomes.

Volume Effect of PTCA on AMI versus Non-AMI Patients

We first examine the effects of each hospital's number of PTCA procedures on all patients including both AMI and non-AMI patients. We include dummy variables representing indications of AMI and unstable angina. This is because AMI patients are, arguably, more likely to die than patients with other diseases, including unstable angina.

We estimate three functional forms as in the main text: linear, log-linear, and quadratic. The results (not shown) are that in each of the three models, hospital PTCA volume does not significantly affect the hazard ratio, although an indication of AMI, the number of occlusions, and an occlusion in the left main trunk significantly raise the hazard ratio. These results justify our strategy of analyzing only AMI patients, leaving out non-AMI patients.

Detailed Risk Adjustment and Higher Hospital Volume

Henceforth we concentrate on AMI patients. We estimate a parametric hazard function using three functional forms: linear, log-linear, and quadratic. Table 5A.1 shows the results. None of the volume variables in the linear, log-linear, or quadratic models are statistically significant. Among the risk factors, the number of occlusions and AMI severity index are highly statistically significant.

These results are obtained with detailed risk adjustment and higher hospital volumes. Therefore, our results in the main text are robust to risk adjustment methods and hospital volume.

Emergency CABG as an Alternative Indicator of Quality

As in the main text, we estimate a multinominal logit model that describes the probabilities of discharge alive, death after PTCA, and emergency

32. When we include IABP or primary PTCA, we find that IABP is strongly statistically significant, but primary PTCA is not.

Table 5A.1 Hospital volume effect on mortality of AMI patients

Independent variables	Linear model			Log-linear model			Quadratic model		
	Hazard ratio[a]	Standard error[b]	p-value	Hazard ratio[a]	Standard error[b]	p-value	Hazard ratio[a]	Standard error[b]	p-value
Volume variables									
Hospital PTCA volume	0.998 (−0.002)	0.001 (0.001)	0.155	0.753 (−0.284)	0.207 (0.275)	0.302	1.000 (−0.000)	0.005 (0.005)	0.924
Hospital PTCA volume squared							1.000 (−0.000)	0.000 (0.000)	0.733
Risk adjustment									
Age	0.735	0.137	0.097	0.733	0.142	0.108	0.729	0.144	0.109
Age squared	1.003	0.002	0.083	1.003	0.002	0.097	1.003	0.002	0.095
Sex	0.740	0.510	0.662	0.732	0.504	0.651	0.735	0.505	0.654
Right coronary artery	3.768	5.146	0.331	3.316	4.967	0.423	4.029	5.609	0.317
Left anterior descending coronary artery	6.238	9.526	0.231	5.472	8.961	0.299	6.607	10.132	0.218
Left circumflex coronary artery	1.778	1.554	0.510	1.445	1.269	0.675	1.866	1.619	0.472
Left main trunk	45.841	136.407	0.199	41.678	130.094	0.232	48.878	140.191	0.175
Number of occlusions	2.766	1.056	0.008	2.760	1.104	0.011	2.755	0.978	0.004
AMI severity index	32.745	31.446	0.000	30.652	31.876	0.001	34.765	35.018	0.000
Number of observations	544			544			544		
Log likelihood	−122.731			−122.956			−122.695		

[a]Coefficients in parentheses.

[b]Standard errors of coefficients in parentheses.

CABG. The dependent variable takes the value zero if the patient is discharged alive without emergency CABG, 1 if he or she died without emergency CABG, and 2 if he or she underwent emergency CABG with or without dying. The sample for this analysis consists of AMI patients who underwent PTCA first.

Table 5A.2 reports the results, where only the results for hospital PTCA volume are shown. In the linear model, PTCA volume is not significant in

Table 5A.2   **Emergency CABG as a quality indicator: Multinominal logit models Chino data**

Independent variables	Hospital volume		
	Hazard ratio[a]	Standard error[b]	p-value
A. Linear model			
Died			
PTCA volume	0.998	0.001	0.111
	(−0.002)	(0.001)	
CABG			
PTCA volume	0.996	0.005	0.430
	(−0.004)	(0.005)	
Number of observations		547	
Log likelihood		−94.324	
B. Log-linear model			
Died			
PTCA volume	0.630	0.134	0.030
	(−0.463)	(0.213)	
CABG			
PTCA volume	0.441	0.257	0.160
	(−0.819)	(0.584)	
Number of observations		547	
Log likelihood		−94.096	
C. Quadratic model			
Died			
PTCA volume	0.995	0.003	0.121
	(−0.005)	(0.003)	
PTCA volume squared	1.000	0.000	0.378
	(0.000)	(0.000)	
CABG			
PTCA volume	0.987	0.006	0.033
	(−0.013)	(0.006)	
PTCA volume squared	1.000	0.000	0.013
	(0.000)	(0.000)	
Number of observations		547	
Log likelihood		−93.581	

[a]Coefficients in parentheses.

[b]Standard errors of coefficients in parentheses.

either the first equation concerning the probability of death or in the second equation on the probability of emergency CABG.

In the log-linear model, hospital volume is a significant predictor in the death equation, but not in the emergency CABG equation. In the quadratic model, hospital volume is significant in the emergency CABG equation, but not in the death equation.

These results are somewhat inconsistent with the results of the survival analysis estimating parametric hazard function with the same JSIC data set and the results in the main text. In view of the fact that hospital volume is not consistently significant across various specifications, we cannot say definitely that hospital volume has significant effects on mortality or emergency CABG. However, in the case of emergency CABG, considering the problems identifying emergency CABG in our data set, we may give more faith to the results obtained in the JSIC data set than in our data set.

References

American College of Cardiology/Society for Cardiac Angioplasty and Interventions. 2001. Guidelines for Percutaneous Coronary Intervention. *Journal of the American College of Cardiology* 37 (8): 2239i–lxvi.

Berwick, Donald. 1996. A primer on leading the improvement of systems. *British Medical Journal* 312:619–22.

Birkmeyer, John, Therese Stukel, Andrea Siewers, Philip Goodney, David Wennberg, and Lee Lucas. 2003. Surgeon volume and operative mortality in the United States. *New England Journal of Medicine* 349:2117–27.

Canto, John, Nathan Every, David Magid, William Rogers, Judith Malmgren, Paul Frederick, William French, Alan Tiefenbrunn, Vijay Misra, Catarina Kiefe et al. 2000. The volume of primary angioplasty procedures and survival after acute myocardial infarction. *New England Journal of Medicine* 342:1573–80.

Chino, Masao, Narumoto Nakanishi, and Takaaki Isshiki. 2000. The first nationwide database for cost analysis of percutaneous transluminal coronary angioplasty (PTCA) in Japan part 1: Registry and basic characteristics [in Japanese]. *Japanese Journal of Interventional Cardiology* 15:407–12.

Chino, Masao, Narumoto Nakanishi, Takaaki Isshiki, and Hideki Hashimoto. 2001. The JSIC nationwide database for cost analysis of percutaneous transluminal coronary angioplasty (PTCA) in Japan part 2: Multivariate analysis of initial in-hospital charge and the inter-hospital difference [in Japanese]. *Japanese Journal of Interventional Cardiology* 16:401–07.

Doucet, Michael, Mark Eisenberg, Lawrence Joseph, and Louise Pilote. 2002. Effects of hospital volume on long-term outcomes after percutaneous transluminal coronary angioplasty after acute myocardial infarction. *American Heart Journal* 144:144–50.

Ellis, Stephen, Nowamagbe Omoigui, John Bittl, Michael Lincoff, Mark Wolfe, Georgiana Howell, and Eric Topol. 1996. Analysis and comparison of operator-specific outcomes in interventional cardiology. *Circulation* 93:431–39.

Ellis, Stephen, William Weintraub, David Holmes, Richard Shaw, Peter Block, and

Spencer King. 1997. Relation of operator volume and experience to procedural outcome of percutaneous coronary revascularization at hospitals with high intervention volumes. *Circulation* 95:2479–84.

Ferguson, T. Bruce, Eric D. Peterson, Laura P. Coombs, Mary Eiken, Meghan Carey, Frederick Grover, and Elizabeth DeLong. 2003. Use of continuous quality improvement to increase use of process measures in patients undergoing coronary artery bypass graft surgery. *Journal of the American Medical Association* 290:49–56.

Fujita, Takashi, and Toshihiko Hasegawa. 1999. Technology agglomeration of cardiovascular operations and its evaluation [in Japanese]. *Byoin Kanri* 36:76.

———. 2000. Technology agglomeration of treatments of AMI patients and its evaluation [in Japanese]. *Byoin Kanri* 37:106.

Fujita, Takashi, Yuki Hasegawa, and Toshihiko Hasegawa. 2001. An analysis of treatments of AMI patients in the second medical area [in Japanese]. *Nihon Eiseigaku Zasshi* 56:195.

Fujita, Takashi, Hisayoshi Kondo, Yuki Hasegawa, and Toshihiko Hasegawa. 2000. An analysis of operation on cancer patients II [in Japanese]. *Nihon Eiseigaku Zasshi* 55:222.

Halm, Ethan, Clare Lee, and Mark Chassin. 2000. How is volume related to quality in health care? A systematic review of the research literature. In *Interpreting the volume-outcome relationship in the context of health care quality,* Maria Hewitt for the Committee on the Quality of Health Care in America and the National Cancer Policy Board. Washington, DC: Institute of Medicine, National Academy Press. http://books.nap.edu/catalog/10005.html.

Hamilton, Barton, and Vivian Ho. 1998. Does practice makes perfect? Examining the relationship between hospital surgical volume and outcomes for hip fracture patients in Quebec. *Medical Care* 36 (6): 892–903.

Hannan, Edward, Michael Racz, Thomas Ryan, Ben McCallister, Lewis Johnson, Djavad Arani, Alan Guerci, Julio Sosa, and Eric Topol. 1997. Coronary angioplasty volume-outcome relationships for hospitals and cardiologists. *Journal of the American Medical Association* 279:892–98.

Harrell, Frank. 2001. *Regression modeling strategies.* New York: Springer-Verlag.

Hasegawa, Yuki, Toshihiko Hasegawa, and Takashi Fujita. 2000. An analysis of operation on cancer patients I [in Japanese]. *Nihon Eiseigaku Zasshi* 55:223.

Ho, Vivian. 2000. Evolution of the volume-outcome relation for hospitals performing coronary angioplasty. *Circulation* 101:1806–11.

Hougaard, Philip. 2000. *Analysis of multivariate survival data.* New York: Springer-Verlag.

Jollis, James, Eric Peterson, Charlotte Nelson, Judith Stafford, Elizabeth DeLong, Lawrence Muhlbaier, and Daniel Mark. 1997. Relationship between physician and hospital coronary angioplasty volume and outcome in elderly patients. *Circulation* 95:2485–91.

Kalbfleisch, John, and Ross Prentice. 2002. *The statistical analysis of failure time data.* 2nd ed. Hoboken, NJ: Wiley.

Kawabuchi, Koichi, and Shigeru Sugihara. 2003a. Hospital- and physician-specific effects on outcomes of PTCA for AMI patients. Mimeograph.

———. 2003b. Hospital-specific effects on after-discharge outcomes of PTCA for AMI patients. Mimeograph.

———. 2003c. The quality and costs of PTCA procedures on AMI patients in Japan. Mimeograph.

Kimmel, Stephen, William Sauer, Colleen Brensinger, John Hirshfeld, Howard Haber, and Russell Localio. 2002. Relationship between coronary angioplasty laboratory volume and outcomes after hospital discharge. *American Heart Journal* 143:833–40.

Klein, John, and Melvin Moeschberger. 1997. *Survival analysis.* New York: Springer-Verlag.

Kumbhakar, Subal, and Knox Lovell. 2000. *Stochastic frontier analysis.* Cambridge: Cambridge University Press.

McGrath, Paul, David Wennberg, John Dickens, Adrea Siewers, Lee Lucas, David Malenka, Mirle Kellett, and Thomas Ryan. 2000. Relation between operator and hospital volume and outcomes following percutaneous coronary intervention in the era of the coronary stent. *Journal of the American Medical Association* 284:3139–44.

Shortell, Stephen M., Charles L. Bennett, and Gayle R. Byck. 1998. Assessing the impact of continuous quality improvement on clinical practice: What it will take to accelerate progress? *Milbank Quarterly* 76:593–624.

Takeshita, Akira. 2000. *Survey of hospitals on cardiovascular intervention in Japan* [in Japanese]. Tokyo: Ministry of Health, Labor and Welfare.

Thiemann, David, Josef Coresh, William Oetgen, and Neil Powe. 1999. The association between hospital volume and survival after acute myocardial infarction in elderly patients. *New England Journal of Medicine* 340:1640–48.

Tsuchibashi, M., Hiroyuki Tsutsui, Hideo Tada, Miwako Shihara, Suminori Kono, and Akira Takeshita. 2003. The volume-outcome relation for hospitals performing angioplasty for acute myocardial infarction: Results from nationwide Japanese registry [in Japanese]. Mimeograph.

Vakili, Babak, Robert Kaplan, and David Brown. 2001. Volume-outcome relation for physicians and hospitals performing angioplasty for acute myocardial infarction in New York State. *Circulation* 104:2171–76.

Market Concentration, Efficiency, and Quality in the Japanese Home Help Industry

Yanfei Zhou and Wataru Suzuki

6.1 Introduction

Aging is one of the most challenging problems facing contemporary Japanese society. According to the 2000 population census, the elderly (aged sixty-five and over) as a fraction of the population reached 17.4 percent in 2000. The elderly fraction is projected to accelerate and reach 27.0 percent in 2017, meaning that the elderly will make up more than one-quarter of the Japanese population.[1] Although aging increases the demand for nursing care services, until quite recently the family network played the traditional primary role in providing care for the frail elderly. However, changes in the social structure, such as weakening community ties, nuclearization of the family, and feminization of the workforce, have made the financial and psychological burdens of family-based care for the aged unbearably large.

In response to the expanding elderly population and the increasing demand for social nursing care services, the Public Nursing Insurance Act (*Kaigo Hoken Ho*) was formally enacted in September 1997. Under this legislation, the Ministry of Health, Labor and Welfare (MHLW) introduced a new public long-term care insurance system in April 2000. This new system aims to respond to society's major concerns about aging and

Yanfei Zhou is a research fellow at The Japan Institute for Labour Policy and Training. Wataru Suzuki is an assistant professor in the Department of Education at Tokyo Gakugei University.

We are grateful to David Wise, David Cutler, Naohiro Yashiro, Reiko Suzuki, Koichi Kawabuchi, Haruko Noguchi, and Chapin White for their helpful comments on our earlier version. We also appreciate Bank of Japan for permitting us to use their microdata.

1. The source is the medium variant projection of the National Institute of Population and Social Security Research (January, 2003).

to assure citizens that they will receive care, if necessary, and be supported by society as a whole.[2]

According to the MHLW statistics, the supply of care services expanded after implementing the insurance system.[3] However, the effects of market-oriented reform on service quality and efficiency are unknown. More specifically, we do not know whether introducing competition by expanding the number of providers in an area can simultaneously improve the quality of service and management efficiency.

Due to the lack of microlevel panel data spanning the transition period, this paper will use cross-sectional data to investigate the effect of market concentration on the quality and cost of home help services.[4] We choose to focus our analysis on home help services because the reforms in this market have been dramatic, and the proportion of for-profit providers[5] is one of the highest among the at-home nursing care businesses.

The number of home help service providers (henceforth referred to as care providers) per thousand elderly will be employed as an index of market concentration. To evaluate the impact of market-oriented reform on service quality and efficiency, it is important to know whether care providers in unconcentrated (i.e., highly competitive) markets have a higher level of quality and efficiency than those in highly concentrated markets. This information is also helpful for determining the appropriate number and scale of operations of care providers in each district.

No academic studies have been done on the relationship between market concentration and quality of service or management efficiency among home help providers in Japan.[6] According to the Survey of Nursing Care Management[7] (*Kaigo Jigyo Keei Jita Chosa*) 2002 by MHLW, the higher the market competition (or, the fewer users per care facility) the higher the costs per care plan. This suggests that competition among care providers may lead to higher management costs, which is reminiscent of the "medical arms race hypothesis" in hospital industry research. This paper shows that this finding does not hold in the context of the home health industry when we use an appropriate econometric framework to control for the effect of other related factors such as the quality of service.

2. See Abe (2003) for a detailed description of the nursing care system.
3. For example, from April 2000 to February 2002, the number of providers registered in WAM-NET doubled, from 9,185 to 18,389.
4. Home help service is one of the most important categories of at-home nursing care services. See appendix A for an introduction to the institutional setting of the at-home nursing care business.
5. According to the Survey of Nursing Care Facilities 2000 by the MHLW, 30.3 percent of home help providers were for-profit companies in December 2000.
6. Shimizutani and Suzuki (2002) investigated the impact of ownership and years in operation on cost and quality using a data set similar to ours.
7. According to the survey results, cost per care plan varies with the number of users per facility. The average cost per care plan in facilities with fewer than 20 users was 12,955 yen, while for those in a facility with more than 200 users, it was only 7,606 yen (41 percent less).

The paper proceeds as follows. Section 6.2 provides a theoretical background and reviews previous empirical research on quality and efficiency issues. Section 6.3 describes the survey data used in this study. Section 6.4 develops the econometric method for estimating the quality and cost functions. Section 6.5 presents empirical results. Specifically, after proposing a set of indices to measure the quality of services, it explores the relationship between market concentration and the quality of services. Section 6.5 also evaluates the effect of market concentration on management after adjusting for quality of services and other related factors. Section 6.6 concludes. Appendix A outlines a set of original indices for measuring quality of care services. Appendix B presents a brief description of the institutional setting of the at-home nursing industry in Japan.

6.2 Previous Research

Theoretically, market concentration in an otherwise perfectly competitive market is generally understood to weaken competition and to have undesirable effects on service quality and management efficiency. However, it is also frequently argued that consumers do not necessarily benefit from competition among service providers. The medical care industry is one relevant example. It differs from traditional industries in three aspects: insurance coverage (for most services), the prevalence of nonprofit providers, and the agency role of physicians and medical care staff. Consequently, hospitals tend to compete with each other on nonprice aspects. This wasteful competition is colloquially referred to as the "medical arms race" (MAR).[8] According to the MAR hypothesis, hospitals compete by providing too many high-technology medical services and hiring excess staff. At the same time, unnecessary duplication of services may cause the quality of care to drop as providers fail to take advantage of the scale of learning effect[9] (Robinson and Luft 1985; Robinson 1988; Hersch 1984; Luft et al. 1986). Zwanziger and Melnick (1988) find evidence consistent with the MAR hypothesis and infer that, as a result, hospitals compete on quality instead of price.

Although most of the nonprice competition literature falls into the preceding categories, there are some exceptions. After taking into consideration local population structure and market structure, the model of Dranove, Shanley, and Simon (1992) casts doubt on claims that hospital mergers increase efficiency by reducing competition. In addition, Shortell and Hughes (1988) employ in-hospital mortality as an index of quality of service and find no significant association between quality of service and

8. For a more comprehensive review, see Dranove and White (1999).
9. "The scale of learning effect" refers to the inverse relationship between an organization's size and the cost of organizational knowledge. Hence, a market with only one supplier maximizes the scale of learning effect.

market concentration. Kessler and McClellan (1999) even find a negative relationship between heart attack mortality and the Herfindahl index in United States since 1990, suggesting that competition led both to substantially lower costs and to significantly lower rates of adverse outcomes.

Literature on the effect of market concentration on the cost of nursing home care is quite limited. Assuming the presence of endogenous and unobserved quality, Gertler and Waldman (1992) investigate the effect of cost-saving public policies on the quality of nursing homes using the survey data of New York State. They find that the increases in competition are associated with higher levels of both quality and cost, and that a 1 standard deviation reduction in competition will reduce costs by about 20 percent but reduce quality by only 2.5 percent. Nyman (1994), on the contrary, finds that policies designed to control government expenditure by limiting the number of nursing home beds in an area may result in excess demand and discourage effort by nursing homes to improve management efficiency. Because higher prices may cause private patients to exhaust their financial resources and become Medicaid patients sooner than they otherwise would, policies that limited competition may have had indirect cost-increasing consequences.

Few empirical studies have examined the effects of Japan's new "deregulation" policies on the quality and cost of home help services. It should be emphasised, however, that even with the new deregulation policies, the prices of home help services are largely fixed in Japan, resulting in a market that is far from perfectly competitive.[10] Because providers are unable to attract customers with lower prices, competition for customers centers on advertising or kickbacks to administrative organizations, leading to higher cost without commensurate benefits such as improvement of service quality (Nanbu 2000). Thus, in the case of Japan's home help industry, although we expect a positive effect of market competition on service quality, we cannot predict whether market competition will drive up costs. Hence, it is extremely important and worthwhile to examine these phenomena empirically.

6.3   Data

The sample is drawn from the Survey of the Environment Surrounding Home Help Providers, conducted by the Bank of Japan and one of the authors (Suzuki) in August 2000. First, 1,200 providers in Kanto district were selected by the method of population weighted stratified random sampling.[11] Then questionnaires were sent to each of 1,200 selected providers,

---

10. The prices of nursing care services are set in detail by the MHLW. The standard prices vary with the type of service, time of day, qualifications of the home helper, and municipality.
11. The distribution of samples by prefectures is as follows: Ibaragi: 80; Gunma: 61; Tochii: 62; Chiba: 174; Saitama: 201; Tokyo: 372; and Kanagawa: 250.

and 445 valid responses were collected (response rate 37.1 percent). Although some providers are running subsidiary businesses such as at-home bathing or day service, the survey gathered information on management costs and outputs relating solely to the home help business.

The 445 providers in the sample are classified by ownership, with the results summarized in table 6.1. The ownership composition in our data is very similar to data obtained from the nationwide provider census, with the one difference being that providers in our sample consist of relatively more for-profit providers and nonprofit providers such as co-ops, agriculture cooperatives, and nonprofit organizations (NPOs). In addition, the share of social welfare associations and medical corporations is somewhat lower in our sample than in the nationwide data.

Table 6.1   **Distribution of providers by ownership category**

| | Our survey | | |
Ownership	No. of observations	Percent	Nationwide (%)
For-profit providers			
Stock corporations and limited			
private companies	204	46.7	40.4
Individuals	4	0.9	
Public providers			
Local public organizations[a]	2	0.5	2.3
Social welfare associations[b]	96	22.0	20.1
Nonprofit providers			
Social welfare corporations (excluding			
social welfare associations)[c]	46	10.5	18.2
Medical corporations[d]	20	4.6	10.0
Civil corporations[e]	16	3.7	1.9
Other nonprofit organizations	49	11.2	7.0
Total	437	100.0	100.0

Source: Nationwide data are derived from the census data conducted by Ministry of Health, Labor and Welfare in July 2000.

[a]Local public organizations are corporations run by local governments directly.

[b]Social welfare associations are a kind of social welfare corporations that are run by local public organizations. Social welfare associations generally have some advantages in achieving agential jobs or underlying subsidies from the local government but they must afford to embrace redundant staffs from local government as an exchange.

[c]Social welfare corporations, established by individuals or organizations, are permitted to run social welfare business only. Although social welfare corporations can enjoy equipment subsidies from the government and receive certain tax benefits, they are prohibited to make profit or own estates in personal equipment subsidies from the government and receive certain tax benefits, they are prohibited to make profit or own estates in personal name.

[d]Medical corporations are nonprofit organizations run by hospitals.

[e]Civil corporations run public welfare businesses under the supervision of the regulatory authorities. Civil corporations may enjoy certain tax benefits but generally can not receive any subsidies from the government.

Our data include detailed information for each home help provider on subsidiary businesses, scale of operations, balance sheets, employee composition, length of operation, and operation costs. We construct three measures of the output of home help services: total hours[12] of physical nursing service, total hours of housework assistance service, and total hours of combination service (including both physical nursing service and housework assistance service). We also construct a systematic index to measure the quality of services of each home help provider. Table 6.2 presents basic descriptive statistics on the variables used in the analysis.

6.4   Theoretical Models

In this section, we develop two models, the first model focusing on providers' choice of quality and the second focusing on the costs of production and efficiency. Specifically, let the care demand function be

$$(1) \qquad Y = Y(P, Q, \mathbf{Z}),$$

where P is the price charged, Q is quality, $\mathbf{Z}$ is a vector of exogenous variables that shift the demand curve, such as the competitiveness and demographic characteristics of the care provider's local market. The cost function is

$$(2) \qquad C = C(Y, Q, \mathbf{W}),$$

where Y is the output of a specific care provider, and $\mathbf{W}$ is a vector of exogenous factor input prices faced by the provider. In this analysis, output Y is classified into three categories: hours of physical nursing service (A), hours of housework assistance service (B), and hours of combination service (C). The input vector $\mathbf{W}$ includes labor cost (labor cost/overall employment hours) and administrative cost[13] (administrative cost/overall employment hours).

Hence, care providers choose price and quality to maximize profits I

$$(3) \qquad I = P \cdot Y(P, Q, \mathbf{Z}) - C(Y, Q, \mathbf{W}).$$

The corresponding first-order conditions are

$$(4) \qquad \frac{\partial I}{\partial Q = 0} \rightarrow P \cdot \frac{\partial Y}{\partial Q} = \frac{\partial C}{\partial Q}.$$

We assume that output Y is exogenous[14] and that prices P are fixed under the Japanese nursing care price system. Therefore, the equations (1),

---

12. Total hours = (number of users per month) × (visits per user per month) × (hours per visit).

13. Administrative cost includes the cost of renting office space, the cost of water and heating, as well as the maintenance cost of automobiles.

14. Strictly speaking, Y is not exogenous even in the case of Japanese nursing care market. To make the model as simple as possible, we assume Y to be exogenous.

Table 6.2   **Descriptive statistics**

Variables	Number of observations	Mean	Standard deviation
Total cost (in 10,000 yen)	399	1,034.52	1,952.70
Wage (= labor cost/overall employment hours, in yen)	344	1,172.04	238.44
Administrative cost (= administrative cost/overall employment hours, in yen)	386	5,468.03	14,177.37
Total hours of physical nursing service provided	427	192.77	304.40
Total hours of housework assistance service provided	427	307.13	613.51
Total hours of hybrid services provided	427	273.94	576.04
Predicted service quality in terms of the total score (Qhat1)	439	8.71	0.72
Predicted service quality in terms of the score of the first principle factor (Qhat2)	439	0.01	0.41
Length of operation (in years)	433	7.11	14.76
Percentage of branch office	445	30.6	0.46
Percentage of providers in region 1	445	37.3	0.48
Percentage of providers in region 2	445	16.4	0.37
Percentage of providers running medical facility business simultaneously	445	2.0	0.14
Percentage of providers running at-home assistance business simultaneously	445	62.9	0.48
Percentage of providers running at-home bathing business simultaneously	440	13.6	0.34
Percentage of providers running day care business simultaneously	445	14.4	0.35
Percentage of providers running sales and lending business of welfare equipment simultaneously	445	7.9	0.27
Percentage of providers running food delivery business simultaneously	445	1.1	0.11
Percentage of providers running short-stay business simultaneously	445	4.7	0.21
Percentage of providers running at home nursing and rehabilitation business simultaneously	445	2.0	0.14
Percentage of regular customers	400	836.1	2.42
Percentage of customers secured before the start of reform	410	404.7	3.63
Percentage of customers in need of nursing care certified as band 3 or over	419	350.1	2.16
Percentage of newer providers	437	56.0	0.50
Percentage of for-profit providers	437	46.7	0.50
Percentage of nonprofit providers	437	40.7	0.49
Percentage of public providers	437	10.8	0.31
Number of providers per thousand elderly	439	44.8	0.22

Note: Minus values of Qhat2 have been transformed to suit for a log form.

(2), and (4) can be solved for the endogenous variable Q in terms of exogenous variables Y, $\mathbf{W}$, and $\mathbf{Z}$:

(5) $$Q = Q(Y, \mathbf{W}, \mathbf{Z})$$

We choose to represent the equilibrium quality function (5) using the following functional form:

(6) $$Q_i = \alpha_0 + \alpha_1 L_i + \alpha_2 Y_i + \mathbf{Z}\rho + u_i$$

where L_i is the total labor hours, and $\mathbf{Z}$ is a vector of exogenous variables for each care provider that includes the market competition level and dummy variables for whether the provider is nonprofit, public, new, or a branch office and dummy variables for region.[15]

Turning to the estimation of the cost function, this analysis employs a quality-adjusted translog cost function. By using the translog cost function, we can make inferences about the principal economic effects without imposing restrictive assumptions on elasticities of substitution among inputs or on returns to scale. The empirical counterpart of equation (2) is the following translog cost function:

$$
\begin{aligned}
\text{(7)} \quad \log C = {} & \alpha_0 + \alpha_y \log Y + \alpha_q \log Q + \sum_{i=1}^{n} \alpha_{wi} \log \mathbf{W}_i + \frac{1}{2}\beta_{yy}(\log Y)^2 \\
& + \frac{1}{2}\beta_{qq}(\log Q)^2 + \frac{1}{2}\sum_i \sum_j \beta_{ij} \ln \mathbf{W}_i \ln \mathbf{W}_j + \beta_{yq} \log Y \log Q \\
& + \sum_i \beta_{yw} \log Y \log \mathbf{W}_i + \sum_i \beta_{qw} \log Q \log \mathbf{W}_i + \sum_i \varepsilon_i \log \mathbf{W}_i \\
& + \mathbf{Z}\gamma + u
\end{aligned}
$$

Because we are interested in the effect of $\mathbf{Z}$, particularly market concentration, on cost, we employ $\mathbf{Z}$ as a vector of exogenous variables in the cost function as well. To be consistent with economic theory, the cost function should be linearly homogenous in input prices, and the cross-coefficients must be symmetric, which implies the following restrictions on equation (7):

$$\sum_i \alpha_{wi} = 1, \quad \sum_i \beta_{ij} = \sum_j \beta_{ji} = 0, \quad \sum_i \beta_{yw} = 0, \quad \sum_i \beta_{qw} = 0$$

Using Shephard's Lemma, the optimal demand for the ith input is obtain by differentiating the cost function with respect to the price of the ith input ($\mathbf{W}_i$), that is, the price of labor. Letting s_i denote the cost share of in-

---

15. There are three region dummies, defined to reflect details of the public long-term-care payment system.

put i and differentiating the cost function of equation (3) with respect to $\mathbf{W}_i$ yields the following structure of the cost shares:

$$(8) \qquad s_i = \alpha_{wi} + \sum_j \beta_{ij} \log \mathbf{W}_j + \beta_{yw} \log Y + \beta_{qw} \log Q + \varepsilon_i,$$

where j denotes the price of inputs other than labor. The cost equation (7) is estimated jointly with the preceding share equation (8) using nonlinear methods subject to the restrictions imposed previously. In particular, Q will be treated as an observed and endogenous variable to emphasize its role as a quality variable. Its predicted value (Qhat) obtained from the estimation of quality function, will be employed as an explanatory variable in the cost function.[16]

6.5   Empirical Results

6.5.1   Quality Comparisons

Currently no uniformed criteria exist for determining the quality of nursing services in Japan. For example, it is well known that the cities of Kobe and Yokohama and Hokkaido prefecture have designed their own sets of local quality criteria and used them in assessment activities. The questionnaire we used[17] includes fourteen indexes that could be measured objectively and precisely. For analytic convenience, we divided these fourteen indexes[18] into four categories: quality management, service convenience, information service, and the skills of the home help staff.

In the following we compare the average quality of services among care providers in a highly concentrated local market[19] with their counterparts in a sparsely concentrated local market. It should be noted that the local market concentration is computed as the number of care providers per thousand elderly (age sixty-five or over), the elderly being the potential users of nursing care services in the area. Table 6.3 employs the four subindexes listed in appendix A to compare the mean scores of providers in the two different types of markets. Areas where the number of providers per thousand elderly is less than the median are categorized as highly concentrated (less-competitive) markets.

We prepared two sets of scores to measure the overall quality of care.

16. Gertler and Waldman (1992) treat quality as endogenous, unobservable variable.

17. Shimizutani and Suzuki (2002) have used an even more comprehensive index derived from a survey performed by the Cabinet Office of the Japanese government in 2001.

18. See appendix A for detailed descriptions about the fourteen subindexes.

19. The common assumption of local market is the municipality in which the care provider is located. There are certainly a few users whose care provider is located in a neighboring municipality, but we assume most users in Japan are using facilities inside their residence municipality.

Table 6.3   Comparison of quality of services by market concentration level

Subindex of quality of services	All providers	Providers in low-concentrated market	Providers in highly concentrated market	Relative score[a]
Quality management	2.20	2.24	2.10	+*
Service convenience	2.84	2.89	2.74	+
Information service	1.65	1.63	1.69	−
Ability of the home help staff	1.88	1.87	1.92	−
Total score	8.69	8.77	8.55	+
Score of the first principle factor	0.000	0.037	−0.069	+

Notes: We define markets where the number of care providers are less than the average level as highly concentrated (less-competitive) market, or we define the markets as low-concentrated (more competitive) ones.

[a]In the last column of each score, "+" implies that the average score of providers in the low-concentrated market is higher than that in the highly concentrated market, while "−" refers to the reverse.

*Significant at the 10 percent level.

The "total score" is calculated by simply adding the scores for each subindex, and hence each query is equally weighted. The "score of the first principal factor" is estimated by principal factor analysis, where each index was assigned different weights. In table 6.3, a "+" ("−") indicates that the average score of providers in highly competitive (low-concentration) markets is higher (lower) than that of the providers in less-competitive markets.

According to the results in table 6.3, for half of the subindexes the sign on the differences between types of markets supports the hypothesis that care providers in highly competitive markets are providing better services. Comparisons using the total score and the scores of the principal component, which are more comprehensive indices of quality, are in accordance with our expectation. The magnitudes of the quality gaps are quite small, however, and only the quality management subindex differs significantly between providers in high-concentration markets versus low-concentration markets.

The results in table 6.3 are informative but lack statistical significance and ignore important information because the market concentration variable is treated as a binary variable (above or below average). Furthermore, given that the service quality of care providers could be influenced by other factors besides market concentration, it is important to control for their separate effects using multiple regression.

The quality function in equation (6) is estimated with ordinary least squares (OLS) using a Huber-White Sandwich estimator of the variance, which accounts for heteroscedasticity to some extent. Table 6.4 highlights the estimated coefficients on the market competition ratio (which equals

Table 6.4   **Estimation of service quality functions**

	Competition level ratio		
	Coefficient	t-value	Adjusted R^2
Case 1: Quality management	−0.131	−0.58	0.173
Case 2: Service convenience	−0.031	−0.12	0.087
Case 3: Information service	0.273**	2.37	0.088
Case 4: Ability of the home help staff	0.122	1.17	0.110
Case 5: Total score	0.110	0.29	0.117
Case 6: Score of the first principle factor	0.097	0.56	0.180

Notes: Estimations are based on the following equation:

$$Q = \beta(0) + \beta(1) \cdot \text{ratio} + \beta(2) \cdot \text{nonprofitdummy} + \beta(3) \cdot \text{publicproviderdummy}$$
$$+ \beta(4) \cdot \text{newproviderdummy} + \beta(5) \cdot \text{regiondummies} + \beta(6) \cdot \text{branchdummy}$$
$$+ \beta(7) \cdot \text{laborhours} + u,$$

where Q is the dependent variable that is the score of each subindex (cases 1 to 4), or the total scores (case 5), or the principle component scores (case 6), and ratio is the number of care providers per thousand people in the population. This table highlights the estimated parameters of ratio only. The equation in case 1 is estimated by OLS with a Haber-White Sandwich estimator of variance, and hence the heteroskedasticity of residuals is adjusted.
**Significant at the 5 percent level.

the number of care providers per thousand population). The estimation results present a somewhat different image from the descriptive statistics in table 6.3. Contrary to the results in table 6.3, the competition ratio has a positive effect on the third index of service quality, after controlling the effects of other covariates such as ownership dummy and region dummy. In other words, with all else held constant (scale of operations, region, and ownership), home help providers' information services improve as market competition rises. However, the competition ratio has no effect on the other three subindexes or the two comprehensive indexes. In sum, the effect of market concentration on service quality, if one exists, is quite limited.

6.5.2   Efficiency

Table 6.5 reports results of the translog cost function analysis, where case 1 employs the sum of total scores as an index of the quality of services, and case 2 employs the score of the first principal component as a proxy for quality of service.

As shown in table 6.5, although there are some differences in the magnitude of coefficients and t-values, we find no substantial differences between the parameter estimates across the two cases. For the market concentration variable, which is our focus, both cases 1 and 2 indicate that an increase in competition is associated with lower cost. In other words, the statistically significant negative coefficient on the market concentration index indicates that the number of care providers per thousand elderly is negatively associated with cost. This result is in accordance with that of Nyman (1994),

Table 6.5 **Estimation of translog cost functions**

	Case 1: Quality = total score		Case 2: Quality = first PC	
	Coefficient	t-value	Coefficient	t-value
ln (Total hours of physical nursing service) – A	1.1850**	2.40	0.9120**	2.51
ln (Total hours of physical nursing service)^2	0.0076***	3.17	0.0062***	2.69
ln (Total hours of house work assistance service) – B	0.6675	0.86	0.8485*	1.66
ln (Total hours of house work assistance service)^2	0.0015	0.61	0.0010	0.43
ln (Total hours of hybrid services) – C	−0.0816	−0.11	−0.5506	−1.06
ln (Total hours of hybrid services)^2	0.0074***	2.97	0.0062**	2.54
ln (A) · ln (B)	0.0004	0.17	0.0017	0.72
ln (B) · ln (C)	0.0036	1.54	0.0049**	2.12
ln (C) · ln (A)	0.0022	0.88	0.0031	1.30
ln (Wage) or ln (W)	2.2347***	3.59	1.4320***	4.92
ln (Wage)^2	−0.0345	−1.57	−0.0310	−1.47
ln (Admin. cost) or ln (AC)	−1.2347**	−1.98	−0.4320	−1.49
ln (AC)^2	0.0508***	12.58	0.0494***	12.70
ln (W) · ln (AC)	−0.0164	−0.70	−0.0184	−0.82
ln (A) · ln (W)	−0.0322	−0.60	−0.0764	−1.39
ln (B) · ln (W)	0.0056	0.11	−0.0106	−0.21
ln (C) · ln (W)	0.0149	0.21	0.0682	0.95
ln (A) · ln (AC)	0.0022	0.58	0.0023	0.60
ln (B) · ln (AC)	0.0051	1.61	0.0063**	2.05
ln (C) · ln (AC)	0.0043	0.37	0.0103	0.96
ln (Qhat)	79.5113***	4.45	46.1283***	5.18
ln(Qhat)^2	−12.4044***	−3.13	−8.4008***	−2.79
ln (Qhat) · ln (A)	−0.3935*	−1.82	−0.2020	−1.27
ln (Qhat) · ln (B)	−0.3095	−1.14	−0.5321***	−2.84
ln (Qhat) · ln (C)	0.0294	0.11	0.1172	0.60
ln (Qhat) · ln (W)	−0.9191***	−3.05	−0.8286***	−4.51
ln (Qhat) · ln (AC)	0.9191***	3.05	0.8286***	4.51
Length of operation	0.0016	0.50	0.0016	0.52
Branch office dummy	−0.7974***	−6.36	−1.3453***	−8.81
Dummy for region 1	−0.7129***	−5.71	−0.5752***	−5.06
Dummy for region 2	−1.0610***	−7.21	−0.7165***	−5.70
Dummy for medical facilities	0.2362	0.79	0.1609	0.56
Dummy for at-home assistance business	−0.0218	−0.24	−0.0048	−0.05
Dummy for at-home bathing business	−0.0004	0.00	0.0334	0.30
Dummy for day care business	0.1115	0.78	0.1815	1.30
Dummy for sales and lending business of welfare equipments	−0.1727	−1.19	−0.1826	−1.31
Dummy for food delivery business	−0.7331	−1.45	−0.7025	−1.44
Dummy for short-stay business	0.0486	0.23	0.0099	0.05
Dummy for at home nursing and rehabilitation business	0.0713	0.24	0.0181	0.06
Proportion of regular users	−0.0089	−0.47	−0.0173	−0.93
Proportion of users secured before 2000	0.0092	0.57	0.0075	0.49
Proportion of users in need of nursing care band 3 or over	0.0056	0.24	0.0140	0.63

Table 6.5   (continued)

	Case 1: Quality = total score		Case 2: Quality = first PC	
	Coefficient	t-value	Coefficient	t-value
Dummy for newer provider	0.4581***	3.79	−0.1088	−1.01
Dummy for nonprofit provider	0.6459***	4.62	0.7016***	5.21
Dummy for public provider	0.3718**	2.17	1.1954***	6.10
Index of market concentration	−0.2815*	−1.65	−0.3813**	−2.31
Constant	−108.1708***	−5.23	−42.0996***	−6.17
R^2	0.7022		0.7193	
Number of observations	306		306	

Notes: The dependent variable is the logarithm of the total expenditure (ln [C]) of individual provider. Index of market concentration refers to the number of care providers per thousand in each area. First principle factor has been transformed to suit for a log form.
***Significant at the 1 percent level.
**Significant at the 5 percent level.
*Significant at the 10 percent level.

but as we mentioned in the introductory section, it is contradicted by the descriptive results of MHLW.

The estimation of the cost function has some other interesting implications. First, among the three kinds of home help services, only physical nursing service is significantly associated with higher cost in both cases. This result is consistent with the notion that physical nursing care is the most costly service among the three kinds of home help service. Second, running subsidiary businesses imposes no significant effect on cost. This result is somewhat surprising but suggests a lack of compensatory benefits between home help and other at-home nursing care businesses. Third, branch offices have lower costs than headquarters in both cases, with the possible reason being that the branch office requires lower costs for advertising, information collection, or employee training. Fourth, newer care providers are less cost-efficient than the older care providers (case 1 only), after controlling for ownership effect and quality of services. This result is quite natural because the newer providers require more initial investment cost than the older ones. In addition, coefficients on the nonprofit provider dummy and public provider dummy are positive and significant in both cases.[20] This outcome is quite plausible because it is well known that nonprofit or public providers generally lack incentives to minimize costs. Finally, the coefficient on quality is positive and statistically significant, which implies that a tradeoff relationship exists between quality and cost.

20. Shimizutani and Suzuki (2002), on the contrary, have reported a significantly negative relationship between public provider dummy and cost.

6.6   Concluding Remarks

Because of the dramatic aging of Japan's population, the nursing care system in Japan has been reformed in order to stimulate the supply of care services and improve quality. This analysis focuses on the home help industry and investigates whether market competition improves quality or reduces costs.

This analysis contributes to Japan's nursing care literature in the following aspects: first, it is the first study to use cross-section data to probe the relationships among market concentration, cost, and quality in an econometric framework. Second, it estimates the cost function while controlling for the effect of quality, an observable and endogenous variable in our model. Hence, our analysis provides statistically reliable results. Third, it develops a set of comprehensive and systematic indices to evaluate the quality of nursing services, which could be a useful reference for government decision-making.

Our major findings are summarized as follows:

1. Holding constant the scale of operations, region, and ownership, we find a positive relationship between market competition and quality of services only in the case of information services. This result shows that the impact of market competition on the quality of care service, if any, was quite limited in 2000.

2. Contrary to the impression created by the descriptive results from the survey by MHLW, this analysis shows that competition is associated with lower costs. In other words, market competition induces cost savings in the home help care market.

3. We also find that there is a tradeoff between quality and cost, running a subsidiary business has few cost-saving premiums, branch offices have lower costs than headquarters, and new providers and nonprofit providers incur higher costs than their counterparts.

Turning to policy implications, although we hesitate to generalize our findings beyond the home help business,[21] this paper suggests that there are no foundations for the concern that market-oriented reforms will sacrifice quality in the name of cost savings.

---

21. Because the amount of competition in different areas may be correlated with unobserved characteristics that in turn affect cost and quality, we need some further tests to determine whether cross-sectional analysis can be interpreted as informative on any causal relationship between competition and cost and quality.

Appendix A

Table 6A.1   Measurement of the quality of service

Subindex	Item 1	Item 2	Item 3	Item 4
			Items in each subindex	
Quality management	Has your establishment acquired silver mark or ISO approval?	Does your establishment have a standard manual for home help service?	Does your establishment regularly hold information exchange meetings, case study meetings, or care conferences?	Does your establishment provide your own regular staff training?
Service convenience	Is your establishment settling no lower limits for utilization hours?	Can your establishment provide nursing service late in the early morning or late at night?	Can your establishment always meet emergency needs?	Can your establishment provide services on holidays?
Information service	Does your establishment designate staff to process claims from customers?	Does your establishment promulgate its service content through brochures or home pages on the web?		
Ability of home help staff	Is the proportion of staff with the qualification of social welfare counselor, welfare caretaker, professional physical therapist (PTCA), or operational therapist (OT) higher than the sample average?	Is the proportion of qualified staff higher than the sample average?	Is the proportion of staff with more than five years' experience as a home helper higher than the sample average?	Is the proportion of staff with less than one year of experience as a home helper lower than the sample average?

Note: "Qualified staff" refers to those who hold at least a certified qualification of second band home helper.

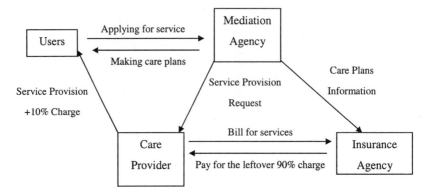

Fig. 6B.1   Flow of money and service provision
Source: Ito (2001, 175).

Appendix B

Institutional Setting of At-Home Nursing Care Business in Japan

In Japan, at-home nursing care services include a total of thirteen categories: home help service, at-home bathing help, at-home nursing help, at-home rehabilitation help, outpatient rehabilitation help, at-home medical care, management counseling, day-service, short-stay service, group homes for the elderly with dementia, long-term care at private home for the elderly, lending care equipment, and home alteration to meet care needs.

Generally, users afford only 10 percent[22] of the total cost as long as they do not break the upper limit of use rights, and other expenses are covered by premium incomes (50 percent), central government subsidy (25 percent), prefecture subsidy (12.5 percent) and municipality subsidy (12.5 percent).[23] Flow of money and provision of service is summarized in figure 6B.1. In other words, at-home nursing business happens when eligible users apply for service through a mediation agency (care manager). Care providers serve the users based on the care plan made by the care manager and receive payment from both users and insurance agencies.

22. There are upper limits for users' burdens.
23. To improve social welfare, some municipalities have additional subsidy for care providers, which we define as government subsidies in the analysis.

References

Abe, A. 2003. *Social security in Japan.* Tokyo: National Institute of Population and Social Security Research.

Dranove, D., M. Shanley, and C. Simon. 1992. Is hospital competition wasteful? *RAND Journal of Economics* 23 (2): 247–62.

Dranove, D., and W. D. White. 1999. *How hospitals survived: Competition and the American hospital.* Washington, DC: American Enterprise Institute for Public Policy Research.

Gertler, P. J., and D. M. Waldman. 1992. Quality-adjusted cost function and policy evaluation in the nursing home industry. *Journal of Political Economy* 100 (6): 1232–56.

Ito, S. 2001. *Readdressing nursing care system* [in Japanese]. Tokyo: Chikuma Shinsho.

Hersch, P. L. 1984. Competition and the performance of hospital markets. *Review of Industrial Organization* 1 (4): 324–40.

Kessler, D. P., and M. B. McClellan. 1999. Is hospital competition socially wasteful? NBER Working Paper no. 7266. Cambridge, MA: National Bureau of Economic Research, July.

Luft, H. S., J. C. Robinson, D. Garnick, S. Maerki, and S. McPhee. 1986. The role of specialized clinical services in competition among hospitals. *Inquiry* 23:83–94.

Nanbu, T. 2000. Economic consequences of the introduction of public long-term care insurance system into long-term care industry in Japan [in Japanese]. In *Analysis of health care and long-term care industry,* ed. National Institute of Population and Social Security Research (IPSS), 151–67. Tokyo: Tokyo University Press.

Nyman, A. J. 1994. The effects of market concentration and excess demand on the price for nursing home care. *Journal of Industrial Economics* 42 (2): 193–204.

Robinson, J. C. 1988. Market structure, employment, and skill mix in the hospital industry. *Southern Economic Journal* 55 (2): 315–25.

Robinson, J. C., and H. Luft. 1985. The impact of hospital market structure on patient volume, average length of stay, and the cost of care. *Journal of Economics* 3:1–24.

Shimizutani, S., and W. Suzuki. 2002. The quality and efficiency of at-home long-term care in Japan: Evidence from micro level data. Discussion Paper Series no. 18. Tokyo: Economic and Social Research Institute, Cabinet Office.

Shortell, S. M., and E. F. Hughes. 1988. The effect of regulation, competition and ownership on mortality rates among hospital inpatients. *The New England Journal of Medicine* 318:1100–07.

Zwanziger, J., and G. Melnick. 1988. The effects of hospital competition and the Medicare PPS program on hospital cost behavior in California. *Journal of Health Economics* 7:301–20.

7

A Comparison of the Quality of Health Care in the United States and Japan
Treatment and Outcomes for Heart Attack Patients

Haruko Noguchi, Yuichiro Masuda, Masafumi Kuzuya, Akihiko Iguchi, Jeffery Geppert, and Mark McClellan

7.1 Introduction

Heart disease is the leading cause of death in the United States, and acute myocardial infarctions (AMIs), or, more colloquially, "heart attacks," are directly or indirectly responsible for most of these deaths. In Japan, as in the United States, heart disease has become one of the significant causes of death. Approximately more than one-third of those with heart diseases died of AMI in 1998 (the death ratios per 0.1 million caused by AMI are 43.3 for males, 34.3 for females, and 38.7 for both sexes; Health and Welfare Statistics Association 2000). Though death from AMI remains less common in Japan than in the United States, the increasing incidence of AMI and the overall aging of Japanese society suggests that heart

Haruko Noguchi is an associate professor in the Faculty of Social Sciences at Toyo Eiwa University. Yuichiro Masuda is a medical doctor in the Department of Geriatrics, Graduate School of Medicine, Nagoya University. Masafumi Kuzuya is a medical doctor and professor in the Department of Geriatrics, Graduate School of Medicine, Nagoya University. Akihiko Iguchi is a professor in the Graduate School of Medicine, Nagoya University. Jeffery Geppert is a senior research associate at Social Policy and Health Economics Research and Evaluation (SPHERE) and a member at Acumen, LLC, as well as a senior research analyst at the Center for Health Policy at Stanford University. Mark McClellan is the administrator of the Centers for Medicare and Medicaid Services, an associate professor of economics and of medicine at Stanford University, and a research associate of the National Bureau of Economic Research.

This project received substantial financial support from the Pfizer Health Research Foundation, the Japan Foundation Center for Global Partnership (through Japan Center for Economic Research), the Health Care Financing Administration (through California Medical Review, Inc.), and the National Institute on Aging. We greatly appreciate all the medical facilities that collaborated in this project. The project was approved by these medical facilities and the Ethics Committee of the Department of Geriatrics, Nagoya University. All errors are our own.

attacks may become a significant health problem in the future, much as cancer is now.

This study had several main objectives. The first was to create a data set containing information on treatments and outcomes among AMI patients in Japan, comparable to the Cooperative Cardiovascular Project (CCP)[1] in the United States. The CCP is a major policy initiative to improve the quality of care for Medicare beneficiaries with AMI undertaken by the Health Care Financing Administration (currently called the Center for Medicare and Medicaid Services). The second objective was to investigate variation between the United States and Japan in the quality of health care for elderly patients (age sixty-five or over) with AMI, with respect to treatments and outcomes and controlling for chart-based detailed clinical information. In this study, we divide medical procedures performed on AMI patients into high-tech and low-tech treatments. We define *high-tech treatments* as those with large fixed or marginal costs and *low-tech treatments* as those with relatively low fixed and marginal costs. Low-tech treatments, in principle, could be provided by virtually any medical facility (McClellan and Noguchi 1998). Both types of procedures are used widely enough to contribute substantially to patient outcomes and hospital expenditure.

This paper is organized as follows. Section 7.2 reviews related previous research. Section 7.3 justifies the empirical specification we use in this study. Section 7.4 describes the data on patient characteristics and treatments received. Section 7.5 uses a bivariate probit procedure to investigate the determinants of patient outcomes and hospital expenditure, mainly focusing on treatment differences. Section 7.6 discusses our findings and concludes.

7.2   Previous Research

Cardiac catheterization, a procedure that visualizes blood flow to the heart muscle through continuous radiologic images of the flow of dye injected into the coronary arteries, is the first step for an important set of high-tech intensive treatments for heart attack. If this procedure detects substantial blockages, it may be followed by a revascularization procedure

1. During the national phase of the CCP project, HCFA conducted standardized abstractions of the medical records of all Medicare beneficiaries hospitalized with AMI over an eight-month period at essentially all hospitals in the United States that had not participated in a four-state pilot phase. The eight-month sampling frame was continuous at each hospital, and all sampling occurred between April 1994 and July 1995. Marciniak et al. (1998) provide more details on CCP goals, sampling and data collection strategy, and methods used to assure standardization and completeness of the medical record reviews. Altogether, charts were abstracted for approximately 180,000 AMI patients. These data were linked to Medicare administrative records (enrollment and hospitalization files), which have been used in previous observational studies of AMI practices and outcomes but do not include the clinical details present in the medical record abstracts. The enrollment files include comprehensive all-cause mortality information from Social Security records.

intended to improve blood flow to the heart. The two common revascular-ization procedures are angioplasty (PTCA, or percutaneous transluminal coronary angioplasty), which involves the use of a balloon (or stent, re-cently) at the end of a catheter to eliminate blockages, and bypass surgery (CABG, or coronary-artery bypass graft surgery), a major open-heart sur-gical procedure to bypass the area of blockage.

Despite the importance of heart attacks for population health and the importance of these intensive procedures for health care resources use, the procedures have been studied in only a limited number of randomized clin-ical trials. Several trials examined the effectiveness of bypass surgery in the early 1980s and angioplasty in the following years. In general, these trials found limited mortality benefits in a few subgroups of patients treated. Tri-als of bypass surgery versus no intensive procedures included Brown et al. (1981), Takekoshi, Murakami, and Nakajima (1983), and Koshal et al. (1988). Trials of angioplasty included Erbel et al. (1986), Simmoons et al. (1988), TIMI Study Group (1989), and Zijlstra et al. (1993). But most of these studies focused primarily on the immediate use of angioplasty, rather than on its use at all during the episode of treatment for heart attack. Re-flecting changes in expectations about treatment benefits, recent trials have focused on narrower questions about use of the intensive procedures, such as the timing of catheterization (e.g., Califf and TAMI VA Study Group 1991), the choice between angioplasty and bypass surgery, and the use of catheterization in very narrow subsets of patients (e.g., VANQWISH Study Group 1998).

Nonetheless, the procedures have become much more widely used in heart attack patients for several reasons. First, the equipment quality and personnel skill involved in the procedure has improved substantially since the time of the trials, leading to much lower complication rates. Second, tri-als on many types of heart disease patients, such as women and the elderly, were regarded as too costly to justify additional studies given the previous trial results. Third, as experience accumulated, fewer and fewer patients were willing to be randomized for such an important decision as an inten-sive cardiac procedure. As with many other intensive medical technologies, these heart procedures are now used in a much broader range of patients than have been explicitly supported by randomized trials.

Consequently, these procedures have been studied frequently using ob-servational methods. In Japan, there have also been several observational studies on the effects of intensive procedures on patient outcomes, that is, by the Japanese Society of Interventional Cardiology. Studies based on di-rect comparisons of treated and nontreated patients have generally found that intensive cardiac procedures like bypass surgery were associated with significant and substantial mortality reductions in these additional pa-tients, even after accounting for observational difference. For example, us-ing the propensity-score methods reviewed in the following, Rosenbaum and Rubin (1984) estimate a large improvement in functional status and in survival for patients with heart disease undergoing bypass surgery. In contrast, observational studies using new statistical methods, such as instrumental variables (IV; e.g., McClellan, McNeil, and Newhouse 1994; McClellan and Newhouse 1997; McClellan and Noguchi 1998, 2001) and general method of moments (GMM; e.g., McClellan and Staiger 2000a,b) have found small mortality effects that appear to be due at least in part to other associated treatments. The estimation methods appear to matter for the results in this case, and the source of the discrepancy in the results—either in differences in biases or differences in the subpopulations included in the effect estimates—is unclear. These sorts of inconsistencies have plagued observational studies of treatment effects and limited their relevance for clinical practice and policies intended to influence it. Either IV or GMM is appropriate for population-based data with enough variation among patients and medical facilities such as the CCP, but not for data with a small number of observations and little variation, like the data we collected in Japan for this project.

First, therefore, we use a bivariate probit procedure in order to examine the effects of cardiac catheterization as a high-tech procedure on patient outcomes and hospital expenditures. Second, we will also focus on low-tech treatments during hospitalizations, such as aspirin, beta-blockers, calcium channel blockers, and smoking cessation. Unlike high-tech treatments, these drug treatments have been studied in a large number of randomized clinical trials since the 1980s (e.g., Lewis, Davis, and Archibald 1983; ISIS-2 Collaborative Group 1988; Kober et al. 1995; MERIT-HF 1999; and CIBIS-II 1999). The recent update of the 1999 ACC/AHA (American Heart Association/American College of Cardiology) guidelines originally released in 1996 collected scientific evidence regarding the benefits and risks of these drugs, including both randomized trial and observational studies. The ACC/AHA guidelines for AMI patients recommend aspirin use and smoking cessation during hospitalization, and aspirin, beta-blockers, and angiotensin converting enzyme (ACE) inhibitors at discharge. The ACC/AHA states that encouraging these procedures will contribute to improving survival probabilities in the population. This statement is consistent with conclusions from several studies based on the CCP (e.g., Jencks et al. 2000; Frances et al. 2000; Shilipak et al. 2001; Shlipak et al. 2002).

Using the exclusion and inclusion criteria for these treatments from the ACC/AHA guidelines (table 7A.1), we will examine how many patients were identified as good candidates for aspirin, beta-blockers; calcium channel blockers; and smoking cessation during hospitalization and how they were actually treated.[2]

---

2. For thrombolytic drugs—IV nitrogen and ACE inhibitors—the complete indicators for exclusion or inclusion criteria to determine ideal or good candidates are not available in our Japanese data.

7.3   Empirical Specification and Measurements

In this section, we explain our empirical specification for estimating the effects of high-tech and low-tech treatments after hospitalization on outcomes and medical expenditures and for investigating the variation in the quality of care across countries. Cardiac catheterization can be considered as the entry procedure for further intensive revascularization procedures. The mean and median durations between hospital admission and catheterization in our data are eight days and twenty-four hours, respectively. Thus, we use seven-day catheterization to measure the effects of high-tech procedures on outcomes and expenditure.

We will apply a bivariate probit procedure for evaluating the impacts of seven-day catheterization on the following dichotomous dependent variables: thirty-day and one-year mortality, and ninety-day and one-year hospital readmission for any cause. A seemingly unrelated regression method is used for the continuous dependent variables: ninety-day and one-year medical expenditures and length of stay from the first hospital admission[3] (Maddala and Lee 1976; Maddala 1983; Greene 1993, 1998). We use these dependent variables as measures for evaluating the quality of care for AMI patients. In addition to seven-day catheterization, we include five low-tech procedures into our model as explanatory variables: use of thrombolytics, aspirin, beta-blockers, and ACE inhibitors and smoking cessation during hospital stay. We expect these low-tech procedures to be highly correlated with aggressive high-tech procedures. All regressions are controlled for patient demographic and chart-based comorbidity and severity measures.

There are a couple of major reasons for adopting a bivariate probit procedure in this study: (a) we suspected that the simple least squares procedure would produce inappropriate estimates because the dependent variables are binominal (0 or 1); (b) for estimating the effects of seven-day catheterization on patient outcomes and hospital expenditure, one single regression analysis including catheterization as an explanatory variable will be inappropriate and statistically biased as whether a patient undergoes cardiac catheterization within seven days after admission is endogenous. Seven-day catheterization would be highly correlated with patient characteristics and other drug use so that the independence among explanatory variables cannot be assumed to hold in the simple least squares method. Therefore, it is appropriate to assume a bivariate distribution for two probabilities: the likelihood a patient undergoes seven-day catheterization and the likelihood a patient dies or is readmitted within a certain period after discharge.

---

3. As regards the length of hospital stay, like hospital expenditure, ninety-day and one-year total durations of stay are ideal as measuring patient outcomes. However, the lengths of hospital stay after the first readmission are available only for limited number of patients in Japanese data.

The key regression formulas are the following:

(1) $\qquad y_1^* = \beta_1 X_1 + \varepsilon_1 \quad y_1 = 1$ if $y_1^* > 0, 0$ otherwise

(2) $\qquad y_2^* = \beta_2 X_2 + \varepsilon_2 \quad y_2 = 1$ if $y_2^* > 0, 0$ otherwise,

where $\varepsilon_1 \sim N(0,1)$, $\varepsilon_2 \sim N(0,1)$, $\mathrm{cov}(\varepsilon_1, \varepsilon_2) = \rho$; y_1^* and y_2^* show unobserved underlying index determining seven-day catheterization and patient outcomes; y_1 and y_2 are the observed patterns of seven-day catheterization and patient outcomes; and, finally, X_1 and X_2 include patient demographic characteristics, comorbidity, severity, and drug treatments. The dependent variables, y_1^* and y_2^* themselves cannot be directly observed. However, with respect to regression formula (1), y_1 equals 1 if the patient underwent seven-day catheterization and 0 otherwise. Also, with respect to regression formula (2), y_2 equals 1 if the patient dies or is readmitted to the hospital within a certain period after discharge and 0 otherwise. The independent variables, X_1 and X_2, include patient demographic characteristics; severity and comorbid measures; and drug use such as thrombolytics, aspirin, beta-blockers, and ACE inhibitors; and smoking cessation during hospital stay. The residuals from the two regressions, ε_1 and ε_2, were assumed to have the standard normal distribution. In other words, we assumed the expected values were $E(\varepsilon_1) = E(\varepsilon_2) = 0$, and the distributions were $\mathrm{Var}(\varepsilon_1) = \mathrm{Var}(\varepsilon_2) = 1$. The covariance of ε_1 and ε_2 was to be $\mathrm{Cov}[\varepsilon_1, \varepsilon_2] = \rho$. We introduce the bivariate predicted probabilities as follows:

Φ_{11}: seven-day catheterization ($y_1 = 1$) and the patient dies or is readmitted ($y_2 = 1$)

Φ_{10}: seven-day catheterization ($y_1 = 1$) and the patient does not die or is not readmitted ($y_2 = 0$)

Φ_{01}: no seven-day catheterization ($y_1 = 0$) and the patient dies or is readmitted ($y_2 = 1$)

Φ_{00}: no seven-day catheterization ($y_1 = 0$) and the patient does not die or is not readmitted ($y_2 = 0$)

The log-likelihood function to be maximized in terms of β_1, β_2, and ρ is

$$(3) \quad \ln L(\beta_1, \beta_2, \rho) = \sum y_1 y_2 \ln \Phi_{11} + \sum y_1 (1 - y_2) \ln \Phi_{10}$$
$$+ \sum (1 - y_1) y_2 \ln \Phi_{01} + \sum (1 - y_1)(1 - y_2) \ln \Phi_{00}.$$

Note that because the hospital expenditure variable is continuous, we will utilize a seemingly unrelated regression procedure that assumes a bivariate probability distribution based on a linear regression rather than the bivariate probit procedure.

7.4 Data

Charts were abstracted for 371 AMI patients admitted to ten medical facilities located in an urban area of Aichi prefecture in Japan. Charts were carefully reviewed by research nurses and physicians, with all sampling taking place between January and December 1995. The CCP includes Medicare enrollees, most of whom are sixty-five years and older. The population in this study was comparable, with 190 patients (out of 371) age sixty-five years and older. The median number of patients admitted to each medical facility within the study period was 23, and the median number of catheterizations performed was eighteen. We followed standardized procedures for abstracting medical records, similar to those used by the Health Care Financing Administration (HCFA) for the CCP. The record abstracts contain over 100 comorbidity and severity measures. The CCP's expert advisory panel believed that these measures collectively summarize all of the major associated diseases, functional status impairments, and aspects of AMI severity that would influence the appropriateness of major AMI treatment decisions and health outcomes.

For the U.S. sample, we extracted 889 patients from sixteen hospitals. These patients were chosen out of approximately 180,000 CCP patients with the goal of making the U.S. sample comparable to the Japan sample. First, we selected five metropolitan statistics areas (MSAs) in the United States with rates of AMI incidence similar to Aichi prefecture (between 190 and 200 per 100,000 per year). Second, because the Japanese data only includes catheterization facilities, we excluded noncatheterization hospitals (defined as hospitals that performed fewer than four catheterizations per year, the minimum number of catheterizations in the Japanese data). Thus, we extracted patients hospitalized in medical facilities providing care with a similar level of technology in both countries. The median number of CCP patients admitted to each hospital was eighty, and the median number of catheterizations performed at each hospital was thirty-three. Therefore, the number of patients and catheterizations per year in each hospital are several times larger in the United States. Sampling for the CCP occurred between April 1994 and July 1995 at essentially all hospitals in the United States, which is slightly different than the sampling time frame for the Japanese data. A major technological change—the aggressive use of stent for PTCA or percutaneous coronary intervention (PCI)—occurred in 1996 to 1997 in both countries, but the difference in time frames between the studies would not likely affect our results. Note that all the results obtained in this study are not necessarily generalizable because all the included hospitals are high-volume catheterization hospitals in urban areas. Also, note that the following statistical analyses of the CCP data are weighted by the number of patients in each MSA.

7.4.1 Patient Heterogeneity

Table 7.1 illustrates the data elements in record abstracts from the CCP and Japanese data. This highlights some of fundamental problems in observational analyses based on direct comparisons of treated and nontreated patients. The table shows that the fraction of patients who underwent catheterization was approximately 45 percent in the United States and 78 percent in Japan. In the United States, catheterized patients were more likely to be younger and male, although the gender gap of treatments in the Japanese data is trivial. This may explain why there are so few studies on the effect of gender on disease outcomes in Japan (e.g., Oe et al. 2002) or on treatment differences by gender. In contrast, the gender gap in the treatment of coronary artery disease in the United States has been widely explored, although the reasons for the disparity remain inconclusive. (See, for example, Harrold et al. 2003; Bertoni et al. 2004; Weisz, Gusmano, and Rodwin 2004; Hochman et al. 1999; and Rodwin and Gusmano 2002.) Demographic differences between treated and nontreated patients were described in previous studies based on less-detailed administrative records (e.g., McClellan, McNeil, and Newhouse 1994). Rates of some of the additional comorbidity and severity variables are also reported; treated and nontreated patients differ substantially in almost all of these dimensions, with catheterized patients generally appearing to be in better health. Catheterized patients are much more likely than noncatheterized patients to be in good functional status (e.g., independent mobility). Also, they are generally less likely to have serious comorbid diseases like prior heart failure, posterior vitreous detachment (PVD) or claudication, cerebral hemorrhage, renal failure, and liver failure. The only exception is in the prevalence of chest pain due to heart problems prior to the AMI, which is a common indication for catheterization. Patients undergoing catheterization were much more likely to be alert and oriented on initial admission, to have no signs of serious heart failure (e.g., high heart rate or low blood pressure), and to have good kidney function as shown by nonelevated blood nitrogen. With literally hundreds of variables that describe patient characteristics, interpreting the cumulative consequences of the differences for outcomes is difficult. For this reason, we constructed a summary indicator of disease comorbidity and severity. The Killip class is based on a number of clinical characteristics related to the extent of heart failure in an AMI patient. This measure has been shown to provide a reliable predictor of short-term AMI mortality. Killip classes 3 and 4 indicate moderate and severe heart failure, while Killip classes 1 and 2 indicate relatively mild heart failure. As table 7.1 shows, catheterized patients in both countries are much more likely to be in the lowest Killip class. These results provide clear evidence that patient heterogeneity is a fundamental challenge for

Table 7.1   Key variable definitions and summary statistics for patient characteristics

	United States						Japan					
	Total		No 7-day cath		7-day cath		Total		No 7-day cath		7-day cath	
	Mean	Standard deviation	Mean	Standard deviation	Mean	Standard deviation	Mean	Standard deviation	Mean	Standard deviation	Mean	Standard deviation
Demographic characteristics												
Female	0.460	(0.499)	0.514	(0.500)	0.388	(0.488)	0.332	(0.472)	0.333	(0.475)	0.331	(0.472)
Black	0.127	(0.333)	0.163	(0.370)	0.079	(0.270)	—	—	—	—	—	—
Age in years	73.904	(9.653)	76.028	(9.945)	71.073	(8.469)	73.379	(6.494)	75.470	(7.766)	72.266	(5.416)
Severity measures												
Killip class 1	0.529	(0.499)	0.437	(0.497)	0.651	(0.477)	0.771	(0.421)	0.600	(0.494)	0.867	(0.341)
Killip class 2	0.125	(0.331)	0.138	(0.345)	0.108	(0.310)	0.052	(0.223)	0.091	(0.290)	0.031	(0.173)
Killip class 3	0.319	(0.467)	0.398	(0.490)	0.215	(0.412)	0.131	(0.338)	0.236	(0.429)	0.071	(0.259)
Killip class 4	0.027	(0.162)	0.028	(0.164)	0.026	(0.160)	0.046	(0.210)	0.073	(0.262)	0.031	(0.173)
Treatment measures												
Catheterization during stay	0.450	(0.498)	0.037	(0.190)	1.000	(0.000)	0.779	(0.416)	0.364	(0.485)	1.000	(0.000)
1-day catheterization	0.168	(0.374)	0.000	(0.000)	0.391	(0.489)	0.589	(0.493)	0.000	(0.000)	0.903	(0.297)
7-day catheterization	0.429	(0.495)	0.000	(0.000)	1.000	(0.000)	0.653	(0.477)	0.000	(0.000)	1.000	(0.000)
30-day catheterization	0.445	(0.497)	0.030	(0.169)	1.000	(0.000)	0.737	(0.442)	0.242	(0.432)	1.000	(0.000)
90-day catheterization	0.445	(0.497)	0.030	(0.169)	1.000	(0.000)	0.768	(0.423)	0.333	(0.475)	1.000	(0.000)
1-year catheterization	0.445	(0.497)	0.030	(0.169)	1.000	(0.000)	0.768	(0.423)	0.333	(0.475)	1.000	(0.000)
angioplasty during stay	0.169	(0.375)	0.012	(0.108)	0.378	(0.486)	0.537	(0.500)	0.152	(0.361)	0.742	(0.439)
1-day angioplasty	0.078	(0.268)	0.000	(0.000)	0.183	(0.387)	0.411	(0.493)	0.000	(0.000)	0.629	(0.485)
7-day angioplasty	0.159	(0.366)	0.002	(0.044)	0.371	(0.484)	0.489	(0.501)	0.030	(0.173)	0.734	(0.444)
30-day angioplasty	0.164	(0.370)	0.010	(0.099)	0.371	(0.484)	0.516	(0.501)	0.106	(0.310)	0.734	(0.444)
90-day angioplasty	0.164	(0.370)	0.010	(0.099)	0.371	(0.484)	0.532	(0.500)	0.152	(0.361)	0.734	(0.444)
1-year angioplasty	0.164	(0.370)	0.010	(0.099)	0.371	(0.484)	0.532	(0.500)	0.152	(0.361)	0.734	(0.444)

(continued)

Table 7.1 (continued)

	United States						Japan					
	Total		No 7-day cath		7-day cath		Total		No 7-day cath		7-day cath	
	Mean	Standard deviation	Mean	Standard deviation	Mean	Standard deviation	Mean	Standard deviation	Mean	Standard deviation	Mean	Standard deviation
Cardiac bypass surgery during stay	0.111	(0.315)	0.002	(0.044)	0.257	(0.438)	0.011	(0.102)	0.000	(0.000)	0.016	(0.126)
1-day cardiac bypass surgery during stay	0.010	(0.100)	0.000	(0.000)	0.024	(0.152)	0.000	(0.000)	0.000	(0.000)	0.000	(0.000)
7-day cardiac bypass surgery during stay	0.083	(0.276)	0.000	(0.000)	0.194	(0.396)	0.000	(0.000)	0.000	(0.000)	0.000	(0.000)
30-day cardiac bypass surgery during stay	0.111	(0.315)	0.002	(0.044)	0.257	(0.438)	0.000	(0.000)	0.000	(0.000)	0.000	(0.000)
90-day cardiac bypass surgery during stay	0.111	(0.315)	0.002	(0.044)	0.257	(0.438)	0.000	(0.000)	0.000	(0.000)	0.000	(0.000)
1-year cardiac bypass surgery during stay	0.111	(0.315)	0.002	(0.044)	0.257	(0.438)	0.000	(0.000)	0.000	(0.000)	0.000	(0.000)
Angiotensin-converting-enzyme during stay	0.369	(0.483)	0.385	(0.487)	0.349	(0.477)	0.315	(0.466)	0.230	(0.424)	0.358	(0.482)
Warfarin during stay	0.183	(0.387)	0.155	(0.362)	0.220	(0.415)	0.166	(0.373)	0.032	(0.177)	0.237	(0.427)
Heparin > 4000 U during stay	0.707	(0.455)	0.573	(0.495)	0.885	(0.320)	0.897	(0.305)	0.823	(0.385)	0.934	(0.249)
Thrombolytics during stay	0.158	(0.365)	0.103	(0.304)	0.231	(0.422)	0.315	(0.466)	0.210	(0.410)	0.370	(0.485)
Aspirin during stay	0.753	(0.432)	0.629	(0.484)	0.916	(0.278)	0.711	(0.455)	0.574	(0.499)	0.782	(0.415)
IV nitrogen during stay	0.551	(0.498)	0.433	(0.496)	0.709	(0.455)	0.757	(0.430)	0.734	(0.445)	0.769	(0.423)
Beta-blocker during stay	0.428	(0.495)	0.323	(0.468)	0.567	(0.496)	0.062	(0.242)	0.017	(0.131)	0.084	(0.279)

	(1)	(2)	(3)	(4)	(5)	(6)
Angiotensin-converting-enzyme at discharge	0.321 (0.467)	0.370 (0.484)	0.270 (0.445)	0.297 (0.459)	0.236 (0.429)	0.330 (0.473)
Warfarin at discharge	0.199 (0.399)	0.192 (0.395)	0.206 (0.405)	0.153 (0.361)	0.000 (0.000)	0.229 (0.423)
Aspirin at discharge	0.668 (0.471)	0.571 (0.496)	0.770 (0.422)	0.686 (0.465)	0.482 (0.504)	0.784 (0.413)
Beta-blocker at discharge	0.314 (0.464)	0.259 (0.439)	0.371 (0.484)	0.083 (0.276)	0.073 (0.262)	0.088 (0.284)
Calcium channel blocker at discharge	0.428 (0.495)	0.484 (0.500)	0.368 (0.483)	0.404 (0.492)	0.382 (0.490)	0.414 (0.495)
Smoking cessation during stay	0.074 (0.262)	0.065 (0.247)	0.087 (0.282)	0.079 (0.272)	0.138 (0.351)	0.029 (0.171)
Outcome measures						
Died within 1 day	0.066 (0.249)	0.102 (0.303)	0.018 (0.134)	0.042 (0.201)	0.061 (0.240)	0.032 (0.177)
Died within 7 days	0.143 (0.350)	0.201 (0.401)	0.066 (0.248)	0.068 (0.253)	0.106 (0.310)	0.048 (0.215)
Died within 30 days	0.198 (0.399)	0.278 (0.448)	0.092 (0.289)	0.121 (0.327)	0.197 (0.401)	0.081 (0.273)
Died within 1 year	0.318 (0.466)	0.445 (0.497)	0.150 (0.357)	0.289 (0.455)	0.318 (0.469)	0.274 (0.488)
In-hospital death from 1st admission	0.182 (0.386)	0.250 (0.433)	0.092 (0.289)	0.158 (0.366)	0.288 (0.456)	0.089 (0.285)
90-day total expenditure in PPP$	11841.520 (13761.830)	9427.900 (12093.490)	15059.680 (15141.540)	24.503 (17.207)	14.699 (12.054)	28.354 (17.560)
1-year total expenditure in PPP$	15180.470 (17928.130)	13056.990 (16696.120)	18011.780 (19107.910)	28.938 (17.977)	21.330 (15.760)	31.790 (18.102)
90-day readmission	0.292 (0.455)	0.294 (0.456)	0.289 (0.454)	0.425 (0.498)	0.250 (0.444)	0.491 (0.505)
1-year readmission	0.421 (0.494)	0.438 (0.497)	0.397 (0.490)	0.712 (0.456)	0.450 (0.510)	0.811 (0.395)
Length of stay from 1st hospital admission	8.514 (100.819)	7.902 (97.621)	9.332 (103.970)	32.314 (30.267)	36.424 (45.256)	30.144 (17.786)
Number of observations	889	508	381	190	66	124

Notes: For United States, tables gives weighted mean values by the number of patients in each metropolitan statistical area. PPP = purchasing power parity.

observational studies that rely on direct comparisons of catheterized and noncatheterized patients.

7.4.2   Treatment Heterogeneity

Table 7.1 also shows that outcomes may differ between catheterized and noncatheterized patients due to differences in treatments other than catheterization. Our medical reviews include substantial information on a range of treatments besides cardiac procedures, especially drug treatments, which might influence outcomes.

First, regarding high-tech treatments, the table shows that Japanese patients tend to be more aggressively treated than the CCP patients. Among the CCP patients, 45 percent receive an angioplasty and 17 percent are catheterized, whereas the rates of these intensive treatments among the Japanese patients are 78 percent and 54 percent, respectively. Also, the timing of clinical decision making for intensive procedures is much earlier in Japan than in the United States. Within twenty-four hours after hospital admission, almost 60 percent of patients in Japan were treated by catheterization, and 40 percent were treated with angioplasty; the comparable rates among CCP patients were only 17 percent and 8 percent, respectively. Our findings are consistent with previous studies showing that, compared to other developed countries, angioplasty has rapidly spread in Japan since it was first performed in 1980 (Sasakuri et al. 1997), and rates of PCI following cardiac catheterization are much higher in Japan (e.g., Nippon Shinkekkan Intervention Gakkai Gakujutsu Iinkai 1993; Endo and Koyanagi 1994). These previous studies also found that the ratio of angioplasty to cardiac bypass surgery is much higher in Japan. Our results are consistent with the previous results. We find that in the United States, 17 percent of patients were treated with angioplasty and 11 percent with bypass surgery, whereas the rates in Japan were 54 percent and only 1 percent, respectively.[4] This extremely high ratio may be caused by alarmingly high mortality from cardiac bypass surgery in the early stage of diffusing bypass technology in Japan (Sezei et al. 1970; Hayashi 1972; Asada et al. 1970) and more-attractive reimbursement for angioplasty than bypass surgery (Yoshikawa et al. 2002).

Table 7.1 shows that patients who receive catheterization are more likely to receive a variety of other beneficial treatments in both countries. For example, during hospitalization they are much more likely to receive aspirin, which has been directly shown to reduce AMI mortality (92 versus 63 percent in the United States and 78 versus 57 percent in Japan); they are more

---

4. Previous studies (e.g., Nippon Shinkekkan Intervention Gakkai Gakujutsu Iinkai 1993; Endo and Koyanagi 1994) found that the ratio of angioplasty to bypass surgery is almost 5 to 1, on average, but it varies among regions—4 to 1 in the eastern region of Japan and 8 to 1 in the western region. Therefore, the results based on the data from collaborative medical centers in this study are extremely biased, with respect to the use of cardiac bypass surgery.

likely to receive thrombolytic or "clot-busting" drugs, which help dissolve the blood clot that causes the AMI (23 versus 10 percent in the United States and 37 versus 21 percent in Japan); and they are more likely to receive beta-blockers, which reduce the workload of the heart (57 versus 32 percent in the United States and 8 versus 2 percent in Japan). Catheterized patients in both countries are also more likely to receive protective drug treatments after discharge that might improve long-term outcomes, including aspirin and beta-blockers. But, in the United States, catheterized patients are slightly less likely to receive ACE inhibitors both during hospitalization and at discharge. These drugs are used primarily in patients with chronic heart failure (that is, patients who have had more severe AMIs). In the Japanese data, catheterized patients are more likely to receive them. In addition to these observed treatments, there are probably many other unobserved treatments and environmental influences that might differ for catheterized versus noncatheterized patients and also contribute to outcome differences.

7.4.3 Outcome Differences

The final section of table 7.1 shows the consequences of catheterization as well as of these differences in individual characteristics and treatments for patient outcomes. Not surprisingly, the differences are large, yet these differences are much larger in the United States than Japan. Noncatheterized patients have one-year mortality rates 31 percentage points higher (46 versus 15 percent) in the United States and 5 percentage points higher (32 versus 27 percent) in Japan. Large mortality differences appear at one day (10 percent versus 2 percent in the United States and 6 percent versus 3 percent in Japan) and increase steadily. These results suggest that catheterized patients have much lower mortality risks for all time intervals after AMI than noncatheterized patients, but many other treatment differences may also contribute to the observed mortality differences.

Although patients we focus on in this study are sixty-five and older and so are covered by similar fee-for-service reimbursement systems in both countries, medical facilities in the Japanese data have weaker incentives for cost containment. One-year hospital expenditures, calculated using purchasing power parity, are higher for catheterized patients in both countries ($18,011 versus $13,057 in the United States, $31,790 versus $21,330 in Japan). In general, the mean length of stay from the first hospital admission is much shorter in the United States than in Japan (nine days versus thirty-two days). The longer length of hospital stay is one of the major causes of higher expenditures in Japan versus the United States. Further, seven-day catheterization has a reverse effect on the length of hospital stay between the CCP and Japanese patients. A CCP patient who undergoes an intensive procedure tends to stay in a hospital longer by approximately one day compared to the one who does not, while the hospital stay for a patient in Japan is six days shorter. In our Japanese data, almost 60 percent of patients underwent catheterization immediately after hospital admission. Patients who do not undergo seven-day catheterization tend to suffer from more-severe heart attacks so that they are expected to stay in hospitals longer than catheterized patients, probably for clinical reasons.

Like the health outcome differences, however, these differences may simply reflect differences in patient characteristics or treatments other than the effect of catheterization. For example, because catheterized patients are more likely to survive, they may have higher medical expenditures independent of catheterization use. Hence, we have to examine carefully the effects of seven-day catheterization on patient outcomes and hospital expenditures, controlling for both patient and treatment heterogeneity.

7.5   Results

Table 7.2 shows the marginal effects calculated based on the results of a bivariate probit analysis for each country. Panel A of table 7.2 indicates the results of regression equation (1), with the binomial dependent variable equaling 1 when a patient underwent seven-day catheterization and 0 otherwise. Also, panel B shows the results of regression equation (2), with the binomial dependent variable equaling 1 when a patient died or was readmitted to the hospital within a certain period after discharge and 0 otherwise. Each panel in table 7.2 shows only the treatment variables of interest, and all regressions include controls for detailed patient characteristics.

7.5.1   Effects of High-Tech Procedure on the Quality of Care

First, we discuss the effects of high-tech interventions on patient outcomes, hospital expenditures, and length of stay. As shown in the panel B of table 7.2, both the CCP and Japanese data suggest that seven-day catheterization contributes to a decrease the probabilities of both mortality and readmission for all time intervals, although the impacts on ninety-day readmission is not statistically significant in either country. The effects of seven-day catheterization on mortality are much larger in the United States than in Japan. However, the difference in impacts of seven-day catheterization on thirty-day versus one-year mortality rates are almost the same in both countries (approximately 6 percentage points at one year). Further, seven-day catheterization decreases one-year readmission rates by 21 and 32 percentage points for the CCP and Japanese patients, respectively.

Figures 7.1 and 7.2 illustrate the adjusted probability of seven-day catheterization and patient outcomes by biprobit model in the United States and Japan, respectively. These figures show that the adjusted probabilities of thirty-day and one-year mortality conditional on seven-day

Table 7.2   Effects of seven-day catheterization on patient outcomes by bivariate probit analysis

	United States[a]							Japan						
	30-day mortality	1-year mortality	90-day readmission for any cause	1-year readmission for any cause	90-day expenditure	1-year expenditure	Length of hospital stay	30-day mortality	1-year mortality	90-day readmission for any cause	1-year readmission for any cause	90-day expenditure	1-year expenditure	Length of hospital stay
A. First equation for 7-day cath														
Thrombolytics use during stay	0.107** (0.043)	0.136** (0.145)	0.097 (0.043)	0.133 (0.044)	0.077** (0.426)	0.077** (0.426)	0.068** (0.041)	1.124** (0.074)	0.883** (0.081)	0.416** (0.075)	0.591** (0.076)	0.159*** (0.072)	0.159*** (0.072)	0.156*** (0.072)
Aspirin use during stay	0.574*** (0.034)	0.609*** (0.123)	0.881*** (0.038)	0.917*** (0.038)	0.251*** (0.376)	0.251*** (0.376)	0.249*** (0.037)	0.731*** (0.079)	1.518 (0.165)	0.407*** (0.077)	0.555** (0.077)	0.218*** (0.076)	0.218*** (0.076)	0.207*** (0.077)
Beta-blocker use during stay	0.149*** (0.033)	0.136*** (0.108)	0.193*** (0.033)	0.227*** (0.033)	0.083*** (0.322)	0.074*** (0.322)	1.221*** (0.031)	0.042 (0.160)	0.278 (0.085)	1.152 (0.080)	0.124 (0.164)	0.124 (0.158)	0.133 (0.158)	0.024 (0.159)
ACE inhibitor use during stay	-0.035 (0.031)	0.006* (0.110)	0.091 (0.032)	0.025 (0.032)	0.014 (0.320)	0.014 (0.320)	0.039 (0.031)	-0.094 (0.084)	-0.350 (0.083)	0.908 (0.154)	0.032 (0.083)	0.030 (0.079)	0.030 (0.079)	0.024 (0.079)
Smoking cessation	-0.263 (0.052)	-0.222 (0.189)	-0.193 (0.065)	-0.022 (0.066)	-0.045 (0.567)	-0.045 (0.567)	0.010 (0.062)	-1.538** (0.232)	-1.318* (0.237)	-1.290** (0.215)	-1.865** (0.222)	-0.399** (0.208)	-0.399** (0.208)	-0.393* (0.208)
B. Second equation for patient outcomes														
7-day cath	-0.339*** (0.062)	-0.398* (0.078)	-0.173 (0.454)	-0.206* (0.255)	5160.540*** (1035.491)	5634.330*** (1339.860)	1.645*** (0.552)	-0.141*** (0.071)	-0.196** (0.093)	-0.314 (0.139)	-0.320** (0.122)	2145.305 (1565.115)	3028.147 (2006.289)	-9.046** (4.930)
Thrombolytics use during stay	-0.001 (0.036)	-0.265 (0.044)	-0.014 (0.058)	-0.023 (0.062)	-981.344 (1316.630)	-1108.269 (1710.970)	1.085* (0.677)	-0.241 (0.043)	-0.217 (0.096)	0.476 (0.067)	0.769 (0.072)	-5074.712*** (1563.686)	-4974.383*** (2094.374)	6.785 (4.935)
Aspirin use during stay	-0.811*** (0.054)	-0.585 (0.067)	-0.725 (0.089)	-0.262 (0.092)	1364.137 (1189.678)	3902.250*** (1415.314)	0.897* (0.618)	-1.178*** (0.059)	1.202 (0.094)	0.278 (0.081)	0.641* (0.105)	-2149.844 (1682.250)	-5199.518*** (2253.177)	-7.251 (5.310)
Beta-blocker use during stay	-0.242 (0.030)	-0.204 (0.036)	-0.293** (0.050)	-0.103 (0.051)	598.790 (996.926)	-30.244 (1306.556)	0.097 (0.518)	-0.405 (0.072)	0.821** (0.077)	0.077 (0.086)	0.102 (0.127)	525.981 (3418.078)	-4595.684 (4578.117)	-7.472 (10.807)
ACE inhibitor use during stay	0.254 (0.031)	0.197 (0.039)	-0.203* (0.054)	-0.324*** (0.054)	335.949 (987.849)	806.030 (1297.685)	2.625*** (0.517)	0.610 (0.058)	-0.650 (0.089)	0.750 (0.128)	-0.080 (0.094)	-1653.425 (1700.296)	583.776 (2277.349)	10.267*** (5.400)
Smoking cessation	-2.921 (0.052)	0.008 (0.064)	-0.058 (0.099)	0.215 (0.101)	-2682.285* (1750.316)	-1695.446 (2287.076)	-0.194 (1.021)	-0.122 (0.095)	-0.279 (0.119)	-4.559 (0.118)	-12.649 (0.160)	-4844.199 (4523.262)	-6110.899 (6058.381)	2.115 (14.280)
Rho	-0.938*** (0.161)	-0.861*** (0.238)	-0.998*** (0.036)	-0.101*** (2.764)				0.791 (0.023)	0.942 (0.794)	0.635 (2.123)	0.170** (1.850)			
Log likelihood	-558.936	-591.000	-654.000	-725.000	-10194.701	-10449.257	-3443.423	-74.500	-172.1966	-158.0251	-144.000	-2031.413	-2079.705	-989.014

Notes: Standard errors in parentheses. For biprobit analyses, the marginal effect of each explanatory variable is calculated as $f(\beta_z X̄)$ · coefficient for panel A; and $f(\beta_z X̄)$ · coefficient for panel B. Each equation is controlled for patient demographic characteristics, comorbidity and severity measures. For medical expenditure, seemingly unrelated regression method is used, since dependent variables are continuous.

[a]For United States, weighted biprobit by the number of patients in each metropolitan area.
***Significant at the 5 percent level.
**Significant at the 10 percent level.
*Significant at the 15 percent level.

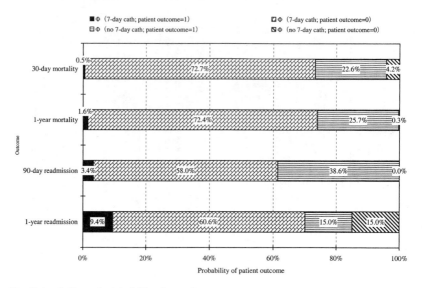

Fig. 7.1   Adjusted probability for patient outcomes conditional on seven-day
catheterization by biprobit model (United States)

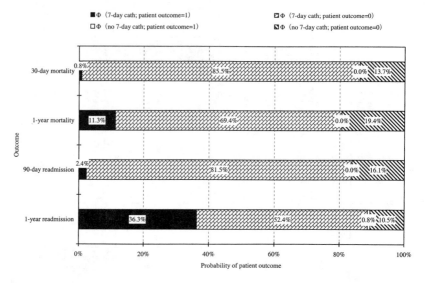

Fig. 7.2   Adjusted probability for patient outcomes conditional on seven-day
catheterization by biprobit model (Japan)

catheterization are approximately 1 percent and 2 percent for CCP patients
and 1 percent and 11 percent for Japanese patients. The adjusted probabilities of thirty-day and one-year readmission conditional on seven-day
catheterization are approximately 3 percent and 9 percent for CCP patients
and 2 percent and 36 percent for Japanese patients. Therefore, among

those who undergo intensive procedures within one week, the risks of dying and being readmitted to a hospital are about the same in both countries over a relatively short time interval, but they become much larger at one year after the first hospital admission in the Japanese data compared to the CCP patients. On the other hand, the adjusted probabilities of thirty-day and one-year mortality conditional on no seven-day catheterization are approximately 23 percent and 26 percent for CCP patients and 0 percent and 0 percent for Japanese patients. As regards adjusted probabilities of thirty-day and one-year readmission conditional on no seven-day catheterization, they are approximately 39 percent and 15 percent for CCP patients and 0 percent and 1 percent for Japanese patients. Thus, among those without seven-day catheterization, the risks of dying and readmission are much larger in the CCP patients than the Japanese patients for any time interval, though the adjusted probability of readmission for the CCP patients without seven-day catheterization are dramatically improved from thirty days through the one-year time interval.

These results could be affected by the difference in the timing of clinical decision making for intensive procedures between both countries. The aggressive and quick clinical choice of intensive procedures (Sasakuri et al. 1997; Nishida, Endo, and Koyanagi 1997) tends to improve patients' outcomes over shorter intervals, while it may lead to increased risks over longer intervals. On the other hand, over all intervals, the CCP patients without intensive procedures face much higher risks of death and readmission, compared to Japanese patients without seven-day catheterization.

After adjusting for patient chart-based characteristics, seven-day catheterization increases one-year hospital expenditures by \$5,634 in the United States and by \$3,028 in Japan. The significantly positive impacts of such high-tech treatments may partially account for the current high health care costs in both countries. The influence of a high-tech treatment on hospital expenditures is much larger for the CCP patients. However, note there are few observations for which hospital expenditure data are available in Japan, which makes it difficult to make the correct clinical policy implications. On the other hand, seven-day catheterization tends to have an opposite effect on the length of hospital stay in the two countries. High-tech treatments increase the length of stay from the first admission by about two days for the CCP patients and decrease it by nine days for Japanese patients, which is consistent with the results from the descriptive statistics. Adjusting for patient and treatment heterogeneity tends to enlarge the effect of intensive procedures on Japanese patients' length of stay, implying that unobserved factors such as other patient characteristics and medical centers cost constraint incentives affect the results.

7.5.2 Effects of Low-Tech Treatments on the Quality of Care

Similar to table 7.1, panel A in table 7.2 shows that drug use is highly correlated with high-tech treatments. For the CCP patients, the use of thrombolytics, aspirin, and beta-blockers during a hospital stay have significantly positive correlations with seven-day catheterization. We also observe that, for Japanese patients, thrombolytics and aspirin use (but not beta-blockers) are positively correlated with high-tech treatments. Interestingly, smoking cessation is negatively related to seven-day catheterization in Japan. This suggests that those who are treated by intensive procedures are more likely to receive some low-tech treatments, and there exists treatment heterogeneity among patients. In order to adjust for the heterogeneity, we apply a bivariate probit procedure in this study. We observe that correlations calculated based on the covariance of residuals between the first and second equations, $Cov(\varepsilon_1, \varepsilon_2) = \rho$, are statistically significantly different from 0 for the CCP patients, but that this is not the case for Japanese patients. This implies that the effect of treatment heterogeneity is much larger among the CCP patients.

As regards the effects of drug use on patient outcomes, aspirin use is seen to decrease thirty-day mortality rates by approximately 80 and 120 percentage points in the United States and Japan, respectively. The use of beta-blockers and ACE inhibitors also contributes to a decrease in the CCP patients' readmission rates, but this is not the case for Japanese patients. Rather, using beta-blockers and aspirin has a positive effect on one-year mortality and readmission rates, respectively, in the Japanese data.

For the CCP patients, aspirin use seems to increase one-year hospital expenditures by $3,900 and the length of hospital stay by about one day. In contrast, it is interesting that aspirin use dramatically decreases one-year hospital expenditure in Japan. Also, use of thrombolytics contributes to a decrease in both ninety-day and one-year medical expenditures. In both countries, ACE inhibitor use tends to length the duration of hospital stay.

Although most effects of drug use are not statistically significant and vary among patient outcomes as dependent variables, they appear to be more significant for CCP patients than for Japanese patients. Next, we examine which patients can be defined as good candidates for receiving aspirin, beta-blockers, no calcium channel blockers, and smoking cessation during their hospitalization and how they are actually treated. Patients are defined as good candidates according to exclusion and inclusion criteria from the ACC/AHA guidelines (table 7A.1). This tests the appropriateness of the low-tech treatments. Note that we define *ideal* or *good candidates* for not receiving calcium channel blockers, as many studies demonstrate harmful impacts on AMI patients and their use has been decreasing in the United States (Rogers et al. 1996; McClellan et al. 2001).

Table 7.3 summarizes the fraction of patients who are ideal or good candidates for each drug based on clinical records and the probability that ideal or good candidates were actually treated. Figure 7.3 illustrates the probability, among ideal or good candidates, of receiving various treatments. Table 7.3 shows that the rates of ideal or good candidates vary

Table 7.3   Ideal/good candidates for medications during stay

Variable	United States Mean	United States Standard deviation	Japan Mean	Japan Standard deviation
Ideal/good candidate for aspirin	0.481	(0.500)	0.684	(0.466)
Actually treated by aspirin	0.799	(0.401)	0.732	(0.445)
Ideal/good candidate for beta-blocker	0.256	(0.437)	0.637	(0.482)
Actually treated by beta-blocker	0.408	(0.493)	0.088	(0.284)
Ideal/good candidate for no calcium channel blocker	0.328	(0.470)	0.826	(0.380)
Actually treated by calcium channel blocker	0.421	(0.495)	0.426	(0.496)
Ideal/good candidate for smoking cessation	0.127	(0.333)	0.405	(0.492)
Actually treated by smoking cessation	0.372	(0.485)	0.179	(0.390)
Candidate for CLASS I	0.408	(0.492)	0.121	(0.327)
Actually treated by catheterization	0.554	(0.498)	0.783	(0.422)
Candidate for CLASS IIa but not CLASS I	0.341	(0.474)	0.879	(0.327)
Actually treated by catheterization	0.356	(0.480)	0.778	(0.417)
Candidate for CLASS IIb only	0.096	(0.294)	0.000	(0.000)
Actually treated by catheterization	0.387	(0.490)	0.000	(0.000)
Number of observations	974		190	

Note: For United States, table shows weighted mean values by the number of patients in each metropolitan area.

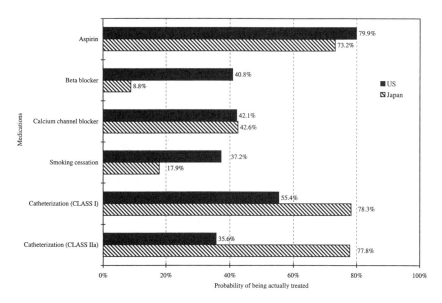

Fig. 7.3   Probability of being actually treated by medications among ideal or good candidates (United States and Japan)

widely between the two countries. Note that the disparity between the two countries in the fraction of individuals who are ideal or good candidates may be caused by missing information on exclusions and inclusion criteria. For aspirin, beta-blockers, no calcium channel blockers, and smoking cessation, the rates of ideal or good candidates tend to be much higher for Japanese patients than for CCP patients: 68 percent versus 48 percent, 64 percent versus 26 percent, 83 percent versus 33 percent, and 41 percent versus 13 percent, respectively. The fraction of patients actually treated, among those identified as ideal or good candidates, is very alike, except the use of beta-blockers and smoking cessation.

For Japanese patients, the underuse of beta-blockers and smoking cessation, relative to CCP patients, is noticeable, although the fraction of patients identified as ideal or good candidates tends to be large in Japan. Previous studies have explained the underuse of beta-blockers in Japan in various ways. Provocative vasomotor studies of Japanese patients found a higher incidence of inducible spasm and greater vasoconstriction of nonspastic segments than Caucasian studies (Beltrame, Sasayama, and Maseri 1999; Pristipino et al. 2000). Therefore, in Japan, cardiologists may avoid using beta-blockers that could lead to an incidence of inducible spasm in order to avoid unnecessary critical complications. On the other hand, Wang and Stafford (1998) emphasized the effects of nonclinical factors on beta-blocker use, such as age, unnecessary fear of complications without medical evidence, and regional and physicians' characteristics. Also, Wang and Stafford (1998) pointed out that uninsured patients are more likely to undergo beta-blocker treatments that cost much less than other treatments in the United States. Because we focus on elderly patients at age sixty-five and older in this study, both CCP and Japanese patients are reimbursed by similar fee-for-service reimbursement systems in both countries. Therefore, the underuse of beta-blockers would be expected partly because of the weaker incentives for cost containment in Japan.

Finally, compared to drug use, it would be difficult to justify criteria for identifying ideal or good candidates for high-tech treatments. However, according to guidelines by ACC/AHA (table 7A.1), we define three types of candidates for catheterization: usually indicated, always acceptable and considered useful/effective (CLASS I); acceptable, of uncertain efficiency and may be controversial, weight of evidence in favor of usefulness or efficacy (CLASSIIa); and acceptable, of uncertain efficiency and may be controversial, not well established by evidence, can be helpful and probably not harmful (CLASSIIb). In the data, almost all patients are classified into either CLASS I or CLASSIIa. While the fraction of patients identified as CLASS I, that is, relatively ideal candidates, is higher for the CCP than Japanese patients (41 percent versus 12 percent), the fraction in CLASS-IIb, that is, good candidates, is higher for Japanese patients (88 percent versus 34 percent). For patients classified into either CLASS I or CLASSIIa, figure 7.3 shows that Japanese patients are 1.5 to 2 times as likely to be catheterized than the CCP patients.

Therefore, we conclude that the patterns of ideal or good candidates for drug use according to ACC/AHA guidelines are very alike between two countries. The CCP patients are more aggressively treated by beta-blockers than Japanese patients, and we observe that collaborative medical centers in the data tend to perform intensive procedures more often.

7.6   Discussion

The CCP is the first major undertaking of the Health Care Quality Improvement Program (HCQIP) from 1992 to 1998 administered by the HCFA. Under this project, peer review organizations in all states encouraged health care providers to improve their systems of care for given quality indicators for patients with AMI. The new data collected by the HCQIP show that the quality of care for each clinical indicator varies from state to state and region to region. As regards AMIs, the data suggest that prescribing beta-blockers and aspirin for patients who have had a heart attack would be a course of action that could save hundreds to thousands of lives each year. One sign of the success of the CCP pilot project in Alabama, Connecticut, Iowa, and Wisconsin was an increase in the use of beta-blockers for heart attack patients, following dissemination of the study's results, from 47 percent to 68 percent (Centers for Medicare and Medicaid Services 2000).

The HCQIP and the CCP are considered models of public health policy. The HCQIP identified twenty-four process-of-care measures[5] that are strongly supported by clinical science and are widely accepted standards of care. These standards relate to primary prevention, secondary prevention, or the treatment of the six medical conditions including AMI, breast cancer, diabetes, heart failure, pneumonia, and stroke. Therefore, the purpose of this study is to help improve health care policies in Japan where there has not yet been established a system for collecting nationwide–individual-level clinical data.

We create a database comparable to the CCP, and we focus our investi-

---

5. For measurements indicating the quality of care for patients with AMI, the following indexes are used: administering aspirin to a beneficiary within twenty-four hours of the beneficiary's admittance to a hospital (national median is 84 percent); prescribing aspirin when a beneficiary is discharged (national median is 85 percent); administering a beta-blocker to a beneficiary within twenty-four hours of the beneficiary's admittance to a hospital (national median is 64 percent); prescribing beta-blockers when a beneficiary is discharged (national median is 72 percent); prescribing ACE inhibitors for patients with decreased left ventricular ejection fraction (national median is 71 percent); providing smoking cessation counseling to patients in the hospital (national median is 40 percent); the length of time before a patient receives angioplasty in minutes (national median is 120 minutes); and the length of time before a patient receives thrombolytic therapy in minutes (national median is 40 minutes; Jencks et al. 2000).

gation on the variation in the quality of health care with respect to treatments and outcomes between the United States and Japan, controlling for chart-based detailed clinical information on elderly patients, sixty-five years old and over, with AMI. Our main conclusions are as follows.

First, we found that there is significant heterogeneity among patients and in treatments that could influence the quality of care among elderly AMI patients. In both the United States and Japan, catheterized patients were more likely to be younger and in better health. Interestingly, the differences in treatment between men and women in Japan are trivial, as compared with treatment differences by gender in the United States. Also, Japanese patients tend to be more aggressively treated by angioplasty following catheterization than the CCP patients.

Comparison of national health systems may provide an insight into the effects of health system characteristics on the different treatment patterns in the United States and Japan. In the United States, inpatient care for older persons is only partially covered by Medicare, and beneficiaries could not receive prescription drug coverage for ambulatory care until recently, unless they had beforehand purchased supplemental insurance or hold coverage from a former employer. Medicare's diagnosis-related group (DRG) payment system for hospitals fixes the payment at the time a patient is admitted to the hospital. Thus, since DRG was adopted in 1984, it might appear to provide strong incentives to providers to limit costs. On the other hand, under the Japanese universal health insurance system, all medical facilities are reimbursed on a fee-for-service basis according to an official fee schedule (*shinryo hoshu*). Manipulation of the fee schedule serves as one of the primary mechanisms by which the Ministry of Health, Labour and Welfare regulates the supply of medical care, utilization rates, and aggregate health care expenditure. So far, in Japan, medical providers have no socioeconomic incentive to distinguish treatments for female from male patients. Also, the upward trend in reimbursement for intensive cardiac treatment has translated into increased availability of the procedures and has motivated health care providers to utilize the high-tech procedures.

Second, after adjusting for chart-based patient characteristics and variation in treatments, we observe that high-tech treatments would significantly improve patient outcomes and would increase hospital expenditures but that the effects are much larger for the CCP patients than the Japanese patients.

Third, the aggressive and quick clinical choice to use an intensive procedure tends to improve patients' outcomes in the shorter time interval, but it may lead to increased risks in the longer time period.

Fourth, a CCP patient who undergoes an intensive procedure tends to stay in a hospital longer compared to the one who does not, while a patient who undergoes an intensive procedure in Japan is inclined to stay in the hospital for a shorter period. This apparent difference between Japan and the United States may be a result of patient characteristics that are unobserved in the data, as well as the economic incentives of the respective health care systems. In the Japanese data, almost 60 percent of patients underwent catheterization immediately after hospital admission. Those who were not treated by seven-day catheterization are typically in very critical condition, leading to longer hospital stays. Also, under the universal coverage system in Japan, patients may have an economic incentive to stay longer in hospitals, particularly when they have no informal or unpaid caregivers (such as relatives) or sufficient financial resources to afford formal home care. Lately, in order to shorten the length of hospital stay and decrease medical expenditure, the Ministry of Health, Labour and Welfare raised the coinsurance rate for insured care services from 10 percent to 15 percent when a patient occupies an acute-care bed for more than 180 days.

Fifth, the patterns of ideal or good candidates according to ACC/AHA guidelines are very similar between the two countries, except beta-blocker use, smoking cessation, and catheterization. The CCP patients are more aggressively treated with beta-blockers and smoking cessation than Japanese patients, while we observe that collaborative medical centers in the Japanese data tend to perform intensive procedures more often. The underuse of beta-blockers in Japan was also found by previous studies and was attributed to clinical and socioeconomic causes.

The data collected for this study may not be representative of the AMI population in Japan, as the data only contain patients admitted to high-volume and high-tech hospitals in a specific region. The statistically insignificant results mentioned in the preceding reveal the shortcomings of the current data. In order to overcome these shortcomings, our goal is to expand the hospitals and patients covered by this project in the future.

Appendix

Table 7A.1   Exclusions and inclusions criteria for various medications eligibility during hospitalization

Variable	Definition	Variable	Definition
IG_ASA	Good candidate for aspirin If XC31809 = 1 or XBSTOOL = 1 or XBLEED = 1 or XPLT1 = 1 or XCOAGULP = 1 or XC11806 = 1 or XPLT1 = 1 or XDXLIV = 1 or XULCER = 1 or XHEMAC = 1 or XYLCRE91 = 1 or XCANCER = 1 or XTERMIL then excluded from ideal/good candidates for aspirin during hospitalization.	XC31809 XBSTOOL XBLEED XCOAGULP XC11806 XPLT1 XDXLIV XULCER XHEMAC XYLCRE91 XCANCER XTERMIL	Allergy to aspirin Evidence of bleeding on admission or during hospitalization History of internal bleeding Coagulopathy (history of bleeding disorder or INR > 1) Warfarin on admission Platelet count $< 100K$ Chronic liver disease Peptic ulcer disease Hematocrit $< 30\%$ or hemoglobin (Hgb) $< 10g$ Highest creatinine $> 3mg/Dl$ Metastatic cancer Terminal illness
IG_BBK	Good candidate for beta blocker If XSHOCK = 1 or XSYST = 1 or XCOND = 1 or XASTHMA = 1 or XBRDYPLS = 1 or XLVEF1 = 1 or XLVEF2 = 1 or XCHF = 1 or XCOPD = 1 or XDEMENT = 1 or XC18004 = 1 or XC1225 = 1 or XCANCER = 1 or XTERMIL = 1 then excluded from ideal/good candidates of beta-blocker during hospitalization. Note: If XCOND1 = 1 or XCOND2 = 1 or XCOND3 = 1 or XCOND4 = 1 then XCOND = 1	XSHOCK XSYST XCOND1 XCOND2 XCOND3 XCOND4 XCOND XASTHMA XBRDYPLS XLVEF1 XLVEF2 XCHF XCOPD XDEMENT	Hypotension or shock during hospitalization Systolic blood pressure on admission $< 100mmHg$ RBBB, any EKG, and left fascic block, any EKG RBBB and left fascic blocks RBBB, any EKG, and left fascic blocks RBBB and any left fascic blocks Conduction disorder Asthma during hospitalization Bradycardia or pulse on admission < 60 beats/min. LVEF $< 35\%$ LVEF $< 50\%$ Pulmonary edema or CHF unless LVEF $> 50\%$ History of COPD Dementia

IG_CBK	Good candidate for no CA+ If XANYFIB = 1 or X@$CHST = 1 then excluded from and if XLVEF5 = 1 or XSHOCK = 1 or CBKINC1 = 1 or XCOND = 1 or XBRADY = 1 then included to ideal/good candidates of no calcium channel blockers with low LVEF during hospitalization.	XC18004 XC12225 XCANCER XTERMIL XANYFIB X24CHST XLVEF5 XSHOCK CBKINC1 XCOND XBRADY	Antidepressant on admission Insulin on admission Mestastatic cancer Terminal illness Any atrial fibrillation Recurrent chest pain Inclusion: LVEF < 40% Inclusion: Hypotension or shock during hospitalization Inclusion: Pulmonary edema or CHF unless LVEF $\geq$ 50% Inclusion: Conduction disorder Inclusion: Bradycardia
ID_SMK	Ideal candidate for smoking cessation If XSMOKE = 1 then excluded from good candidates of smoking cessation during hospitalization.	XSMOKE	Not a current smoker
CCLASS1A[a]	Candidate for CLASS I If CCLASS1 = 1 then included in good candidates for CLASS I	CCLASS1	Inclusion: Recurrent chest pain or ischemia by stress test
CCLASS1B[b]	Candidate for CLASS IIa but not CLASS I If CHF = 1 or XLEVF4 = 1 or CHF = 1 or P_REVAC = 1 then included as ideal candidates for catheterization.	XLVEF4 CHF P_REVAC	Inclusion: LVEF $\leq$ 40% Inclusion: CHF Inclusion: Pre-revascularization
CCLASS1C[c]	Candidate for CLASS IIb only If CCLASS1 = 1 then included in good candidates for CLASS IIb.	XQWAVEMI	Inclusion: Non Q wave Mis.

Source: Ryan et al. (1999).

[a]CLASSI = usually indicated, always acceptable and considered useful/effective.

[b]CLASSIIa = acceptable, of uncertain efficiency and may be controversial; weight of evidence in favor of usefulness/efficacy.

[c]CLASSIIb = acceptable, of uncertain efficiency and may be controversial; not well established by evidence, can be helpful and probably not harmful.

References

Asada, S., K. Ogawa, S. Tsushima, K. Nakamura, and S. Hashimoto. 1970. Shinkinkosoku setsujo no ichirei-sobo benchikan shijutsu ga dojini shinko sareta chikenrei ni tsuite [Results of open heart surgery in severe cases of heart diseases and discussion on the improvement of operative results]. *Kyobu Geka* 23 (12): 847–59.

Beltrame, J. F., S. Sasayama, and A. Maseri. 1999. Racial heterogeneity in coronary artery vasomotor reactivity: Differences between Japanese and Caucasian patients. *Journal of the American College of Cardiology* 33 (6): 1442–52.

Bertoni, A. G., D. E. Bonds, J. Lovato, D. C. Goff, and F. L. Brancati. 2004. Sex disparities in procedure use for acute myocardial infarction in the United States, 1995 to 2001. *American Heart Journal* 147 (6): 1054–60.

Brown, C. A., A. M. Hutter, Jr., R. W. DeSanctis, H. K. Gold, R. C. Leinbach, A. Roberts-Niles, W. G. Austen, and M. J. Buckley. 1981. Prospective study of medical and urgent surgical therapy in randomizable patients with unstable angina pectoris: Results of in-hospital and chronic mortality and morbidity. *American Heart Journal* 102 (6): 959–64.

Califf, R. M., and TAMI VA Study Group. 1991. Evaluation of combination thrombolytic therapy and timing of cardiac catheterization in acute myocardial infarction. *Circulation* 83:1543–56.

The Cardiac Insufficiency Bisoprolol Study (CIBIS-II). 1999. CIBIS-II: A randomized trial. *Lancet* 353:9–13.

Centers for Medicare and Medicaid Services. 2000. Medicare gets first database measuring quality of medical care delivered to beneficiaries. http://www.cms.hhs.gov/media/press/release.asp?Counter=385.

Endo, M., and H. Koyanagi. 1994. CABG: Sekai no Doko to Honpo no Jittai [CABG: The world trends and the Japanese realities]. *Nihon Rinsho* 52 (Suppl. Pt. 1): 961–69.

Erbel, R., T. Pop, K. J. Henrichs, K. Von Olshausen, C. J. Shuster, H. J. Rupprecht, C. Steuernegel, and J. Meyer. 1986. Percutaneous transluminal coronary angioplasty after thrombolytic therapy: A prospective controlled randomized trial. *Journal of the American College of Cardiology* 8:485–95.

Frances, C., H. Noguchi, W. Browner, B. Bassie, and M. McClellan. 2000. Are we inhibited? Renal insufficiency should not preclude the use of ACE inhibitors for patients with acute MI and depressed left ventricular function. *Archives Internal Medicine* 160 (17): 2645–50.

Greene, W. H. 1993. *Econometric analysis.* 2nd ed. New York: Macmillan.

———. 1998. Gender economics courses in liberal arts colleges: Further results. *Journal of Economic Education* 29 (4): 291–300.

Harrold, L. R., D. Lessard, J. Yarzebski, J. H. Gurwitz, J. M. Gore, and R. J. Goldberg. 2003. Age and sex differences in the treatment of patients with initial acute myocardial infarction: A community-wide perspective. *Cardiology* 99 (1): 39–46.

Hayashi, H. 1972. Kyoshinsho ni tisuru kankekka chokusetsu hogoho ni yoru ichi chikenrei [Present status and the future of coronary surgery]. *Kokyu To Junkan* 20 (5): 377–83.

Health and Welfare Statistics Association. 2000. *Journal of Health and Welfare Statistics* Tokyo: Health and Welfare Statistics Association.

Hochman, J. S., J. E. Tamis, T. D. Thompson, W. D. Weaver, H. D. White, F. Van de Werf, P. Aylward, E. J. Topol, and R. M. Califf for the Global Use of Strategies to Open Occluded Coronary Arteries in Acute Coronary Syndromes IIb Investigators. Sex, clinical presentation, and outcome in patients with acute coronary syndromes. *New England Journal of Medicine* 341 (4): 226–32.

Second International Study of Infarct Survival (ISIS-2) Collaborative Group. 1988. Randomized trial of intravenous streptokinase, oral aspirin, both, or neither among 17,187 cases of suspected acute myocardial infarction. *Lancet* 2 (8607): 349–60.

Jencks, S. F., T. Cuerdon, D. R. Burwen, B. Fleming, P. M. Houck, A. E. Kussmaul, D. S. Nilasena, D. L. Ordin, and D. R. Arday. 2000. Quality of medical care delivered to Medicare beneficiaries: A profile at state and national levels. *Journal of the American Medical Association* 284:1670–76.

Kober, L., C. Torp-Pedersen, J. E. Carlsen, H. Bagger, P. Eliasen, K. Lyngborg, J. Videbaek, D. S. Cole, L. Auclert, and N. C. Pauly. 1995. A clinical trial of the angiotensin-converting-enzyme inhibitor trandolapril in patients with left ventricular dysfunction after myocardial infarction. Trandolapril Cardiac Evaluation (TRACE) Study Group. *New England Journal of Medicine* 333 (25): 1670–76.

Koshal, A., D. S. Beanlands, R. A. Davies, R. C. Nair, and W. J. Keon. 1988. Urgent surgical reperfusion in acute evolving myocardial infarction: A randomized controlled study. *Circulation* 78 (3 Pt. 2): I171–I178.

Lewis, H. D., J. W. Davis, and D. G. Archibald. 1983. Protective effects of aspirin against acute myocardial infarction and death in men with unstable angina: Results of a Veterans Administration cooperative study. *New England Journal of Medicine* 309 (7): 396–403.

Maddala, G. S. 1983. *Limited-dependent and qualitative variables in econometrics.* Cambridge, UK: Cambridge University Press.

Maddala, G. S., and L. F. Lee. 1976. Recursive models with qualitative endogenous variables. *Annals of Economic and Social Management* 5 (4): 525–45.

Marciniak, T., E. Ellerbeck, M. J. Radford, T. F. Kresowik, J. A. Gold, H. M. Krumholz, C. I. Kiefe, R. M. Allman, R. A. Vogel, and S. F. Jencks. 1998. Improving the quality of care for Medicare beneficiaries with acute myocardial infarction. *Journal of the American Medical Association* 297 (17): 1351–57.

McClellan, M., N. Every, A. M. Garber, P. Heidenreich, M. Hlatky, D. P. Kesseler, J. Newhouse, and O. Saynina. 2001. Technological change in heart attack care in the United States. In *Technological change in health care,* ed. M. McClellan and D. Kessler, 21–54. Ann Arbor: University of Michigan Press.

McClellan, M., B. J. McNeil, and J. Newhouse. 1994. Does more intensive treatment of acute myocardial infarction reduce mortality? Analysis using instrumental variables. *Journal of the American Medical Association* 272 (11): 859–66.

McClellan, M., and J. Newhouse. 1997. The marginal costs and benefits of medical technology. *Journal of Econometrics* 77 (1): 39–64.

McClellan, M., and H. Noguchi. 1998. Technological change in heart-disease treatment: Does high tech mean low value? *The American Economic Review* 88 (2): 90–96.

———. 2001. Validity and interpretation of treatment effect estimates using observational data: Treatment of heart attacks in the elderly. Stanford University. Unpublished Manuscript.

McClellan, M., and D. Staiger. 2000a. Comparing hospital quality at for-profit and not-for-profit hospitals. In *The changing hospital industry: Comparing not-for-profit and for-profit institutions,* ed. D. Cutler, 93–112. Chicago: University of Chicago Press.

———. 2000b. Comparing hospital quality of health care providers. In *Frontiers in health policy research,* ed. A. Garber, 113–36. Boston: MIT Press.

Metoprolol CR/XL Randomized Intervention Trial in Congestive Heart Failure

(MERIT-HF). 1999. Effect of metoprolol CR/XL in chronic heart failure. *Lancet* 353:2001–07.

Nippon Shinkekkan Intervention Gakkai Gakujutsu Iinkai. 1993. Iinnkai anketo hokoku kekka ni tsuite [Report on the survey conducted by the Japanese Intervention Association in 1993]. *Shinkekkan* 8:465.

Nishida, H., M. Endo, and H. Koyanagi. 1997. Nippon no gejo wo domiruka [What can we think of the current status of treatments for patients with cardiovascular disease in Japan?] *Mebio* 14 (12): 25–34.

Oe, K., M. Shimizu, H. Ino, M. Yamaguchi, H. Terai, K. Hayashi, M. Kiyama, K. Sakata, T. Hayashi, M. Inoue, et al. 2002. Effects of gender on the number of diseased vessels and clinical outcome in Japanese patients with acute coronary syndrome. *Circulation Journal* 66 (5): 435–40.

Pristipino, C., J. F. Beltrame, M. L. Finocchiaro, R. Hattori, M. Fujita, R. Mongiardo, D. Cianflone, T. Sanna, S. Sasayama, and A. Maseri. 2000. Major racial differences in coronary constrictor response between Japanese and Caucasians with recent myocardial infarction. *Circulation* 101 (10): 1102–08.

Rausenbaum, P., and D. Rubin. 1984. Reducing bias in observational studies using subclassification on the propensity score. *Journal of the American Statistical Association* 79:516–24.

Rodwin, V. G., and M. K. Gusmano. 2002. The World Cities Project: Rationale, organization, and design for comparison of megacity health systems. *Journal of Urban Health* 79:445–63.

Rogers, W. J., N. C. Chandra, W. French, J. M. Gore, C. T. Lambrew, and A. J. Tiefenbruunn. 1996. Trends in the use of reperfusion therapy: Experience from the Second National Registry of Myocardial Infarction (NRMI2). *Circulation* 194 (8): Abstract.

Ryan, T. J., E. M. Antman, N. H. Brooks, et al. 1999. ACC/AHA guidelines for the management of patients with acute myocardial infarction: 1999 update: A report of the American College of Cardiology/American Heart Association task force on practice guidelines. http://www.acc.org.

Sasakuri, S., Y. Hosoda, T. Watanabe, K. Takazawa, I. Hayashi, T. Yamamoto, K. Minami, H. Miyagawa, and T. Fukuda. 1997. Graft selection in coronary artery bypass surgery in the aged. *Nippon Kyobu Gaka Gakkai Zasshi* 45 (3): 384–86.

Sezai, Y., A. Yamazaki, H. Inoue, S. Ogawa, and H. Sakai. 1970. Kandomyaku no chokusetsu shijitsu, ditaidomyakuhen ni yoru jokodaidomyaku-kandomyaku dypass heno ichi shorei [Direct coronary artery surgery—Case report of aortocoronary bypass utilizing femoral artery autograft]. *Koyobugeka* 23 (12): 888–97.

Shilipak, M., C. Frances, H. Noguchi, B. Massie, and M. McClellan. 2001. Comparison of the effects of angiotensin converting-enzyme inhibitors and beta-blockers on survival in elderly patients with reduced left ventricular function after myocardial infarction. *American Journal of Medicine* 110 (6): 425–33.

Shlipak, M., P. Heidenreich, H. Noguchi, B. Warren, and M. McClellan. 2002. Associations of renal insufficiency with treatment and outcomes after myocardial infarction in the elderly. *Annals of Internal Medicine* 137 (7): 555–62.

Simmoons, M. L., A. E. R. Arnorld, A. Betriu, D. P. DeBono, J. Col, F. C. Dougherty, R. Von Essen, H. Lambertz, J. Lubsen, B. Meier, et al. for the European Cooperative Study Group for Recombinant Tissue-Type Plasminogen Activator (rTPA). 1988. Thrombolysis with tissue plasminogen activator in acute myocardial infarction: No additional benefit from immediate percutaneous angioplasty. *Lancet* 1 (8579): 197–203.

Takekoshi, N., E. Murakami, and M. Nakajima. 1983. Clinical characteristics and prognosis of patients with unstable angina treated medically and surgically—results in patients with ST-segment elevation and depression. *Japanese Circulation Journal* 47 (4): 495–502.

Thrombolysis in Myocardial Infarction (TIMI) Study Group. 1989. Comparison of invasive and conservative strategies after treatment with intravenous tissue plasminogen activator in acute myocardial infarction. *New England Journal of Medicine* 320:618–27.

VANQWISH Study Group. 1998. Design and baseline characteristics of the Veterans Affairs Non-Q-Wave Infarction Strategies In-Hospital (VANQWISH) trial. *Journal of the American College of Cardiology* 31 (2): 312–20.

Yoshikawa, A., H. Noguchi, S. Ide, A. Koike, T. Maruyama, N. Uemura, A. Urae, and T. Nambu. 2002. The causes and consequences of technological change in the treatment of acute myocardial infarction in Japan. In *Technological change in health care,* ed. M. McClellan and D. Kessler, 156–83. Ann Arbor: University of Michigan Press.

Wang, T. J., and R. S. Stafford. 1998. National patterns and predictors of β-blocker use in patients with coronary artery disease. *Archives of Internal Medicine* 158 (17): 1901–06.

Weisz, D., M. K. Gusmano, and V. G. Rodwin. 2004. Gender and the treatment of heart disease in older persons in the United States, France, and England: A comparative, population-based view of a clinical phenomenon. *Gender Medicine* 1 (1): 29–40.

Zijlstra, F., et al. 1993. A comparison of immediate coronary angioplasty with intravenous streptokinase in acute myocardial infarction. *New England Journal of Medicine* 328:680–84.

Geography and the Use of Effective Health Care in the United States

Jonathan Skinner

8.1 Introduction

There is a growing concern in the United States about shortfalls in health care quality. One influential Institute of Medicine (IOM) study called attention to problems of underuse, overuse, and misuse in health care quality (IOM 2000). With regard to underuse, there are a wide variety of procedures that are proven to be effective, yet are often used at rates as low as 50 percent for appropriate patients (most recently, see McGlynn et al. 2003). Examples of such effective treatments include the use of beta-blockers and aspirin for appropriate heart attack patients, annual eye examinations for people with diabetes, and mammography examinations for women over age fifty.

By the same token, there is evidence of overuse of procedures where they are not appropriate. For example, 20 percent of antibiotics prescribed in 1992 were used for common colds and respiratory tract infections, illnesses where the effectiveness of such antibiotics is questionable and may even be harmful. By the same token, only about one-third of angioplasties (PTCA) for cardiovascular disease are clearly appropriate, with about one-half uncertain and the remainder inappropriate (Schneider et al. 2001). Technological advances in diagnostic methods to detect appendicitis such as computerized tomography have improved tremendously, but there has been no apparent decline in the rate of inappropriate surgery for appendicitis (Flum et al. 2001). Finally, there is some evidence on the misuse of care, whether that means resulting complications resulting from errors in the

Jonathan Skinner is the John French Professor of Economics and professor of community and family medicine at Dartmouth College, and a research associate of the National Bureau of Economic Research.

treatment of a disease or (more generally) whether it means a poor match between what the patient wants (in terms of risk and side effects) and what the patient actually receives (Wennberg, Fisher, and Skinner 2002).[1]

This paper focuses on the underuse of effective procedures and, in particular, the remarkable variation across regions in the United States with regard to the use of such treatments. Geographical variation in quality of care is of interest for two reasons. First, it provides a snapshot of the degree of technological inefficiency in the health care system; that is, how much do some regions and hospitals lag behind best-practice practiced in other areas? It is not surprising that health care innovations take time to diffuse; physicians need to be trained in the use of new technology (perhaps through residency programs), and their use spreads as the newly trained residents diffuse to new practice areas. What is more surprising is how persistent are the shortfalls in quality across regions.

For example, beta-blockers are used to reduce demands on weakened hearts following acute myocardial infarction (AMI), with well-established benefits in terms of reduced mortality. As Jencks, Huff, and Cuerdon (2003) reported, median state level of use among ideal patients is just 69 percent in 2000 and 2001. Yet beta-blockers have been known to be effective for many years; in 1985, Yusuf et al. concluded that "Long-term beta blockade for perhaps a year or so following discharge after an MI is now of proven value, and for many such patients mortality reductions of about 25% can be achieved" (335). In other words, despite the passage of nearly two decades since beta-blockers had become well established and inexpensive treatment for heart attacks, roughly 30 percent of AMI patients are still not getting appropriate treatment.[2] Similarly, Garg et al. (2002) have found an average of 42 percent of heart attack patients for whom angiography was deemed "necessary" actually received the angiography, with regional rates varying from 24 to 58 percent.

To quantify the degree of technological process inefficiency in the United States, I use data from the *Dartmouth Cardiovascular Atlas of Health Care* (Wennberg and Birkmeyer 2000) that, in turn, is based on a large detailed survey (with chart reviews) of more than 160,000 heart attack patients during 1994 and 1995. I find that the average loss per heart

I am grateful to helpful comments from seminar participants at the conference on health economics in Nikko, Japan in May 2003, and from Elliott Fisher, Douglas Staiger, and John E. Wennberg. This research was supported by a grant from the National Institute on Aging (PO1-AG).

1. Also see chapter 4 in the *Economic Report of the President* (Council of Economic Advisors 2002) for a parallel discussion of these issues.

2. Berwick (2003) makes this point with an analogy to the treatment of scurvy on sea-going ships; despite the fact that James Lancaster proved the effectiveness of vitamin C in the treatment of scurvy in 1601 (with randomization by treating just one ship in his fleet of four), it took more than 200 years before the British Navy enacted rules to ensure proper vitamin C consumption.

attack patient, relative to best-practice care, is between $1,500 and $5,000 per year, depending on the benchmark used, the value of a life year, and other assumptions. The measured inefficiency does not stem from specific skills of the surgeon, but instead largely reflects the use (or nonuse) of pharmaceuticals such as beta-blockers and aspirin.

Geographic variation is used for a second task, to estimate a reduced form model of technology adoption that depends on supply factors that might be expected to lower the cost of adapting the new technology, such as the prevalence of cardiologists—who are presumably most aware of new technologies in the use of health care innovations—and demand factors such as education, income, and the overall incidence of heart disease in the region. Supply factors are less important in explaining technology diffusion than expected, but estimated demand effects are significant both statistically and economically. More cardiologists per capita is not significantly associated with higher rates of beta-blocker use, nor is there an association between cardiologists supply and the *average* quality use rate for beta-blockers, aspirin, reperfusion, and angiotensin converting enzyme (ACE) inhibitors.

In conclusion, there seems to be a missing link between the potentially large benefits of effective care for heart attack patients and financial incentives to pay for them. While beta-blockers may not be reimbursed directly by the Medicare program (and indeed cost just pennies per dose), other procedures with uncertain (or potentially negative) effects on outcomes, such as nonprimary angioplasty or angioplasty for non-Q-wave heart attacks, are paid in full by Medicare.[3] An intriguing question that remains is why physicians working in hospital settings do not comply with quality guidelines, given the large benefits in terms of patient outcome to do so.

8.2   Theoretical Models of Technology Adoption and Quality of Care

Standard economic models begin with the assumption of profit maximization, and it is not surprising that such models predict that firms with the greatest expected gain from adopting new technology should be the ones to do so (e.g., Griliches 1957). In the context of health care, financial incentives are largely determined by the reimbursement policies of insurance programs, most notably the Medicare program. For most measures of effective care, however, the financial costs of adopting pharmaceutical technology is minimal, particularly for beta-blockers and aspirin where costs are measured in cents rather than in dollars.

The exception is reperfusion therapy for heart attack patients, which

---

3. Fisher and Skinner (2001) found a negative correlation between Medicare spending and Medicare quality.

may consist either of primary angioplasty within twenty-four hours of the heart attack, or a regime of thrombolytic drugs, again administered shortly after the heart attack. The surgical approach, angioplasty, involves the use of a small deflated "balloon" inserted through a vein and threaded up to the blockage area, where it is popped open, thus generally restoring blood flow to the oxygen-starved heart muscle. The pharmaceutical approach uses "clot buster" thrombolytics that help to dissolve the platelets and other deposits that contribute to blocking blood flow to the heart; they are generally not used together because the thrombolytics discourages clotting, which can be dangerous during surgery. In this case, Medicare does compensate generously for surgery, thus providing a strong profit motive for investing in the newer technology. However, because the Medicare system is federal, it generally pays similar amounts across regions (albeit adjusted for costs of living, low-income patients, and graduate medical programs). While theoretical models would predict the more rapid diffusion of the most profitable (to hospitals or physicians) technologies, they do not generally predict why some regions would become persistently late adopters (see Skinner and Staiger 2005). Thus, one cannot appeal to differences in reimbursement rates to explain why regions in the United States differ so much with regard to technology adoption, particularly as the technologies I consider in the following are not particularly costly (i.e., aspirin or beta-blockers).

The literature in health care quality improvement is quite different and focuses much less on financial incentives and more on organizations and personalities. Indeed, the dominant model (adopted in turn from the management literature) sorts personalities of the relevant individuals according to whether they are innovators, early adopters, early or late majority adopters, and laggards (for an excellent review, see Berwick 2003). Some of these differences may, of course, stem from the organizational structure of the hospitals or the educational systems whence they emerge. As well, social networks (Coleman, Katz, and Menzel 1966) are another important mechanism for the transmission of medical innovations. These factors may be reflected in peer effects as found by Epstein and Nicholson (2005) and Burke, Fournier, and Prasad (2003).

We therefore consider quite general hypotheses based on a large class of factors on both the supply and demand side of health care markets. On the supply side, cardiologists might be expected to adopt earliest, as their practice is almost exclusively for patients with cardiovascular care, and they have received advanced training in cardiac care. As well, physicians would have the greatest incentive to adopt efficacious care the greater is the overall burden of cardiovascular disease or when urban dense regions increase the potential for specialization. On the other hand, demand-side factors could increase pressure on physicians to innovate; one might hypothesize that higher-educated or higher-income patients would be more familiar with new treatments and play a more active role in their use. (Conversely, they might be less likely to refuse the new treatment.)

This simple model suggests two distinct empirical exercises. The first is to attempt to quantify the gains from adopting more efficient technologies, which in the empirical section I define as the use of beta-blockers, ACE inhibitors, aspirin, and reperfusion in the treatment of AMI. Given those measures, factors (supply or demand) are next considered that may affect the adoption of one of these innovations in particular—both with regard to the use of beta-blockers and with regard to a set of effective treatments for AMI.

8.3   Empirical Measures of Technology Adoption and Quality of Care

In measuring technological diffusion for the treatment of heart attack patients, it is important to note that the technologies considered are not particularly hi-tech: beta-blockers and aspirin have been used for many years in the treatment of other illnesses, but their use for heart attack patients was established conclusively several decades ago (see Yusuf et al. [1985] and Heidenreich and McClellan [2001]). These treatments can be viewed as *efficient* care that is appropriate for nearly 100 percent of the appropriate patient population, regardless of health status or nearly any set of preferences.[4] Problems with measuring health status, or with the true underlying preferences, are therefore greatly reduced, as everyone should demand the treatment, and the right rate does not depend on health status—as it is as close to 100 percent as one can get.

The disadvantage with measuring quality in this way is that it comprises a small fraction of how health care is actually practiced. The vast majority of decisions require much greater degrees of judgment, where a treatment choice may be appropriate and helpful for one patient but inappropriate and even harmful for another. For example, roughly 15 percent of angioplasty (a less invasive approach than bypass surgery to restoring blood flow to arteries in the heart) are deemed inappropriate, and about half are of uncertain benefit (Schneider et al. 2001). As well, treatment for chronically ill patients with diseases such as congestive heart failure, cancer, or pulmonary diseases differ widely across regions in the United States, and assessing how many physician visits are appropriate, or the appropriate level of intensive care unit (ICU) care, is difficult even with detailed clinical data.[5]

Some approaches focus on outcomes measures, such as mortality rates or complication rates, but such measures must first control for possible

4. The terminology here follows Wennberg, Fisher, and Skinner (2002).
5. This type of care, which accounts for nearly all of the variation across regions in the United States, is referred to as *supply sensitive* care because such care tends to be associated with the supply of hospital beds and the per capita supply of physicians.

differences in the initial health status of the patient population. One example of an output measure of quality is the thirty-day or one-year mortality rate following AMI. The advantage of this type of measure is that it is a summary statistic and thus captures the multidimensional vector of inputs including the quality of the surgical team, follow-up care, smoking cessation programs, and the myriad other factors that comprise quality but which are difficult, if not impossible, to measure.

There are several shortcomings with measuring quality in this way, however. The first is simply the small numbers problem. If a hospital admits thirty AMI patients, purely random variation in the health status of the patient may lead to say six deaths in one year and nine deaths the next year. Thus, one cannot clearly determine whether the hospital looks better (or worse) than average because the hospital is better (or worse), or because the hospital had several lucky or unlucky draws. While McClellan and Staiger (1999) have used filtering methods at the hospital level to address this problem, it is still difficult to infer much about quality of care from smaller hospitals.

Another way around this problem is to aggregate individual hospitals into larger regions. This latter method was used in the *Dartmouth Atlas of Health Care* (Wennberg and Cooper 1999), creating 306 hospital referral regions (HRRs) based on the migration patterns of Medicare patients to hospitals (Wennberg and Cooper 1999). Each HRR is required to include at least one major hospital performing cardiovascular surgery and neurosurgery. While the larger size of the region masks the within-region (across-hospital) variation in hospital quality, in practice there is plenty of across-region variation in these measures of output quality. However, it may be difficult to control entirely for differences across HRRs with respect to underlying health status, and so unexplained variations across regions may be due to unmeasured confounding variables rather than quality of care per se. More problematic is the improved detection of enzymes that are markers for AMI, and thus a patient who would be designated with unstable angina in one region could be labeled a non-Q-wave AMI in another region. To the extent these patients are *healthier* than average, the mortality estimates for that region could be biased downward. To avoid such biases, I adopt the process-based quality measures in this paper because at least for the treatment of AMI, they are highly predictive of outcomes.

8.4   The Estimated Cost of Low-Quality Care for AMI

An important study by Heidenreich and McClellan (2001) has attempted to quantify the incremental benefits of treatments for AMI that have proven effectiveness. They identify five treatments with "clear mortality benefit"—aspirin, beta-blockers, thrombolytics, ACE inhibitors, and primary angioplasty (i.e., done within twelve hours of the initial heart attack)—and provide consensus marginal odds ratios (i.e., their additional value conditional on other treatments).[6] As well, they also provide odds ratios at thirty days of the *marginal* effectiveness of each procedure, conditional on the value of other treatments. The approach used here is to predict how mortality would vary across regions solely on the basis of the variations in the use of these effective procedures, multiplied by their effectiveness in expanding survival.

There are two adjustments to the data before deriving predicted mortality values in each region for the same hypothetical patient. The first is that the thirty-day odds ratios are assumed to be the same for one-year odds ratios. At least in the case of beta-blockers, this seems to be the case; the thirty-day odds ratio used in this study is 0.88, while Krumholz et al. (1998) estimated a one-year risk ratio between 0.77 and 0.86.[7] The second adjustment is to combine angioplasty and thrombolytics as reperfusion. These procedures are typically substitutes (because thrombolytics increase the risk of bleeding during the angioplasty procedure), and just reperfusion rates are reported in the HRR-level data. I average their odds ratios to estimate effectiveness.

To estimate predicted mortality based solely on the HRR-level use of these four procedures, I further convert the odds ratios back into coefficients in the logistics regression and then calculate the following linear index:

$$Z_i = \theta + \sum_{}^{4} X_{ij}\gamma_j,$$

where γ_j is the modified coefficient for the *j*th treatment ($j = 1, 2, 3, 4$), θ the constant term, and X_{ij} is the fraction of ideal candidates receiving treatment *j* in HRR *i*. (Strictly speaking, one would like to know each individual and their treatment vector, but that data is not available; thus I make a linear approximation in the context of the index.) Thus, Z_i is the linear index of mortality in HRR *i*, and estimated mortality m_i is $\exp(Z_i)/[1 + \exp(Z_i)]$. The constant term θ is varied to ensure that the predicted mortality matches a 30 percent one-year mortality rate.

Data on use of these procedures is from the Cooperative Cardiovascular Project that collected chart review and outcome data on more than 160,000 heart attack patients during 1994 and 1995. The detailed information allowed researchers to define "ideal" and "appropriate" patients for each of the four treatments. Figure 8.1 shows the distribution of one of these treatments, beta-blocker use among ideal patients, for each of 267 HRRs. (The remaining HRRs were dropped because of small sample sizes.) There is a very large degree of variation across regions, with usage ranging from less than 20 percent to over 80 percent during 1994 and 1995.

---

6. They are aspirin (0.77), beta-blockers (0.88), thrombolytics (0.75), primary angioplasty (0.51), and ACE inhibitors (0.94).

7. Note that odds ratios are typically larger in magnitude than risk ratios.

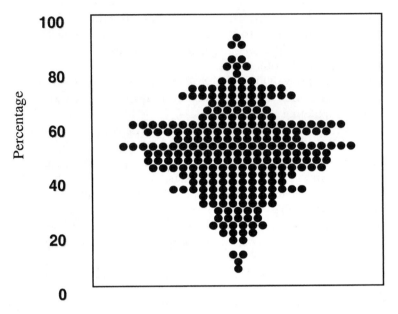

Fig. 8.1   Percent of "ideal" patients receiving beta-blockers at discharge following AMI (1994–1995)

Source: Dartmouth Atlas of Cardiovascular Health Care (Wennberg and Birkmeyer 2000).
Note: Each dot refers to an HRR.

Predicted mortality, based on the variation in the utilization of these four treatments, ranges from less than 28 percent (in Everett, Washington [27.4 percent] and St. Petersburg, Florida [27.9 percent], for example) to more than 33 percent (Oxford, Mississippi [34.1 percent], Hattiesburg, Mississippi [33.3 percent] and Jonesboro, Arkansas [33.1 percent], for example). Using the adjustment from one-year mortality to expected life years used in Cutler et al. (1998) and placing $50,000 as the price tag for the loss of one life year, the average efficiency cost per AMI patient is $3,687 compared to the best performing region, Everett Washington. Compared to a uniform compliance rate of 90 percent across all four dimensions of quality, the average cost rises to $5,106. The extremes, of course, are much greater; for patients living in Oxford, Mississippi who are appropriate candidates for these four treatments, they should be willing to pay $18,584 to be airlifted to Everett, Washington.

These estimated values would be twice as high if one were to use a commonly used benchmark of $100,000 per life year and even larger under some recommendations (Ubel, Hirth, Chernew, and Fendrick 2003). By the same token, however, one can deflate the values by the percentage of patients deemed "ideal" for the procedures. Taking a rough estimate of 39 percent of patients deemed ideal (as in Krumholz et al. [1998] for the case of beta-blockers) and applying this to all treatments yields a smaller mean cost of $1,446 (compared to Everett, Washington) and $1,758 (compared to a 90 percent uniform compliance rate) using the $50,000 per life year price tag. A compromise estimate could be using these adjusted numbers with a $100,000 per life year cost figure, leading to an estimate of approximately $3,000 per person inefficient level, but with some regions showing benefits from better compliance as much as $10,000 per patient. In other words, hospitals located in the poorly performing regions during 1994 and 1995 with 200 heart attack patients per year would have realized a social gain of more than $2 million annually during 1994 and 1995 had they simply adopted best-practice cardiac care for heart attack patients. Any additional costs that would have been incurred would have been either negligible (aspirin, beta-blockers) or reimbursed by Medicare (angioplasty). Given the apparently large benefits associated with the adoption of this technology, I next turn to considering factors affecting its adoption or non-adoption.

8.5   Factors Affecting the Adoption of High-Quality Care

First consider supply factors that might affect the adoption of new technology. Figure 8.2 shows a graph of HRR-level beta-blocker use according

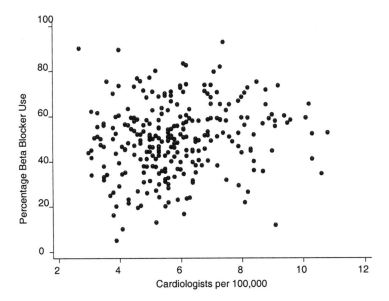

Fig. 8.2   Per capita cardiologist population and beta-blocker use

Source: Dartmouth Atlas of Cardiovascular Health Care (Wennberg and Birkmeyer 2000).

Note: Each dot represents one of the 269 HRRs with sufficient information on beta-blocker use (that is, percentage of patients with AMI who are "ideal" for beta-blockers who get it).

Table 8.1   Regression analysis explaining quality measures for cardiac care by
                   HRR, 1994–1995

	Beta-blocker use[a] (1)	Aspirin use in the hospital[a] (2)	Reperfusion use[a] (3)	Average quality measure[a] (4)
Cardiologist per 100,000[a]	0.84	−0.31	−1.35	−0.20
	(1.5)	(1.8)	(3.6)	(0.8)
Percent college graduate[b]	0.71	0.23	−0.02	0.37
	(4.5)	(4.6)	(0.2)	(5.4)
Poverty rate[b]	−0.82	−0.21	−0.25	−0.36
	(5.2)	(5.0)	(2.4)	(5.3)
Percent urban[b]	−0.16	−0.04	−0.02	−0.09
	(2.7)	(2.2)	(0.5)	(3.6)
Percent cigarette smokers[c]	−0.50	0.24	0.55	0.08
	(1.4)	(2.1)	(2.3)	(0.5)
AMI rate per 1,000[d]	1.61	−0.06	−0.34	0.34
	(4.7)	(0.6)	(1.5)	(2.3)
Constant	29.82	83.27	74.52	61.10
	(2.4)	(20.9)	(8.9)	(11.0)
Adjusted R^2	0.30	0.16	0.10	0.26
Mean of dependent variable (SD)	50.89	86.12	67.00	66.04
	(13.71)	(4.29)	(8.37)	(5.61)

Notes: $N = 267$. Absolute value of t-statistics in parentheses. All regressions weighted by population of Medicare enrollees in 1996.
[a]Source: Wennberg and Birkmeyer (2000).
[b]Source: 1990 Census.
[c]Source: CDC Behavioral Risk Factor database.
[d]Source: Wennberg and Cooper (1999).

to the supply of cardiologists per 100,000 population. There is a modest positive correlation; essentially having more cardiologists helps to ensure that the HRR is not in the "very low" category, with rates under 40 percent. Table 8.1 presents least squares regression results where the dependent variable is the percentage of ideal patients receiving a variety of high-quality treatments as a function of a variety of factors, including an average measure of quality in the rightmost column.

The first column attempts to explain the use of beta-blocker use. The regression estimates imply that increasing the supply of cardiologists from the 10th percentile (4.2 per 100,000) to the 90th percentile (9.0 per 100,000) is predicted to increase the use of beta-blockers by just 4 percentage points, and even that estimate is not significantly different from zero at the 95 percent confidence interval.[8] On the other hand, a greater burden of cardio-

---

8. By way of comparison, the standard deviation for beta-blocker use was 14 percentage points.

Table 8.2	Beta-blocker use in Georgia	
City	Percent of beta-blocker use among ideal patients
Albany	90.0
Rome	68.7
Columbus	53.3
Atlanta	**44.8**
Savannah	35.8
Macon	**21.3**

Source: Wennberg and Birkmeyer (2000).
Note: Medical schools are located in Macon and Atlanta (shown in bold).

vascular disease was associated with higher use of beta-blockers; a shift from the 10th to the 90th percentile in the underlying rate of AMI per 1,000 population of Medicare enrollees over age sixty-five was associated with a 5.6 percentage point increase in the use of beta-blockers. As well, demand factors appeared to exert an influence; shifting from the 10th to the 90th percentile in the percentage of college graduates living in the HRR was associated with a 5.8 percentage point higher rate of beta-blocker use.

Nor does the supply of cardiologists appear to be correlated with rates of aspirin use, reperfusion, or the combined index of cardiac health care quality (columns [2] through [4]). As was observed in the case of beta-blockers, most of the variation in the use of quality appeared associated with factors such as education levels and poverty rates in the region. Interestingly, the population of cardiologists was *negatively* associated with reperfusion rates. While the negative association holds solely for the per capita population of noninterventional cardiologists (that is, those who do not perform angioplasty), it is still somewhat surprising that reperfusion should not be more closely associated even with interventional cardiologists. This is a topic for future research.

To this point, the presence of a medical center has not yet been included in the statistical analysis. However, it may be of interest to consider a state chosen because of the very wide range in beta-blocker compliance, ranging from 21 percent in Macon, Georgia to 90 percent in Albany, Georgia. At least in Georgia, the use of beta-blockers in a community is not positively associated with the presence of a medical school; table 8.2 lists each HRR in Georgia, with the medical schools represented in bold. Indeed, Atlanta and Macon show beta-blocker use well below the state average.

8.6   Conclusion

The starting point for this analysis was the remarkable variation in measured quality of care for the treatment of heart attack patients across regions.

This variation has also been observed in more recent studies across states (Jencks et al. 2000; Jencks, Huff, and Cuerdon 2003), with only a modest degree of convergence over time. The first question addressed in this paper is to quantify the extent of these inefficiencies across regions. The estimates are consistent with an average quality gap of between $1,800 and $5,000 per heart attack patient. These are estimates that are not compared to some hypothetical level of perfection, but instead relative to a region in the United States that has managed to make efficient use of the existing technological treatments for AMI. Nor do these estimates assume that delicate surgical skills can be effortlessly transferred across regions, as most of the gains are realized through pharmaceutical rather than surgical innovations.

We also ask what factors appear to be associated with the adoption of effective technology. The supply of cardiologists appears to be weakly associated with the use of beta-blockers, but not with an average of four quality measures. Instead, quality appears to be a normal good; regions with higher overall income and education levels are more likely to adopt early. As well, regions with a higher prevalence of cardiovascular disease are more likely to adopt beta-blockers and to experience higher average rates of effective care for AMI, suggesting that volume effects—the ability of hospitals to specialize in cardiac care where there are a relatively large number of patients with cardiac disease—may improve organizational environments for adopting newer technologies.

One unanswered question is why the medical profession is so slow to adopt newer technologies, despite the clear benefits of doing so. The traditional (noneconomic) diffusion model distinguishes between the "early adopters," who are most effective at disseminating the successful ideas of innovators to the four-fifths of the remaining population, and the "early majority" and "late majority" group, who, while not entirely laggards, account for the majority of the profession in being very slow to adopt new innovations. For example, Berwick (2003) suggests that

> Medical communities are primarily local in their orientation, are dominated numerically by early and late majority groups, and do not trust remote and personally unfamiliar sources of authority. (1973)

A topic for future research is therefore to identify whether regions that are more effective in adopting new technologies have a "flatter" structure of authority as opposed to a hierarchical one where a "late majority" department chair can implicitly hold up new innovations for decades.

Regions that score well on treatment for AMI are only modestly more likely to score well for other measures of process quality. The correlation coefficient between beta-blocker use and the provision of annual eye examinations for diabetics in the Medicare population is 0.15 ($p < .02$), while the corresponding coefficient with mammography rates is 0.29 ($p < .001$). The low correlation across regions, as well as the low explanatory value of the regressions explaining adoption, are consistent with a model where each physician group, whether cardiologists, cardiac surgeons, internists, or family practice physicians, undergo different processes regarding the adoption of specific technologies for their group.

This is not to say, however, that financial incentives introduced with regard to these specific quality measures may not exert a strong and important impact on their overall use. One of the reasons why the use of beta-blockers grew so rapidly between 1997 and 1998 and 2000 and 2001 is because it was one of the Health Plan Employer Data and Information Set (HEDIS) quality measures used to quantify health care quality at the hospital or provider level. That there is so much latitude in the potential to improve the quality of care (and at such little cost) suggests that the incentives of the Medicare program could be better aligned with improving quality rather than rewarding the quantity of services in the United States.

References

Berwick, D. M. Dissemination innovations in health care. 2003. *Journal of the American Medical Association* 289 (15): 1969–75.

Burke, M., G. M. Fournier, and K. Prasad. 2003. Physician social networks and geographical variation in medical care. The Center on Social and Economic Dynamics Working Paper no. 33. Washington, DC: Brookings Institution.

Coleman, J. S., E. Katz, and H. Menzel. 1966. *Medical innovation: A diffusion study.* Indianapolis, IN: Bobbs-Merrill.

Council of Economic Advisors. 2002. *Economic report of the president.* Washington, DC: Government Printing Office.

Epstein, A., and S. Nicholson. 2005. The formation and evolution of physician treatment styles: An application to cesarean sections. NBER Working Paper no. 11549. Cambridge, MA: National Bureau of Economic Research, August.

Fisher, E., and J. Skinner. 2001. Medicare reform: Don't spend more, spend right. *Providence Journal* (March).

Garg, P. P., M. B. Landrum, S.-L. Normand, J. Z. Ayanian, P. J. Hauptman, T. J. Ryan, B. J. McNeil, and E. Guadagnoli. 2002. Understanding individual and small area variation in the underuse of coronary angiography following acute myocardial infarction. *Medical Care* 40 (7): 614–26.

Griliches, Z. 1957. Hybrid corn: An exploration in the economics of technological change. *Econometrica* 25 (4): 501–22.

Heidenreich, P. A., and M. McClellan. 2001. Trends in treatment and outcomes for acute myocardial infarction 1975–1995. *The American Journal of Medicine* 110: 165–74.

Institute of Medicine (IOM). 2000. *To err is human: Building a safer health system,* ed. Linda T. Kohn, Janet M. Corrigan, and Molla S. Donaldson. Washington, DC: National Academy Press.

Krumholz, H. M., M. J. Radford, Y. Wang, J. Chen, A. Heiat, and T. A. Marciniak. 1998. National use and effectiveness of β-blockers for the treatment of elderly patients after acute myocardial infarction. *JAMA* 280 (7): 623–29.

Jencks, S. F., T. Cuerdon, D. R. Burwen, B. Fleming, P. M. Houck, A. E. Kuss-maul, D. S. Nilasena, D. L. Ordin, and D. R. Arday. 2000. Quality of medical care delivered to Medicare beneficiaries: A profile at state and national levels. *JAMA* 284 (13): 1670–76.

Jencks, S. F., E. D. Huff, and T. Cuerdon. 2003. Change in the quality of care delivered to Medicare beneficiaries. *JAMA* 289 (3): 305–12.

McClellan, M. B., and H. Noguchi. 1998. Technological change in heart-disease treatment: Does high-tech mean low value? *American Economic Review* 88 (2): 90–96.

McClellan, M., and D. Staiger. 1999. The quality of health care providers. NBER Working Paper no. 7327. Cambridge, MA: National Bureau of Economic Research, August.

McGlynn, E. A., S. M. Asch, J. Adams, J. Keesey, J. Hicks, A. DeCristofaro, and E. A. Kerr. 2003. The quality of health care delivered to adults in the United States. *New England Journal of Medicine* 348 (26): 2635–45.

Schneider, E. C., L. L. Leape, J. S. Weissman, R. N. Piana, C. Gatsonis, and A. M. Epstein. Racial differences in cardiac revascularization rates: Does "overuse" explain higher rates among White patients? *Annals of Internal Medicine* 135 (5): 328–37.

Skinner, J., and D. Staiger. 2005. Technological Diffusion from hybrid com to beta-blockers. NBER Working Paper no. 11251. Cambridge, MA: National Bureau of Economic Research, March.

Ubel, P. A., R. A. Hirth, M. E. Chernew, and A. M. Fendrick. 2003. What is the price of life and why doesn't it increase at the rate of inflation? *Archives of Internal Medicine* 163 (14): 1637–41.

Wennberg, D. E., and J. Birkmeyer, eds. 2000. *The Dartmouth atlas of cardiovascular health care.* Chicago: American Hospital Association.

Wennberg, J. E., and M. Cooper, eds. 1999. *Dartmouth atlas of health care 1999.* Chicago: Dartmouth Medical School and American Hospital Association.

Wennberg, J. E., E. Fisher, and J. Skinner. 2002. Geography and the debate over Medicare reform. *Health Affairs* (Web Exclusive): W96–W114.

Yusuf, S., R. Peto, J. Lewis, R. Collins, and P. Sleight. 1985. Beta blockage during and after myocardial infarction: An overview of the randomized trials. *Progress in Cardiovascular Disease* 27 (5): 335–71.

Does Caregiving Affect Work?
Evidence Based on Prior Labor Force Experience

Kathleen McGarry

9.1 Introduction

The aging of a population presents numerous problems with which a country must grapple. Public attention in the United States and around the developed world has focused on the financial solvency of pension programs, the demands placed on the formal health care sector, and the expected increases in aggregate health care costs. However, of perhaps more direct concern to individuals and families, is the prospect of caring for a frail elderly family member, particularly an elderly parent. The United States General Accounting Office estimates that by 2040 there could be as many as 12 million disabled elderly (Walker 2002). Based on current caregiving patterns, the vast majority of these needy individuals will receive care exclusively through informal networks of family and friends, most typically a spouse or child (Department of Health and Human Services 1998). Intuitively one would expect this caregiving to affect the labor market behavior of the provider; caregivers may reduce hours or exit employment entirely in response to the needs of an elderly family member. The loss of trained workers will likely negatively affect the productivity of the economy, a drain made potentially more serious in light of the aging of the population and the declining ratio of workers to retirees.

On an individual level, reductions in labor market activity would be expected to affect later financial well-being. Not only would there be the obvious decline in earnings and thus an expected decline in retirement savings,

Kathleen McGarry is a professor of economics at the University of California, Los Angeles, and a research associate of the National Bureau of Economic Research.

I thank Hui Cao for bibliographic assistance and gratefully acknowledge financial support from the National Institute on Aging.

but future pension benefits may be adversely affected as well. These adverse effects may be especially severe for women as they comprise the majority of caregivers and, perhaps for this reason, the majority of poor elderly.

The concern among lawmakers over the potential impacts of caregiving on employment is evidenced by such policies as the Family Medical Leave Act of 1993 and the Older Americans Act Amendments of 2000.[1] However, despite the expected labor force consequences, the relevant academic literature has not yet provided a definitive examination of the relationship between work and caregiving. Not only is the magnitude of the effect uncertain, but research has differed even on the existence of a negative effect. Several papers have reported strong negative effects of caregiving on work, while others have found little relationship.

Empirical analysis of the work-caregiving trade-off is not straightforward. Market work and caregiving are certainly competing uses of one's time, suggesting a negative relationship between the two. However, it is not clear whether those who provide care do so because they are working fewer hours or if they work fewer hours because of their caregiving chores. In assessing the labor market effects, and the potential policy response, causality is important.

This paper takes advantage of a longitudinal panel of observations on employment and caregiving to begin to address this issue. I examine labor market behavior prior to caregiving and note how it differs for those who subsequently provide care and those who do not. I look both at short-term effects through changes in behavior over a two-year period and at more extended effects over a period of six years. My measures of labor market attachment include employment status, hours worked, and expected retirement. I find surprisingly little relationship between previous employment and later caregiving.

The outline of the paper is as follows: section 9.2 provides a description of the long-term care market, including a discussion of the type of insurance coverage available. Section 9.3 sketches the type of model used to examine the labor/leisure/caregiving decisions and highlights some results from the previous literature. In section 9.4, I discuss the data to be used, and in section 9.5, I present the empirical analysis. A final section concludes and offers direction for future research.

9.2   Background

In the United States, nearly all elderly are eligible for comprehensive medical insurance through the Medicare program. Although Medicare

---

1. The Family Medical Leave Act required that employers with fifty or more employees provide employees with twelve weeks of unpaid leave to care for a new child or a family member with a health condition. The Older Americans Act Amendments of 2000 amended the original 1965 Older Americans Act and, among other provisions, established the National Family Support Program.

provides generous benefits, there are important gaps in coverage.[2] In particular, Medicare does not cover very long hospital stays or prescription drugs. Most important for this analysis, Medicare also excludes much nursing home care and home health care providing coverage in only a restricted set of circumstances.

Care in nursing homes or, more properly, skilled nursing facilities (SNFs), is covered by Medicare to the extent that it is medically skilled care that is needed to "manage, observe, and evaluate care" and not simply assistance with activities of daily living such as dressing, bathing, eating, or what is termed *custodial care.*[3] Furthermore, to be covered by Medicare, this medical need must come within thirty days of a hospital stay that lasted at least three days (or a previous stay at a SNF that was linked to a hospital stay) and must be prescribed and supervised by a doctor or skilled staff. The duration of this care is limited. Medicare covers all costs for the first 20 days, a portion of the cost of days 21 to 100, but nothing beyond 100 days.[4]

There are similar restrictions on the coverage of home health care. Home health care is covered only if the care is prescribed by a doctor and requires skilled nursing care on an intermittent, rather than full-time, basis.[5] Further, in order to be eligible for benefits the insured individual must also be homebound. If these conditions are met, Medicare will pay for a skilled nurse or home health aid to visit the home.[6] The structure of care is then carefully monitored by a doctor who must review the plan of care every sixty days. This requirement assures that the care continues to have the medically needed component.

An important limitation with respect to home care coverage is that Medicare does not pay for help with basic personal needs like dressing, bathing, and toileting, *unless* the patient also needs medical care. This omission thus leaves a large number of elderly who are unable to live independently, but whose long-term care needs are not covered by Medicare.

For the poor elderly, assistance is available through the Medicaid program. Medicaid is a public health insurance program that benefits those elderly who have little in the way of income or assets.[7] It is administered on a state level with some financing from the federal government, and thus the specifics of coverage can vary across states. All states do provide nursing

2. See McGarry (2002) for a discussion of the development of the Medicare program and its current coverage.

3. See CMS (n.d.a) for an easy to follow discussion of benefits.

4. The copayment is approximately $100 per day. This is covered under some Medigap plans. (Medigap plans are privately purchased health insurance plans that fill some of the gaps in the Medicare program.)

5. Intermitted means that the care required is less than eight hours per day and twenty-eight or fewer hours per week.

6. It will also pay for physical therapy, speech pathology, occupational therapy, medical social services, and medical supplies and equipment (CMS n.d.b).

7. Medicaid also covers other ask risk groups, in particular, pregnant women and children.

home coverage and some amount of home health care coverage as well, but the generosity of home health services varies.

Those elderly not eligible for Medicaid and concerned about the potential for future long-term care expenditures may purchase private long-term care insurance that covers home health care or nursing home stays. However, these policies have not proved popular, and only 10 percent or so of the elderly are currently covered by this type of insurance (Finkelstein and McGarry Forthcoming). Numerous explanations have been offered for the relatively small size of the long-term care insurance market, with many of the explanations, and the policy prescriptions, focusing on the cost of this insurance. Costs may be high because of informational asymmetries resulting in problems such as moral hazard or adverse selection or simply because the cost of nursing home care is high and increasing rapidly. Long-term care policies may also be unpopular because many provide only limited coverage with caps on daily or lifetime benefits and little inflation protection.[8]

With limited insurance protection, the elderly requiring long-term care face substantial out-of-pocket costs. A Metropolitan Life Insurance Company survey (2002) estimated that the average cost of a year of care in a nursing home in 1997 was $61,000 for a private room and $52,000 for a semiprivate room. Even home care is expensive, averaging $37 per hour for a licensed practical nurse.

Given the high cost of formal care and the lack of insurance coverage, many elderly rely on unpaid, informal care. Although difficult to quantify, the economic value of this care is likely to be substantial. Arno, Levine, and Memmott (1999) provide an estimate of the approximate value of this care by imputing an average wage per hour and multiplying by an estimate of hours of informal care. They use a single wage for all caregiving but experiment with three different values of this wage. Their preferred estimates are based on a wage rate of $8.18 per hour. At this price, the value of informal caregiving in 1997 totaled $196 billion. At a wage rate of $11.20 per hour—their estimate of the average rate for home health aids—the total value was $288 billion. These totals dwarf the total expenses in the formal sector. As Arno, Levine, and Memmott (1999) report, total spending for nursing home care in the same year was $83 billion, and spending on formal home health care was just $32 billion. Informal care is large in economic terms even relative to health expenditures as a whole. Total medical spending in 1997 was $1,092 billion, just four or five times larger than the imputed value of informal care. The monetary importance of informal care suggests that it could well have important secondary economic effects.

---

8. Brown and Finkelstein (2003) and Finkelstein and McGarry (Forthcoming) provide more detailed analyses of these issues.

9.3   Theoretical Framework

The theoretical framework for analyzing the decision to provide long-term care grows out of the standard labor supply literature. A potential caregiver maximizes a standard utility function by comparing the marginal value of providing an hour of care with the value of an hour spent working or enjoying leisure. Consider an altruistic child who cares about his own consumption of market goods, C_c, his consumption of leisure, L_c, and the well-being of his parent, U_p. The parent's utility in turn is positively related to his or her own consumption, C_p and his or her health status, H_p, Health status is enhanced through the provision of home health care, HC; all else constant, the more needy the parent, the more valuable an hour of care. Providing care is costly to the child, however, in that it requires time and thus enters into the child's budget constraint with a price equal to the opportunity cost of the child's time. The child has a finite number of hours, T, which he or she can allocate to employment (income), leisure, or caregiving. Thus, time spent helping a parent comes at the expense of reduced consumption of goods or hours of leisure.

Formally, the utility maximization problem can be written as

$$\max U_c = U[C_c, L_c, U_p(C_p, H_p)]$$

$$\text{subject to: } wT = wL_c + pC_c + w\text{HC},$$

where w is the child's wage rate (i.e., the opportunity cost of his or her time), T is the total time available, and p is the price of the consumption good. With the standard assumptions about utility functions, one would expect caregiving to be negatively related to the wage so that caregivers ought to have a lower (potential) wage rate (w) than noncaregivers.[9] This prediction is consistent with the greater likelihood of providing care observed for women relative to men and their relatively lower market wages.[10]

Typically in this literature authors estimate a reduced form specification. Some studies have analyzed the decision to provide care with labor market status as an explanatory variable, while others have examined the reverse— labor force participation, or hours worked, as a function of caregiving. The simultaneous nature of the decision process makes it difficult to infer causality from these results.

Furthermore, the empirical relevance of even the apparently straightforward relationship between work and caregiving has been called into question. A number of early studies found a strong negative relationship

9. If one assumes that professional services are a substitute for informal caregiving, then a utility maximizing child could choose to work *more* hours and provide the parent with the financial resources to purchase care for the elderly parent. I do not address this potential substitution in this chapter.

10. In light of this prediction, the strengthening of the attachment of women may signal a change in future patterns of caregiving.

between the two tasks (e.g., Dwyer and Coward 1991; Brody and Schoonover 1986; Boaz and Muller 1992; Stone, Cafferata, and Sangl 1987). However, several more recent papers have not found the expected negative effects (Ettner 1996; Stern 1995; Wolf and Soldo 1994). Both sets of results are primarily cross-sectional in nature and thus have a difficult time in assessing the counterfactual—what would work to absent the necessity of caregiving?[11] Here I draw on longitudinal data to examine labor market behavior prior to the caregiving decision.

9.4 Data

The data for this study are drawn from the Health and Retirement Study (HRS). When appropriately weighted, the HRS is representative of the noninstitutional U.S. population born between 1931 and 1941 and their spouses or partners.[12] The HRS is a panel survey with the first round interviews taking place in 1992. At that time, respondents were approximately fifty-one to sixty-one years old or were married to individuals in that age range. Follow-up interviews took place every other year. The most recently available data are for 2000, and I draw on all waves of data (1992, 1994, 1996, 1998, 2000) for this project.[13]

The HRS is uniquely suited for a study of this type. It is individuals in this age range who are most likely to have parents needing assistance with personal care. The Commonwealth Fund (1999) reports that 13 percent of women age forty-five to sixty-four provided care in 1998 compared to 10 percent of women thirty to forty-four and 7 percent of women age sixty-five or older. Furthermore, whereas many previous studies have been limited to families in which some care was being provided, the HRS contains information on parents and parents-in-law of *all* respondents, regardless of whether the parent needs or is receiving care, as well as information on each of the respondent's siblings. Thus, I am able to examine behavior in both families that do and those that do not provide some care as well as the effect of family structure on the provision of care. In addition, the HRS is a panel survey. This aspect of the data allows me to examine changes in

11. Stern (1995) is an exception. He uses lagged employment status and distance to a parent as instrumental variables in the child's decision to provide care.

12. Individuals in heavily Black and Hispanic areas were oversampled by the survey. In the tables reported in the following, sample means are weighted to account for the oversampling. Frequencies and regressions are not weighted. When weighting observations, I use the household-level weight rather than the respondent-level weight. Individuals who are outside of the target age range (but who are married to an age eligible respondent) have an individual weight of zero. Rather than lose these observations from the analysis, I assign all respondents the (nonzero) household weight. This procedure is based on discussion with the HRS staff at the University of Michigan.

13. More information on the HRS can be obtained from http://hrsonline.isr.umich.edu/ and in Juster and Suzman (1995).

caregiving over time and, importantly, to focus on labor market behavior several years prior to the point at which I measure care.

My measure of caregiving is the response to the following question:

"Have you (or your [husband/partner]) spent 100 or more hours in the past twelve months helping (your parent[s]/stepparents, your husband's/partner's parent[s]/stepparents) with basic personal needs like dressing, eating, and bathing?"

The survey then asks who was helped and how many hours of care the respondent and, separately her spouse provided.[14] One should note that the question asks specifically about help with personal care needs rather than help in general. In the 1992 interview, this was the only question asked about time help. Later interviews also asked about help with household chores. Because I am specifically focusing on the provision of home health care, I restrict my analysis to responses to the questions about help with personal care even in waves in which more information is available.

The questions on the provision of care changed over the interview waves in other ways as well. In the 1994 interview the question was changed to ask about 50 or more hours of care (rather than 100) although the reference period again asked about care over the past twelve months. In 1996, the cutoff point was returned to 100 hours, but the period was changed to the length of time elapsed since the previous interview (or two years for new respondents). Subsequent waves have retained this 100 hours/two-year format. I do not adjust the data for these differences.

The question about labor force participation is more straightforward. I use the response to the question "Are you doing any work for pay?" The hours-worked variable is the sum of usual hours worked on a main job and a second job (if one exists). Earnings are for the previous calendar year (i.e., the 1992 survey collects information on 1991 earnings) and include earnings from a second job, and any bonuses or overtime payments, as well as earnings on the main job.

I place several restrictions on the sample. First, because women are consistently found to be more likely to provide care than men (Coward and Dwyer 1990; Dwyer and Coward 1991; Wolf, Freedman, and Soldo 1997; McGarry 1998), past studies have typically focused on women. I follow this example and restrict my sample to women. I also restrict my sample to those who have a living parent or parent-in-law in at least one wave of the survey. In the latter portion of the analysis, I draw primarily on data from a single wave and use information from earlier time periods as controls. In these exercises I rely on 1998 data rather than data from 2000. The choice

---

14. These questions are asked only once per HRS household. For married couples, these and other questions on family relationships were typically provided by the female respondent.

Table 9.1   **Work and caregiving in 1992**

Variable	All (N = 3,937)[a]		Providing care (N = 243)		Not providing care (N = 3,691)	
	Mean	Standard error	Mean	Standard Error	Mean	Standard error
Works for pay	0.65	0.006	0.60	0.03	66	0.007
Hours of work (positive)	38.4	227	41.7	1.15	38.2	0.23
Earnings (positive)	20,673	289	18,016	984	20,725	304
Provides care (if living parent)	0.06	0.003	1.0	0	0	0
Hours of care (unconditional)	34.4	4.4	592.9	67.7	0	0

[a]Caregiving status is missing for 175 respondents.

of the penultimate year of available data allows me to use lagged values of labor market participation back to 1992, six years prior to the caregiving arrangement I observe, while at the same time avoiding the much larger reduction in sample size that comes from a fall in the number of respondents with living parents when looking out to 2000.[15] This initial sample consists of 3,937 women in 1992.

9.5   Results

9.5.1   Cross-Sectional Examination of Caregiving

The focus of this analysis is on work and caregiving. In simple correlations, many past studies have observed less labor market activity (i.e., lower employment rates or fewer hours worked) among caregivers. Table 9.1 reports the mean probability of working, mean hours of work and earnings (both conditional on having nonzero values), and mean hours of care in 1992 for my sample of 3,937 respondents with a living parent or parent-in-law in that year. Sixty-five percent of these women were working for pay. As is typical of past studies, the probability of working differs by caregiving status: 60 percent of caregivers and 66 percent of noncaregivers were employed. Thus, at first glance, caregivers do appear to have a weaker attachment to the labor force. Conditional on working, however, caregivers ac-

15. By the year 2000, interview respondents are approximately fifty-nine to sixty-nine years old, indicating that their parents would likely be well over eighty. There are thus many fewer respondents with living parents or parents-in-law; the number of female respondents with a living parent or parent-in-law falls from 2,759 in 1998 to 1,633 in 2000. Thus, restricting the sample to those with living parents or parents-in-law in 2000 results in an even more selected group and likely reduces the precision of any estimates.

tually work more hours than noncaregivers, forty-two versus thirty-eight hours on average, a statistically significant difference. However, despite the greater number of hours, caregivers have significantly lower earnings. This result is consistent with a lower opportunity cost of time among caregivers (i.e., lower wage rate). Thus, while caregivers do not appear to be reducing hours worked (conditional on employment) in order to provide care, their lower earnings is consistent with less intensive investment in the job, perhaps with associated smaller raises or bonuses or less overtime.[16]

9.5.2   Transitions between Work and Caregiving

Past studies of caregiving behavior have primarily been limited to this type of point-in-time analysis. However, of perhaps greater interest than simple cross-sectional comparisons is an understanding of causality. Are caregivers less likely to work because they are providing care? Or are they providing care because they have always had a less strong attachment to the labor force than noncaregivers? The latter would be expected if the family were maximizing a joint utility function where the member with the lowest opportunity cost of time would be selected to provide care. By taking advantage of the panel nature of the HRS data set I begin to address this issue. Here I examine transitions into and out of caregiving and observe the employment status of caregivers prior to the actual provision of care.

I begin by simply examining the prevalence of various types of cross-wave transitions. Table 9.2 shows the fraction of the sample of transiting between each of four possible work and caregiving states: not working and not providing care, working and not providing care, providing care and not working, providing care and working. The data from each of the five survey years (1992, 1994, 1996, 1998, and 2000) are stacked together so that an individual may provide multiple observations.[17] I again use the sample of 3,937 women with a living parent or parent-in-law in at least one wave but drop the observation when the woman's last parent or parent-in-law dies. Thus, an individual may not contribute data to the table for all periods 1992 to 2000 even though she responds to the survey in every period. This procedure yields a sample of 11,184 year-to-year observations.[18]

16. An important assumption in this literature, and in the literature on labor supply in general, is that individuals can freely choose the number of hours they work. It should be noted, here and throughout the discussion that follows, that this assumption may not hold. Hurd and McGarry (1993) find that only one-quarter of workers can decrease hours on their current job. Change may therefore be more readily observed in complete departures from the labor force. I will present evidence on both dimensions.

17. Single year-by-year comparisons show similar patterns. I report one such comparison in the following.

18. However, if the individual has more than one living parent or parent-in-law, a particular parent may die between waves and the individual remains in the sample. Some of the transitions to noncaregiving states are likely associated with the death of the parent initially receiving care.

Table 9.2   Transition between work and caregiving: Time t to time $t + 1$

Time t	Time $t + 1$				
	Not working/not caregiving	Working only	Caregiving only	Working/ caregiving	Total
Not working, not caregiving					
Number	2,875	455	320	47	3,697
Percent of row	77.0	12.5	9.2	1.4	100
Working only					
Number	842	5,100	931	457	6,492
Percent of row	13.1	78.6	1.4	6.9	100
Caregiving only					
Number	182	31	181	26	420
Percent of row	45.9	7.6	40.7	5.9	100
Working, caregiving					
Number	61	284	32	198	575
Percent of row	11.1	50.0	5.4	33.5	100
Total	3,960	5,870	626	728	

Note: Percents are weighted values; counts are unweighted.

The working and caregiving state in any period t is denoted on the left (vertical) column of table 9.2, and the state in the following interview; time $t + 1$, is shown in the top row (horizontal). The majority of observations correspond to working only in wave t (row 2); 6,492 out of 11,184 observations fall into this category. Arguably it is this group who is most at risk for changing employment status in response to caregiving, and I will focus most of the discussion on their behavior. Among those in this category, the vast majority, nearly 80 percent, continue to be working only at time $t + 1$, while just 8.3 percent (1.4 + 6.9) begin providing care.

The second most common initial state is not working and not caregiving, containing 3,697 observations. As with the case of the working only row, the majority (77 percent) of this group remain in this same arrangement in the following period. Ex post one would expect those who are not working to have a lower opportunity cost of time and to be more likely to take up caregiving than those who are employed. However, by comparing the first and second set of rows in the table it is apparent that the differences between the two groups in the probability of transitioning to a caregiving state are not large: 10.6 percent (9.2 + 1.4) of the not working and not caregiving sample begins providing care by time $t + 1$, compared to 8.3 percent of the working sample. Furthermore, of the 8.3 percent of working onlys who begin to provide care, only 17 percent (1.4/8.3) discontinue working at the same time. This figure is similar to the 13.1 percent of working onlys who leave the labor force but do not provide care, indicating a potentially weaker than anticipated causal relationship between work and caregiving.

The two final rows of table 9.2 provide evidence on what happens from one period to the next for those who are already providing care. A surprisingly large fraction of those providing care (either with or without work) transit out of the caregiving arrangement. More than 50 percent of those caregiving only in period t were not caregiving in period $t + 1$, and over 60 percent of those who were initially working and caregiving were no longer caregiving in the second period. The transition out of caregiving could arise from an improvement in the health of the needy parent or a switch to an alternative caregiving arrangement (e.g., care being provided by a sibling of the respondent or professional caregiver). However, note that the selection criterion require only that the respondent have at least one living parent or parent-in-law, but there is no requirement that the number of living parents remain constant throughout the observation period. Some of the transitions out of caregiving are therefore likely attributable to the death of the particular parent who was receiving care.

Further evidence of the transitory nature of caregiving is available by examining the average number of years for which care is provided. Although not shown in the table, the average number of surveys for which a respondent reports providing care is below 2 for nearly all cells in the table. The highest value is 2.5 for those caregiving only in both waves. Based on these figures then, caregiving appears to be a relatively temporary state for many women.

Not only were those who were working only relatively unlikely to cease employment in response to the onset of caregiving, but many of those who were caregiving only became employed while maintaining their roles as caregivers. The fraction of caregiving onlys who do start to work, 13.5 percent (7.6 + 5.9), is lower than the fraction of those not working and not caregiving who become employed, 13.9 percent (12.5 + 1.4), but the difference is small.

Table 9.3 parallels table 9.2 but each cell reports the average hours worked, average earnings in wave t, the average change in hours of work between waves, and average hours of care provided in wave $t + 1$. Again I focus first on the second row of the table and examine the behavior of those who were working only at time t. Within this category, those who leave the labor force by time $t + 1$ are initially working significantly fewer hours than those who remain. This result holds regardless of whether the woman transits to not working and not caregiving or to caregiving only. The two groups average just seventeen hours and fifteen hours per week at time t, respectively. In contrast, both those who remain in the working only category and those who take up caregiving along with work report an average of thirty-nine hours of work per week, identical to that worked by those who do not provide care.

Also worth noting are hours of work for those who were initially working and caregiving (bottom set of results). Those who continue to both

Table 9.3   **Degree of labor force attachment: Time t and time $t + 1$**

Time t	Time $t + 1$			
	Not working/not caregiving	Working only	Caregiving only	Working/ caregiving
Not working, not caregiving				
Hours worked t	0.0	0.0	0.0	0.0
Earnings in previous year	2,304	7,788	2,546	6,077
Change in hours	0.0	24.7	0.0	21.1
Hours of care $t + 1$	0.0	0.0	452	240
Working only				
Hours worked t	17.3	39.2	15.1	39.2
Earnings in previous year	17,446	22,743	18,928	22,294
Change in hours	−34.8	−5.0	−31.4	−4.5
Hours of care $t + 1$	0.0	0.0	299	263
Caregiving only				
Hours worked t	0.0	0.0	0.0	0.0
Earnings in previous year	3,075	4,206	1,272	6,480
Change in hours	0.0	17.8	0.0	10.9
Hours of care $t + 1$	0.0	0.0	691	450
Working, caregiving				
Hours worked t	17.4	39.4	9.4	44.2
Earnings in previous year	13,723	22,007	28,038	20,587
Change in hours	−39.5	−5.4	−32.7	−11.3
Hours of care $t + 1$	0.0	0.0	238	458

work and provide care average forty-four hours per week, while those who transit to working only were averaged thirty-nine hours. Thus, those who remain caregivers were actually working a greater number of hours while caregiving than those who discontinue care.

The comparison of earnings across groups yields similar results to the hours comparison.[19] There are no apparent differences in time t earnings by time $t + 1$ caregiving status for those working only at time t. Earnings in the previous year were $22,743 for those who remain in the working only category and $22,294 for those who become workers and caregivers. As was the case with hours worked, those who leave the labor force, either to provide care or not, have lower average values than those who remain employed. Those who are eventually caregiving only average $18,928 per year, and the eventual nonwork and noncaregivers average $17,446.

Earnings are also similar for those who were working and caregiving at time t and who remain employed regardless of whether they continue pro-

19. The earnings reported in the table refer to earnings in the year prior to the time t interview because the survey asks about earnings in the previous year. This explains the nonzero earnings among those not working at time t.

viding care. Those in this group who transit to working only and thus cease providing care averaged $22,007 per year, and those who remained in the working and caregiving classification averaged $20,587. Surprisingly, those who left the labor force and transited to caregiving only had substantially higher period t average earnings of $28,038. However, as shown in table 9.2, there are very few women in this cell, just thirty-two, so one ought to be cautious about putting much weight on this finding.

Not only were labor market positions for noncaregivers and eventual caregivers similar prior to the start of caregiving, but also there is little change resulting from the transition. Among those who were working only, the average change in hours worked across the two waves is negative for both those who begin to provide care and those who do not, falling by 5 hours for those who remain working only and 4.5 for those who work and provide care. Those who stop working obviously have much larger declines in hours.

The hours of care lines in the table 9.3 (the fourth row in each set of results) also provide an interesting insight into behavior. In the working only category, those who take up caregiving provide nearly identical hours of care, on average, regardless of whether they continue working. The caregiving only group supplies an average of 299 hours and the working and caregiving group supplies 263. Again it looks as though the relationship between caregiving and work is weak.

However, among those who were caregiving initially, the hours of care provided are much higher. They average 691 hours among those who are caregiving only at both time t and at time $t + 1$, and 450 among those who transit from caregiving only to working and caregiving. Those who were working and caregiving average fewer hours; 238 for those who stop work and 458 for those who continue to do both tasks. Again, however, the sample sizes are small.

9.5.3   Longer Time Horizon

The lack of a relationship between labor market behavior and caregiving in table 9.2 and table 9.3 may simply be because caregivers have not had sufficient time to adjust their hours of work. To incorporate a longer range view into this framework, I compare behavior in 1992 with that in 1998. The tables are constructed similarly to tables 9.2 and 9.3 but instead of time t and time $t + 1$, I use the individual's status in 1992 and 1998. Caregivers in 1998 could have started providing care at any time after the 1992 interview, but they must still be providing care in 1998 to be classified as such. Thus, the category of caregiving in 1998 will include those new to the chore as well as those who began caring for a parent several periods earlier and who are still providing care. Care provided at some point between 1992 and 1998 but not in either of those years is not observed. Tables 9.4 and 9.5 display the cross-year results.

Table 9.4   Transition between work and caregiving, 1992 to 1988

1992 Status	Not working/not caregiving	Working only	Caregiving only	Working/ caregiving	Total
		1998 Status			
Not working, not caregiving					
Number	541	147	76	21	785
Percent of row	68.8	18.6	9.8	2.8	100
Working only					
Number	367	1,092	64	134	1,657
Percent of row	22.7	65.7	3.7	7.9	100
Caregiving only					
Number	23	6	16	6	51
Percent of row	45.7	9.3	33.6	11.4	100
Working, caregiving					
Number	15	46	7	19	87
Percent of row	15.2	56.9	7.2	20.7	100
Total	946	1,291	163	180	

Note: Percents are weighted numbers; counts are unweighted.

Table 9.5   Degree of labor force attachment, 1992 to 1998

1992 Status	Not working/not caregiving	Working only	Caregiving only	Working/ caregiving
		1998 Status		
Not working/not caregiving				
Mean hours worked t	0.0	0.0	0.0	0.0
Mean earnings in previous year	2,261	5,111	1,206	5,485
Mean change in hours	0.0	31.5	0.0	22.1
Mean hours of care $t + 1$	0.0	0.0	691	317
Working only				
Mean hours worked t	37.3	39.4	35.4	41.6
Mean earnings in previous year	20,032	21,745	17,887	24,666
Mean change in hours	−37.3	−1.2	−35.4	−1.9
Mean hours of care $t + 1$	0.0	0.0	932	544
Caregiving only				
Mean hours worked t	0.0	0.0	0.0	0.0
Mean earnings in previous year	2,138	6,684	1,212	5,819
Mean change in hours	0.0	32.3	0.0	20.1
Mean hours of care $t + 1$	0.0	0.0	1,087	258
Working, caregiving				
Mean hours worked t	39.8	44.0	39.9	51.3
Mean earnings in previous year	16,462	18,067	21,152	18,006
Mean change in hours	−39.9	−6.3	−39.9	−4.7
Mean hours of care $t + 1$	0.0	0.0	1,623	555

As was the case in the year-to-year comparisons, with this long-difference comparison, there are surprisingly similar probabilities of transiting to caregiving for women who are working only and women who are not working/not caregiving. Less than 13 percent (9.8 + 2.8) of those not working and not caregiving in 1992 were caregiving in 1998, and 11.6 percent (3.7 + 7.9) of those who were just working initially were providing care in the later year. Similarly, there are numerous transitions out of caregiving. Fewer than half of those who were caregiving only in 1992 were caregiving (either with or without work) in 1998. Among those who were working and caregiving in 1992, only 20.7 percent were still in this category in 1998, and just 28 percent were providing care at all. Again though, these results do not show whether the respondent has stopped providing care because the parent or parent-in-law has had an improvement in functioning, has found an alternative source of care, or has died.

Comparing initial hours, earnings, and change in hours worked for those working only in 1992 (table 9.5) there are again only very small differences across outcomes. The women in the 1998 working only group and the working and caregiving groups appear to have nearly equal ties to the labor force. If anything, those who are eventually working and caregiving may have had stronger ties. For those who started out as working only, this group averaged 41.6 hours in 1992 compared to an average of 39.4 hours for those who remain working only. Similarly, the 1998 working and caregiving group had higher earnings, $24,666 compared to $21,745. Neither group experiences much in the way of a decline in hours. Those who were working only in 1992 and not working in 1998 averaged 37 and 35 hours per week in 1992 if they did not and did subsequently provide care. Consistent with a strong income effect, these women who leave the labor force had lower earnings than those who remain, and those who leave and provide care have the lowest. Perhaps surprisingly, those who are initially working and caregiving (bottom set of results) have earnings and hours that are similar to those who were initially working only although their slightly greater number of hours, and lower earnings may indicate a lower hourly wage.

9.5.4   Multivariate Analyses of Caregiving and Work

Certainly these women likely differ across categories in measures other than caregiving and labor market behavior, and the observed patterns may reflect these underlying differences as well. The age distribution of caregivers may differ from that of noncaregivers, and their levels of schooling, marital status, number of siblings, and so forth may differ. In particular, women who are in better health may be better able to handle the rigors of working and the rigors of caregiving. I therefore turn to regression analysis to control for these other factors while examining the link between market behavior and caregiving.

I examine the work and caregiving decision in 1998 using a bivariate probit model. In this cross-sectional analysis, I restrict my sample to those individuals who have a living parent or parent-in-law in 1998 and who were not providing care at the start of the survey, so this is a sample of "new" caregivers. It is this group who is of perhaps of most interest to policymakers—women who may be forced prematurely from the labor market in order to provide assistance to an elderly parent. The final sample for the multivariate analyses consists of 2,015 women with a living parent or parent-in-law in 1998.

The results of the estimation are reported in table 9.6. The first pair of columns presents the coefficient estimates and standard errors for the

Table 9.6   **Multinomial analysis of work and caregiving**

Variable	Specification 1	
	Working	Caring
Age		
Less than 55 (omitted)		
55–61	–.26 (.07)	.01 (.10)
62–64	–.85 (.16)	–.02 (.14)
65 and over	–1.38 (.13)	–.05 (.16)
Health status		
Excellent (omitted)		
Very good	.90 (.09)	–.02 (.12)
Good	–.00 (.09)	.09 (.12)
Fair	–.59 (.10)	.11 (.14)
Poor	–1.50 (.16)	–.11 (.19)
Married	–.28 (.09)	–.23 (.11)
Net worth ($1,000s)	–.22 (.06)	–.02 (.06)
Schooling		
Less than high school	–.13 (.08)	–.04 (.11)
High school (omitted)		
Some college	–.08 (.08)	.04 (.19)
College	.19 (.09)	.09 (.33)
White	–.07 (.08)	–.03 (.12)
Family characteristics		
Parent needs care	–.05 (.07)	1.09 (.08)
Number of sisters	–.005 (.02)	–.02 (.03)
Number of brothers	.007 (.02)	.07 (.03)
Number of sisters-in-law	–.000 (.03)	–.01 (.04)
Number of brothers-in-law	–.007 (.03)	–.05 (.04)
Intercept	1.46 (.47)	–2.71 (.64)
Cross-equation correlation	–0.027 (0.049)	
Number of observations	2,271	
Log likelihood	–2,028.18	

Note: Also included are spousal earnings, asset income, other income, number of own children, number of children living at home, marital status, and Hispanic.

probability of working in 1998, and the second shows the probability of providing care. The variables tend to operate in the expected directions. There is a strong negative and monotonic relationship between both age and poor health and working. There do not, however, appear to be significant differences by age in the probability of providing care. Unsurprisingly, being married significantly reduces the probability of employment for this sample of women. Consistent with past studies that have found that unmarried daughters were the most likely caregivers, married women in this sample are less likely to provide care. The standard wealth effect is also observed in that the probability of work is significantly negatively related to assets, but there is no apparent relationship between assets and caregiving. One might have imagined that there would be a negative relationship in this case in that those with more resources could purchase formal care for elderly parents rather than provide their own time.

As expected from studies of women's labor force participation, a college education significantly increases the employment probability. However, it does not have an effect on caregiving. If schooling level is viewed as a proxy for the opportunity cost of a respondent's time, it is surprising that it does not have a more powerful negative effect on caregiving. Race is strongly related to caregiving, with Whites significantly more likely than non-Whites to provide care.

Of particular interest is the variable indicating that a parent or parent-in-law needs care. This variable summarizes responses to questions asking if a particular parent "needs help with basic personal needs like dressing, eating, or bathing." The variable is equal to one if at least one parent needs care.[20] If women were leaving the labor market to provide care, then having a needy parent or parent-in-law should be negatively related to employment. Here, however, although the estimated effect is negative, it is not statistically different from zero, and, in fact, the point estimate is smaller than the standard error. This result is consistent with the finding of tables 9.2, 9.3, 9.4, and 9.5. There is no effect of caregiving on employment probabilities. In contrast, having a parent or parent-in-law who needs care has a large effect on the probability of providing care.

Past research has demonstrated that women are more likely to provide care than men. It is therefore instructive to ask whether the caregiving decisions of women are affected by the sex of their siblings. As shown in table 9.6, the sex distribution of siblings does not affect work behavior, but the number of brothers does have a positive and significant effect on caregiving. Women with more brothers are more likely to provide care, but additional sisters have no effect.

---

20. I experimented with separate indicators for the need of a mother, father, mother-in-law, and father-in-law, but the individual categories are relatively unlikely. For example, 4 percent of the sample reports having a father who needs care, and just 3 percent have a needy father-in-law.

The bivariate probit model allows for a correlation between the error terms for the two equations. An examination of this correlation provides a test for whether unobserved characteristics of the individual that affect work also affect caregiving. For instance, there may be "energetic people" who are more likely to do both, or, conversely, some individuals might specialize in market activity while others specialize in home production. The correlation across regressions in this specification is negative, suggesting an explanation along the lines of the latter story, but the relationship is not significantly different from zero.

9.6   Conclusion

This study has provided a first look at transitions to caregiving. Results from simple transition matrices indicate that eventual caregivers were not less likely to be employed in prior periods than noncaregivers and did not work fewer hours. They also did not appear to have substantially lower earnings. These results are consistent with anecdotal evidence that women appear to cut back on leisure rather than work when providing care to an elderly parent. As Cantor (1983) notes, "the most severe impact [of caregiving] was registered in areas such as free time for oneself and opportunities to socialize with friends, take vacations, have leisure time pursuits, and run one's own house" (600).

The results of a multivariate analysis similarly fail to support a strong relationship between labor market ties and caregiving later in life. Having a parent who needs care does not affect employment behavior, and lagged labor force participation does not affect current caregiving.

Despite these conclusions, many questions remain. Of interest is the extent to which women are able to remain in the labor force because of accommodations made by employers. Stone and Short (1990) found little effect of caregiving on employment in general but significant effects on the likelihood that accommodations were required on the job. If accommodations are important, then the effect of caregiving on labor market behavior would be most severely felt by those with little flexibility on the job. If this flexibility is positively correlated with measures of socioeconomic status, such as schooling and income, then it may be the poor who are most likely harmed. Some of the evidence presented here suggests that caregivers may have lower wage rates, perhaps indicative of less investment on the job or of a cost of any needed accommodations.

Finally, the lack of an employment response does not mean all is well. Numerous studies have reported a high level of stress among caregivers. The task of providing care to an elderly parent may therefore have large negative effects on caregivers in terms of emotional well-being. If psychological stress is associated with deteriorations in health and shorter life expectancy, this could also be costly in economic terms.

References

Arno, Peter, Carol Levine, and Margaret Memmott. 1999. The economic value of informal caregiving. *Health Affairs* 18 (2): 182–88.

Boaz, Rachel, and Charlotte Muller. 1992. Paid work and unpaid help by caregivers of the disabled and frail elders. *Medical Care* 30 (2): 149–58.

Brody, Elaine, and Claire Schoonover. 1986. Patterns of parent care when adult daughters work and when they do not. *The Gerontologist* 21:371–81.

Brown, Jeffrey, and Amy Finkelstein. 2003. Why is the market for private long-term care insurance so small? The role of pricing and Medicaid crowd-out. University of Illinois. Mimeograph.

Cantor, Marjorie. 1983. Strain among caregivers: A study of experience in the United States. *The Gerontologist* 23 (6): 597–604.

Centers for Medicare and Medicaid Services. n.d.a. *Medicare coverage of skilled nursing facility care.* Washington, DC: Centers for Medicare and Medicaid Services.

———. n.d.b. *Medicare and home health care.* Washington, DC: Centers for Medicare and Medicaid Services.

Commonwealth Fund. 1999. FACT SHEET: Informal caregiving, fact sheet from The Commonwealth Fund 1998 Survey of Women's Health. New York: Commonwealth Fund.

Coward, Raymond, and Jeffrey Dwyer. 1990. The association of gender, sibling network composition, and patterns of parent care by adult children. *Research on Aging* 12:158–81.

Department of Health and Human Services (DHHS). 1998. *Informal caregiving compassion in action.* Washington, DC: DHHS, Office of the Assistant Secretary for Planning and Evaluation.

Dwyer, Jeffrey, and Raymond Coward. 1991. A multivariate comparison of the involvement of adult sons versus daughters in the care of impaired parents. *Journal of Gerontology: Social Sciences* 46:S259–S269.

Ettner, Susan. 1995. The impact of "parent care" on female labor supply decisions. *Demography* 32 (1): 63–80.

———. 1996. The opportunity costs of elder care. *The Journal of Human Resources* 31 (1): 189–205.

Finkelstein, Amy, and Kathleen McGarry. Forthcoming. Multiple dimensions of private information: Evidence from the Long-term Care Insurance Market. *American Economic Review.*

Hurd, Michael, and Kathleen McGarry. 1993. The relationship between job characteristics and retirement. NBER Working Paper no. 4558. Cambridge, MA: National Bureau of Economic Research, December.

Juster, Thomas, and Richard Suzman. 1995. An overview of the Health and Retirement Study. *The Journal of Human Resources* 30 (Supplement): S7–S56.

McGarry, Kathleen. 1998. Caring for the elderly: The role of adult children. In *Inquiries in the economics of aging,* ed. David A. Wise, 133–63. Chicago: University of Chicago Press.

———. 2002. Public policy and the U.S. health insurance market: Direct and indirect provision of insurance. *National Tax Journal* 55 (4): 789–827.

Metropolitan Life Insurance Company. 2002. *MetLife market survey on nursing home and home care costs.* Westport, CT: MetLife Mature Market Institute.

Stern, Steven. 1995. Estimating family long-term care decisions in the presence of endogenous child characteristics. *The Journal of Human Resources* 30 (3): 551–80.

Stone, Robyn, Gail Cafferata, and Judith Sangl. 1987. Caregivers of the frail elderly: A national profile. *The Gerontologist* 27 (5): 616–26.

Stone, Robyn, and Pamela Farley Short. 1990. The competing demands of employment and informal caregiving to disabled elders. *Medical Care* 28 (6): 513–26.

Walker, David. 2002. Long-term care: aging baby boom generation will increase demand and burden on federal and state budgets. United States General Accounting Office, Testimony before the Special Committee on Aging, U.S. Senate, March 21, 2002.

Wolf, Douglas, Vicki Freedman, and Beth Soldo. 1997. The division of family labor: Care for elderly parents. *Journals of Gerontology: Social Sciences* 52:102–09.

Wolf, Douglas, and Beth Soldo. 1994. Married women's allocation of time to employment and parental care. *The Journal of Human Resources* 29 (4): 1259–76.

10

Conjoint Analysis to Estimate the Demand for Nicotine Replacement Therapy in Japan

Seiritsu Ogura, Wataru Suzuki, Makoto Kawamura, and Tamotsu Kadoda

10.1 Introduction

Cigarette smoking is associated with such life-threatening illnesses as cancer, ischemic heart disease, cerebrovascular disease, and chronic lung disease. Smoking contributes not only to lung cancer but also to cancers of the pharynx, esophagus, bladder, and many others. It is reported that complications of pregnancy, including low birth weight and miscarriage, are related to smoking. Passive smoking is also a risk factor for such diseases. Cigarette smoking is one of the most serious causes of premature mortality in Japan. Researchers have estimated that about 113,400 Japanese die annually due to smoking-related illnesses, which accounts for 11.8 percent of total deaths (Peto et al. 2004). Estimates of excess medical costs per year due to smoking-related disease range from 1.2 trillion (Institute for Health Economics and Policy 1997) to 3.2 trillion yen (Goto 1995, 1996),[1] or from 5 to 15 percent of national medical expenditures.

In response to the escalating national health care costs, particularly those of lifestyle-related diseases, smoking cessation has become one of the most important national health policy objectives. The Ministry of Health, Labor and Welfare established the Committee on Tobacco Control for the 21st Century in the year 2000 and was committed to a national no-

Seiritsu Ogura is a professor of economics at Hosei University and director general of the Hosei Institute on Aging. Wataru Suzuki is an assistant professor in the Department of Education at Tokyo Gakugei University. Makoto Kawamura is a professor of economics at Hosei University. Tamotsu Kadoda is an assistant professor of economics at Daito Bunka University.

1. It has been estimated that the total social loss including lost gross national product (GNP) as well as medical expenses amounted to between 4 trillion (Institute for Health Economics and Policy 1997) and 5.6 trillion yen (Goto 1995, 1996).

smoking-week campaign. The ministry also established as an objective the provision of support to help smokers stop smoking in all communities. The Japanese Medical Association has also conducted an antismoking campaign since year 2001.

A significant proportion of smokers seriously consider quitting smoking. For example, according to the Survey on Smoking and Health Problems in 1998 by the Japanese government, 26.7 percent of current smokers aged fifteen and over want to quit smoking, and 64.2 percent of them want to quit smoking or cut down smoking. However, only a small fraction of them actually succeed on their own, due to the addictive nature of nicotine (U.S. Department of Health and Human Services 1988, 1995, 1996a; WHO 1993). Recently, however, smoking intervention programs, particularly those using nicotine replacement therapy (NRT), have been shown to be very effective in other countries, such as the United States.

Nicotine replacement therapy is a method of treatment that helps smokers by alleviating the withdrawal symptoms associated with smoking cessation by replacing the nicotine. Researchers have shown that 17 to 50 percent of smokers have succeeded in smoking cessation using those therapies (Momma 1998; Asano 2000; Wasley et al. 1997; Jorenby et al. 1999; Schneider, Jarvik, and Forsythe 1984). Two types of NRT products are available in Japan, nicotine transdermal patches and nicotine gum. Nicotine patches were approved by the Ministry of Health and Welfare in 1994, and nicotine gums were approved in 1999. Despite the effectiveness of those products, they have failed to come into wide use in Japan, as they have been available only by prescription, and their costs have not been covered by the public health insurance.

The government has done nothing to inform the smokers of the availability of NRT, and there were few medical professionals who could give counseling or other therapies for smoking cessation. Things changed completely in September 2001 when the Ministry of Health and Welfare, under the strong pressure to show concrete results of deregulation in health care sector, approved nicotine gum (brand name Nicorette) as an over-the-counter drug. There immediately followed an extensive nationwide campaign by the pharmaceutical company using TV, newspapers, and magazines. As a result, Nicorette is now widely recognized among smokers as well as nonsmokers.

In this paper, we estimate the demand for nicotine gum and examine the smoking cessation assistance policy with NRT using original survey data gathered by the authors in late 2001. Our analysis is the first attempt to estimate the demand for NRT in Japan. Tauras and Chaloupka (2001) assessed the impact of NRT prices and cigarette prices on NRT demand using pooled cross-sectional–time series data for fifty major metropolitan markets in the United States from 1996 to 1999. We could not employ a similar technique because panel data are not available in Japan; nicotine gum has been in the market for a relatively short period of time, and domestic cigarette prices are uniformly set throughout Japan. Therefore, we employed conjoint analysis (CA), a technique that is relatively new to the field of health economics.

Conjoint analysis is one of the techniques belonging to contingent valuation methods (CVM) used to estimate an individual's utilities from responses to hypothetical questions. Conjoint analysis was originally developed in the field of market research and psychometrics. It has been widely used in environmental economics and transport economics, and it has been introduced into health economics.[2] In Japan, CA has been used to estimate the demand for nursing care (Suzuki and Okusa 1999), the choice of medical facilities (Fukuda et al. 1999), and the demand for medical care for minor illness (Suzuki and Okusa 2000).

The stages of CA are detailed as follows. First, hypothetical scenarios and discrete choice questionnaires are presented to individuals. After individuals state their preference, the responses are used to determine utilities. A statistical model is constructed using the hypothetical scenarios and the characteristics of respondents as explanatory variables and stated preferences as the dependent variable. Then the utility function and rate of substitution are calculated.

The methodologies commonly utilized to assess individuals' utilities in health economics have been the standard gamble, time trade-off, and rating scale as well as willingness to pay. These traditional approaches have both theoretical and technical problems. The price obtained from willingness to pay does not properly reflect the real utility level. None of usual approaches—standard gamble, time trade-off, and rating scale—can capture the utility level very well. When we deal with ordinal utility, it can be problematic to compare and add up utility levels among individuals. Unlike these four techniques, CA uses questionnaires asking individuals about their relative preferences instead of directly asking their utility level. Therefore, it can avoid the problem faced by the other methods. Conjoint analysis is also advantageous in that unobservable factors related to the individual can be eliminated as an individual effect.

The remainder of the paper is organized as follows. In section 10.2, the data used for this study are described. Descriptive statistics regarding smoking and awareness of nicotine gum are also provided in this section. In section 10.3, the methods and results using CA are presented. The application of the estimates from CA to cost-benefit analysis is demonstrated in section 10.4. We compare the costs and benefits of a hypothetical subsidy for nicotine gum. Section 10.5 concludes.

---

2. For examples, see Bryan et al. (1998), Freeman (1998), Hakim and Pathak (1999), Ratcliffe and Buxton (1999), Ryan (1999), Ryan and Farrar (1994), Ryan and Hughes (1997), Singh et al. (1998), and Van der Pol and Cairns (1997).

Table 10.1   Descriptive statistics

	N	Mean	Standard deviation	Minimum	Maximum
Age of smoking initiation	499	20.68136	5.032891	12	60
Years of smoking	499	20.28858	12.45703	0	50
Level of nicotine dependence (FTND index)	501	4.966068	2.199283	1	11
Sex	501	0.6267465	0.484152	0	
Age	501	41.00399	13.24915	20	69
Education	501	0.491018	0.500419	0	1
Annual income	487	692.7618	399.5757	50	2000
Logged annual income	487	6.357238	0.6582189	3.912023	7.600903
Number of family	498	3.210843	1.484231	1	12
Heart disease	501	0.0279441	0.1649775	0	1
Diabetes	501	0.0299401	0.1705925	0	1
Disease of circulatory system	501	0.0578842	0.2337578	0	1
Disease of digestive system	501	0.0798403	0.2713167	0	1

Notes: Years of smoking is derived by subtracting age of smoking started from current age. The FTND index is an epidemiological index that measures the level of nicotine dependence (see note in the paper). Annual income is in ten thousands of yen. Education was coded 1 if finished postcollegiate, college, or junior college, 0 otherwise. Each chronic illness was coded 1 if there is any, 0 otherwise.

Table 10.2   Desire for smoking cessation

	N	Percent
In the process	36	7.2
Want to but haven't done anything	239	47.7
Don't want to quit	226	45.1

10.2   Data

The data were collected using the Survey on Smoking that the authors conducted in November 2001. The questionnaire was mailed to 500 smokers aged twenty to sixty-nine who were residing in the Tokyo metropolitan area. They were selected from a list of monitors who had registered with a private research firm. The firm randomly selected their monitors from a national resident-registry list.[3] The response rate was 83.3 percent. The characteristics of individuals included in the analysis are presented in table 10.1.

The survey asked the respondents about their attitude toward and awareness of smoking cessation and nicotine gum before presenting the hypothetical scenarios. Table 10.2 indicates the attitude toward smoking ces-

---

3. It is possible that sample bias arose when people decided whether to be a monitor, but the social research firm made efforts to make the bias as small as possible by adjusting the sample to represent the census distribution in terms of age and other characteristics.

Table 10.3   **A means of smoking cessation**

	Smokers who want to quit		Smokers who attempted smoking cessation	
	N	Percent	N	Percent
Don't use anything	198	72.5	27	75.0
Counseling by medical professionals	0	0.0		
Nicorette	63	23.1	8	22.2
Other	12	4.4	1	2.8

Table 10.4   **Recognition of Nicorette**

	N	Percent
Know of Nicorette	350	70.14
Don't know of Nicorette	149	29.86

Table 10.5   **Opinion of the price of Nicorette**

	N	Percent
Expensive	398	79.8
Appropriate	89	17.8
Inexpensive	12	2.4

sation among smokers. Of particular interest is the fact that 7 percent of smokers were attempting to quit, and 48 percent were contemplating quitting. Thus, more than half of smokers in our sample want to quit smoking. The methods of smoking cessation are presented in table 10.3. Among the smokers who want to quit smoking, a large majority of them (72.5 percent) did not plan to use any particular device or help, but almost one-quarter (23.1 percent) of them mentioned nicotine gum as a device. There were eight respondents who were actually using the nicotine gum, which represents 22.2 percent of those who were actually trying to quit smoking. Table 10.4 shows that already 70.1 percent of respondents were aware of the nicotine gum, and it is clear that the nicotine gum has become widely known, at least in the Tokyo metropolitan area, in a very short period of time after it was introduced into the market. However, nearly 80 percent of respondents viewed Nicorette as expensive, as table 10.5 shows.[4] As a result, only

4. The price was 6,900 yen for sixty pieces and 36,000 yen for a course of smoking cessation. The authors estimated the cost of a course of smoking cessation based on the directions for use and the price from Nicorette's homepage (http://www.nicorette-j.com/).

13.5 percent of respondents were willing to use nicotine gum (table 10.6). We also asked for the reason they were not going to use the gum among those who answered "interested but won't use" or "not interested." About 50 percent of them answered that the nicotine gum was expensive. This suggests that the high price is preventing the diffusion of the nicotine gum.

10.3   Estimation of Demand for Nicotine Gum

10.3.1   Estimation Model

The questionnaires used for CV are presented in table 10.7. Respondents were asked to circle 1 or 2 for each scenario, which indicated "use nicotine gum" and "not use nicotine gum," respectively. The factors that varied across scenarios were the price of nicotine gum, the price of cigarettes, and access to nicotine gum. Several levels were assigned for each attribute. Two different prices were assigned for the nicotine gum: its current price and half the current price. Three different prices were assigned for cigarettes: the current price, double the current price, and five times the current price. Two levels of access were used: status quo and being able to get the gum at

Table 10.6   Interest in Nicorette

	N	Percent
Want to use	67	13.5
Interested but won't use soon	241	48.5
Not interested	189	38.0

Table 10.7   Hypothetical scenarios

If Nicorette is sold at half-price (3,450 yen for 60 tablets; 18,000 yen for a course of smoking cessation)

If Nicorette is sold at half-price and available at a vending machine or at a convenience store

If Nicorette is sold at half-price while tobacco price is doubled (about 500 yen a box)

If Nicorette is sold at half-price while tobacco price is raised to five times as much as current price

If Nicorette is sold at half-price and available at a vending machine or at a convenience store while tobacco price is raised to five times as much as current price

If Nicorette's price stays the same (6,900 yen for 60 tablets; 3,600 yen for a course of smoking cessation) but available at a vending machine or at a convenience store

If Nicorette's price stays the same while tobacco price is doubled

If Nicorette's price stays the same while tobacco price is raised to five times as much as current price

If Nicorette's price stays the same and Nicorette is available at a vending machine or at a convenience store while tobacco price is doubled

If Nicorette's price stays the same and Nicorette is available at a vending machine or at a convenience store while tobacco price is raised to five times as much as current price a vending machine or at a convenience store. The combination of attributes and levels resulted in eleven possible scenarios ($2 \times 3 \times 2 - 1$).

The estimation equation is as follows:

$$G^*_{i,k} = \alpha_0 + \alpha_P P_{i,k} + \alpha_T T_{i,k} + \alpha_R R_{i,k} + \alpha_F F_i + \alpha_Y Y_i + \alpha_S S_i + \alpha_A A_i + \alpha_E E_i$$

$$+ \alpha_I \log I_i + \alpha_J \sum_l \mathbf{J}_{i,l} + v_{i,k}$$

$$G_{i,k} = \begin{cases} 1 & \text{if} \quad G^*_{i,k} > 0 \\ 0 & \text{otherwise} \end{cases}$$

$$v_{i,k} = \varepsilon_{i,k} + u_i,$$

where $G^*_{i,k}$ is a latent variable, which is a difference between the utility from quitting smoking with the nicotine gum and the utility from keeping smoking without it. Explanatory variables were defined as follows: $P_{i,k}$ is price of nicotine gum; $T_{i,k}$ is price of cigarettes; $R_{i,k}$ represents whether nicotine gum is available at a vending machine or at a convenience store (1 if available, 0 otherwise); F_i is the FTND index;[5] Y_i is years of smoking; A_i is age; S_i is sex (1 if male, 0 if female); E_i is categorized years of education (1 if junior college or more, 0 otherwise); $\log I_i$ is logged annual income; $\mathbf{J}_{i,t}$ is a vector of chronic illnesses (1 if they have, 0 otherwise); and H_i is health status (1 if in bad health, 0 otherwise). We employed a random effect probit model (Butler and Moffitt, 1982) because we assumed that an individual had consistent effects regardless of scenarios. We assumed that the individual effect, u_i, was normally distributed as follows:

$$u_i \sim N(0, \sigma^2_u)$$

10.3.2   Results

Table 10.8 reports the results of the estimation. The coefficients of the three policy instruments had the expected signs. The price of nicotine gum had a negative effect on nicotine gum purchase, the price of cigarettes had a positive effect, and access to the gum had positive effects on nicotine gum purchase. Other statistically significant explanatory variables were the Fagerstrom Test for Nicotine Dependence (FTND) index, years of smoking, sex, education, log of annual income, and circulatory illness. The higher FTND index made the nicotine gum demand higher. The more years of smoking, the higher the demand for the gum. Women, people with higher income, and people with higher levels of education had higher de-

---

5. The nicotine dependence index developed by Dr. Fagerstrom was derived from a short paper-and-pencil test (Fagerstrom and Schneider 1989). We employed a revised Fagerstrom Test for Nicotine Dependence index (FTND index) for this study. The actual test is presented in the appendix.

Table 10.8   **Profit estimates for NRT demand**

	Coefficient	Standard error	p-value
Nicorette price	–0.8379***	0.0340	0.000
Tobacco price	0.0021***	0.0001	0.000
Vending machine or convenience store	0.1668***	0.0517	0.001
FTND index	0.2938***	0.0260	0.000
Years of smoking	–0.023**	0.0095	0.016
Sex	–0.6523***	0.1152	0.000
Age	0.0006	0.0086	0.944
Education	0.1935*	0.1099	0.078
Logged income	0.2920***	0.0870	0.001
Heart disease	–0.0812	0.2159	0.707
Diabetes	–0.2906	0.2145	0.176
Disease of circulatory system	1.0400***	0.3642	0.004
Disease of digestive system	0.0424	0.1489	0.776
Constant	–3.0500***	0.5361	0.000

Notes: Nicorette price is in 10,000 yen, and tobacco price is in yen. The number of total samples is 5,820 (485 individuals are included). Log likelihood = –2065.8625.
***Significant at the 1 percent level.
**Significant at the 5 percent level.
*Significant at the 10 percent level.

mand for nicotine gum. People with circulatory disease also had higher demand.

Table 10.9 shows the marginal effect of each attribute. The results indicate that a 10,000 yen (27.8 percent) decrease in the price of nicotine gum would increase its own demand by 16.5 percent, and a 100 yen (40.0 percent) increase in the price of cigarettes would lead to an increase of 4.2 percent in the demand for nicotine gum. It is also revealed that if nicotine gum is made available at a vending machine or a convenience store, the demand for the gum would increase by 3.3 percent.

Our estimation results are basically consistent with the findings of Tauras and Chaloupka (2001) that show that the price of nicotine gum has a negative effect on its demand, while the price of cigarettes has a positive effect.[6] Specifically, using pooled cross-sectional–time-series observational data for fifty major metropolitan markets in the United States, Tauras and Chaloupka showed that the average own-price elasticity of demand for nicotine gum is –1.5, while the average cross-price elasticity for cigarettes is 0.81, which is several times larger in magnitude than our estimates of –0.59 and 0.11, respectively. These differences in price elasticities could be

6. Keeler et al. (2002), however, find that the impact of the price of nicotine gum on demand is not statistically significant in the United States.

Table 10.9   Marginal effects

	Coefficient	Standard error	p-value
Nicorette price	−0.1652***	0.0121	0.000
Tobacco price	0.0004**	0.0000	0.000
Vending machine or convenience store[a]	0.0329***	0.0104	0.002
FTND Index	0.0579***	0.0060	0.000
Years of smoking	−0.0045**	0.0018	0.015
Sex[a]	−0.1419***	0.0274	0.000
Age	0.0001	0.0017	0.944
Education[a]	0.0383*	0.0222	0.086
Logged income	0.0576***	0.0171	0.001
Heart disease[a]	−0.0153	0.0389	0.694
Diabetes[a]	−0.0484	0.0299	0.105
Disease of circulatory system[a]	0.3113**	0.1377	0.024
Disease of digestive system[a]	0.0085	0.0305	0.780

Note: Nicorette price is in 10,000 yen, and tobacco price is in yen. Standard errors are calculated by Delta method.

[a]dy/dx is for discrete change of dummy variable from 0 to 1.

***Significant at the 1 percent level.

**Significant at the 5 percent level.

*Significant at the 10 percent level.

due to the difference in the nature of the data used for the analyses; where they use aggregate market data, we use microconjoint data.

10.4   Cost-Benefit Analysis for a Smoking Cessation Support Policy

Nicotine replacement therapy is costly to the individual because it is not paid for by health insurance, whether it is prescribed or purchased over the counter. We examine whether a government subsidy for nicotine gum would make NRT more available to people who want to quit smoking.

Many epidemiological studies have shown that among ex-smokers, disease incidence decreases dramatically up until five years after smoking cessation and continues to drop thereafter, eventually reaching the same level as nonsmokers after ten to fifteen years (U.S. Department of Health and Human Services 1990, 1996b; Hirayama 1987; Hirayama 1990). If the benefits from smoking cessation go only to smokers, they should be responsible for all the costs associated with NRT. However, Japan has a universal health insurance system, which covers 70 percent of medical expenses, and the nation as a policyholder shares the cost of supporting the health insurance system. If nicotine gum helps to reduce national medical expenditures and health insurance payments, the benefits are considered externalities. In such a case, it could make sense to introduce a subsidy for the nicotine gum. Specifically, we wish to examine how the costs of a sub-

Total costs

Total cost = A (Subsidy per capita) · B (Increased number of smokers who demand the gum after the policy)

A = Average cost for a course of smoking cessation · Subsidy rate (70%)

B = C (Estimated number of smokers) · D (Increased demand ratio due to the policy)

D = Estimated demand elasticity (0.16) · A

Yearly benefits

Yearly benefits = E (Number of smokers who would succeed in smoking cession with policy) · F (Reduced annual insurance payment)

E = B · Success rate by nicotine gum

F = G (Excess health insurance payment per smoker) · H (Rate of medical expense reduction by smoking cessation)

G = Excess annual medical expenditure due to smoking · Health insurance coverage rate (0.7)/C

H = (Mortality of smokers – Mortality of former smokers)/(Mortality of smokers – Mortality of nonsmokers) = (Excess mortality of smokers – Excess mortality of former smokers)/Excess mortality of smokers

Note: Average cost for a course of smoking cessation: 36,000 yen (authors' calculations based upon an explanatory note on the product). Subsidy rate: 0.7. Estimated number of smokers: 33.6 millions (Ministry of Health and Welfare 1999). Estimated price elasticity of demand: 0.16 (table 10.8). Excess annual medical expenditure due to smoking: 1.2 trillion yen (Institute for Health Economics and Policy 1997). Health insurance coverage rate: 0.7. Success rate by nicotine gum: 23% (Asano 2000). Excess mortality of smokers: 23% (Hirayama 1987).

sidy compare to the benefits associated with a reduction in health insurance payments.

Therefore, we have estimated the costs and the benefits associated with the subsidy policy and conducted a cost-benefit analysis. We assumed the subsidy rate to be 70 percent. This was appropriate because if the nicotine gum is covered with health insurance, the coverage rate would be 70 percent.[7] Equations for costs and benefits are presented in table 10.10.

10.4.1   Total Cost

The total cost was calculated by multiplying the subsidy per smoker by the increased number of smokers who demand the nicotine gum due to the policy. The subsidy per smoker is the product of the average cost for a course of smoking cessation (36,000 yen) and subsidy rate (70 percent). The increased number of smokers demanding the nicotine gum after the policy is the product of the estimated number of smokers and increased demand ratio due to the policy (equation [3]). The increased demand ratio due to the policy was derived from the estimates presented in table 10.8. According to the CA results, a 10,000 yen downward shift in the price of a

7. Our assumption is not that insurance coverage would pay 70 percent of the cost, but rather that a subsidy would reduce the price to 30 percent of the current price.

course of treatment is to reduce the demand response by 16 percent. The cost reduction due to the subsidy was 25,200 yen (36,000 yen × 0.7). Therefore, the increased demand ratio due to the policy was 0.40 (D in table 10.10).

10.4.2 Yearly Benefit

The yearly benefit is a product of the number of smokers who succeeded in quitting smoking after the policy and the reduced annual insurance payments due to the policy (E · F in table 10.10). The number of smokers who succeeded in quitting smoking after the policy is derived by multiplying the increased number of smokers demanding the nicotine gum after the policy by the success rate for smoking cessation with the nicotine gum (E in table 10.10). The success rate used in this estimation was 23 percent, which is the mean value from epidemiological studies conducted in Japan (Asano 2000). It is conservative compared to other studies on NRT. The reduced annual insurance payment is, as F in table 10.10 shows, the product of the excess health insurance payment per smoker and the rate of medical expense reduction from smoking cessation. The excess health insurance payment per smoker was derived by dividing the product of excess annual medical expenditure due to smoking (1.2 trillion yen) and health insurance coverage rate (0.7) by the estimated number of smokers (33.6 millions). The 1.2 trillion yen as excess annual medical expenditures is quite moderate, and the actual insurance coverage rate is more than 70 percent. Therefore, the values we used are considered very conservative. We multiplied excess health insurance payment per smoker by the rate of medical expense reduction rate due to smoking cessation in order to adjust the effect of smoking cessation on medical expenses, which was not exactly the same as among nonsmokers. According to Hirayama's study (1987), excess mortality of smokers and excess mortality of former smokers were 23 percent and 4 percent, respectively. We employed these numbers. We divided the difference between 23 percent and 4 percent by 23 percent, then obtained the rate of medical expense reduction due to smoking cessation, which is 82 percent.

10.4.3 Cost-Benefit

Consequently the subsidy would cost the government a total of 352.4 billion yen, and the benefits due to the reduction of health insurance payment would be 67.6 billion yen per year. The benefits would be ongoing even if the subsidy were offered only once. After five years, the government would be able to save 338.5 billion yen (67.6 billion × 5), which is approximately equal to the cost. Given that the benefits could continue for longer than five years, it is highly possible that the benefits of the subsidy policy could meet all of the costs.

10.4.4 Other Factors to Be Considered as Long-Run Effects

The cost-benefit analysis in this section was conducted with very limited information, so it cannot be overemphasized that various other factors

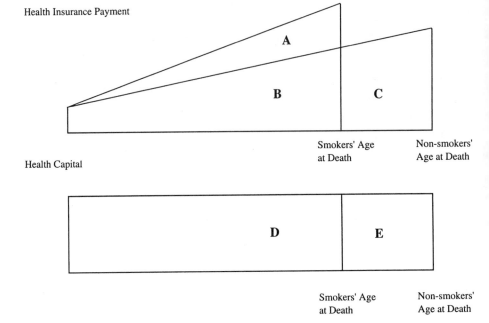

Fig. 10.1   Lifetime health insurance payment and health capital by smoking status

should be taken into consideration for a more precise analysis. One of the most important factors is the part of the health insurance payment corresponding to the life extended by smoking cessation. The concept is shown in the upper part of figure 10.1. It illustrates the insurance payment that increases with age. The lifetime insurance payments of smokers are shown by the area of A + B. The area of B is an insurance payment that is common to both smokers and nonsmokers, and the area of A is a smoker's additional health insurance payment due to health problems. The decrease in the area of A due to smoking cessation represents cost savings. On the other hand, the area of C would be added to costs when the length of life is extended. Therefore, net benefits should be calculated by subtracting the area of C from the area of A.

In order to compute the area of C, two numerical values are required. One is the difference between the average life expectancy among smokers versus nonsmokers. The other is medical expenses associated with longevity. The first number is, unfortunately, unavailable in Japan, but it has been estimated in various countries. The median longevity effect is eight years (Simpson 2000), and we used this number. As for the extra medical expense, it is not overwhelming according to the research by Suzuki and

8. Suzuki and Suzuki (2003) decomposed the medical expenses for the aged into the ordinal care and the terminal care as Lubitz, Beebe, and Baker (1995) did.

Suzuki (2003).[8] Living eight more years makes medical expenses increase only by 3.94 million yen per person because most of the medical expenditure for the old is accounted for by terminal care. We multiplied this 3.94 million yen increase in the insurance payment by 78 million people, which is the number of successful ex-smokers, and obtained the cost presented in the area of C, which is 3,073 billion yen.

The other possible benefit is the increased health capital due to longevity (see figure 10.1). Health capital is a monetary value of life that takes health into consideration. It is defined as follows:

$$\text{health capital} = V\sum_{k=0}^{\infty} \frac{E(H_k)}{(1 + r)^k},$$

where V is the value of the life, which is normally lifetime earnings. H_k is quality of life factor for a year at age k; and r is real discount rate. The value of health capital was estimated by Cutler and Richardson (1997, 1998) in the United States and by Fukui and Iwamoto (2003) in Japan. We can take sum of the implied quality of life age factor from Fukui and Iwamoto (2003) and lifetime earnings (280 million yen) from the Economic Surveys of Japan in 1990. Using a 3 percent real discount rate, like Cutler and Richardson, the benefit associated with an eight-year increase in health capital was 8.54 million yen per person. We multiplied the 8.54 increase in health capital by 78 million people and obtained the benefit represented by the area of E, which is 6,670 billion yen. As a result, the area of C subtracted from E, which is the net benefit associated with the lengthened life, amounts to 3,300 billion yen.

10.5 Conclusions

This paper estimates the demand function for nicotine gum (Nicorette) that has been on the market since it was approved as an over-the-counter drug in September 2001. The estimate obtained from conjoint analysis indicates that a 10,000 yen decrease in the price of nicotine gum would increase the demand for the gum by 16.5 percent, and a 100 yen increase in the price of cigarettes would lead to an increase in the demand for nicotine gum of 4.2 percent. It is also estimated that if nicotine gum were made available at a vending machine or a convenience store, the demand for nicotine gum would increase by 3.3 percent.

A cost-benefit analysis was conducted to estimate the consequence of a subsidy policy for nicotine gum. In the case of a 70 percent subsidy for nicotine gum, it would cost the government 352.4 billion yen. The benefits associated with the subsidy are a decrease in smoking-related illnesses through successful smoking cessation. This would make annual medical insurance payment fall by 67.6 billion yen. After five years, the government would save 338.5 billion yen, which is comparable to the cost.

When we take the change in the lifetime medical insurance payments and health capital accumulation into account, 3,300 billion yen should be added to the benefits in the long run.

The Ministry of Health, Labor and Welfare initiated the national health promotion movement so-called Healthy Japan 21 in the year 2000 and established smoking cessation promotion as one of the most important policy objectives. A subsidy for nicotine gum or insurance coverage for the gum is one possible means of achieving the public health goal.

It is worth noting that the costs and benefits that this study used were based on a demand function estimated using CA, which does not necessarily represent the actual demand function.[9] The net values of CBA should, therefore, be carefully examined. Furthermore, when real transaction data eventually become available, the demand function should be calculated with the real values, and the total costs and benefits should be reexamined.

Appendix

Table 10A.1   Fagerstrom Test for Nicotine Dependence Index

Questions	Answers	Points
1. How soon after you wake up do you smoke your first cigarette?	Within 5 minutes	3
	Within 6–30 minutes	2
	Within 31–60 minutes	1
	After 60 minutes	0
2. Do you find it difficult to refrain from smoking in places where it is forbidden? (e.g., in library, in movie theater)	Yes	1
	No	0
3. Which cigarette would you most hate to give up?	The first one in the morning	1
	Any other	0
4. How many cigarettes a day do you smoke?	31 or more	3
	21–30	2
	11–20	1
	10 or more	0
5. Do you smoke more frequently during the first hours after awakening than during the rest of the day?	Yes	1
	No	0
6. Do you smoke if you are so ill that you are in bed most of the day?	Yes	1
	No	0

9. Suzuki and Okusa (2000) evaluated the magnitude of the bias in CA by comparing the demand function from CA to the actual demand function calculated from transaction data. Tsuji and Suzuki (2002) measured the bias in CVM. Conjoint analysis has relatively small bias compared to other hypothetical market methods, but there is still a discrepancy with the real value. Further research should explore methods to lessen the bias.

References

Asano, M. 2000. Kitsuen to kinen [Smoking and smoking cessation]. *Nihon Kinen Suishin Ishi-shikaishi Renmei Tushin* 3:1–3.

Bryan, S., M. Buxton, R. Sheldon, and A. Grant. 1998. The use of magnetic resonance imaging for the investigation of knee injuries: A discrete choice conjoint analysis exercise. *Health Economics* 7:595–604.

Butler, J., and R. Moffitt. 1982. A computationally efficient quadrature procedure for the one factor multinominal probit model. *Econometrica* 50:347–64.

Cutler, D., and E. Richardson. 1997. Measuring the health of the United States population. *Brookings Papers on Economic Activity, Microeconomics:* 217–71.

———. 1998. The value of health: 1970–1990. *American Economic Review* 88 (2): 97–100.

Fagerstrom, K. O., and N. G. Schneider. 1989. Measuring nicotine dependence: A review of the Fagerstrom Tolerance Questionnaire. *Journal of Behavioral Medicine* 12 (2): 159–82.

Freeman, J. 1998. Assessing the need for student health services using maximum difference conjoint analysis. *Journal of Research in Pharmaceutical Economics* 9 (3): 35–49.

Fukuda, K., H. Kinoshita, S. Takemura, and S. Hachimaki. 1999. Kanja no iryokikan senkou ni kansuru conjoint analysis wo mochiita chosa kenkyu [Analysis of patients' decision to choose medical facilities using conjoint analysis]. Paper presented at the annual meeting of the Japan Hospital Management Association. October, Chiba, Japan.

Fukui, T., and Y. Iwamoto. 2003. Medical spending and the health outcome of the Japanese population. Paper presented at the 2003 spring meeting of the Japanese Economic Association. June, Oita, Japan.

Goto, K. 1995. Kankyo-keizai to korekara no sangyo-shakai [Environmental economic and future industrial society]. *Chuo Koron* 47:125–36.

———. 1996. Tobacco no keizai bunseki [Economic analysis of tobacco]. *Nohon Ishikai Zasshi* 116:370–71.

Hakim, A., and D. Pathak. 1999. Modelling the EuroQol data: A comparison of discrete choice conjoint and conditional preference modelling. *Health Economics* 8:103–16.

Hirayama, T. 1987. *Yobo gan gaku* [A study of cancer prevention]. Tokyo: Medikaru Saiensusha.

———. 1990. *Lifestyle and mortality: A large-scale census based cohort study in Japan,* Vol. 6 of *Contributions to epidemiology and biostatistics.* Basel, Switzerland: Karger.

Institute for Health Economics and Policy. 1997. Heisei 6-8 nendo kosei kagaku kenkyuhi hojo jigyo ni yoru kitsuen seisaku no cost-benefit bunseki ni kakawaru chosa kenkyu houkokusho [A report on cost-benefit analysis of smoking cessation policy]. Tokyo: Institute for Health Economics and Policy.

Jorenby, D. E., S. J. Leischow, M. A. Nides, S. I. Rennard, J. A. Johnston, A. R. Hughes, S. S. Smith et al. 1999. A controlled trial of sustained-release buyprorion, a nicotine patch, or both for smoking cessation. *New England Journal of Medicine* 340:685–91.

Keeler, T. E., T. W. Hu, A. Keith, R. Manning, M. D. Marciniak, M. Ong, and H. Y. Sung. 2002. The benefits of switching smoking cessation drugs to over-the-counter status. *Health Economics* 11:389–402.

Lubitz, J., J. Beebe, and C. Baker. 1995. Longevity and Medicare expenditure. *The New England Journal of Medicine* 332:999–1003.

Ministry of Health and Welfare. 1999. *Survey on smoking and health conditions.* Tokyo: Ministry of Health and Welfare.

Momma, Y. 1998. Nikochin chikan ryoho ni yoru kitsuen no seiseki [Performance of smoking cessation using nicotine replacement therapy]. *Journal of the American Medical Association* (Japanese ed.): August: 62–63.

Peto, R., A. D. Lopez, J. Boreham, and M. Turn. 2004. Mortality from smoking in developed countries: 1950–2000. 2nd ed. Oxford, UK: Oxford University Press.

Ratcliffe, J., and M. Buxton. 1999. Patients' preferences regarding the process and outcomes of life saving technology: An application of conjoint analysis to liver transplantation. *International Journal Technological Assessment Health Care* 15 (2): 340–51.

Ryan, M. 1999. Using conjoint analysis to take account of patient preferences and go beyond health outcomes. An Application to In-Vitro Fertilization, Social Science and Medicine 48:535–46.

Ryan, M., and S. Farrar. 1994. A pilot study using conjoint analysis to establish the views of users in the provision of orthodontic services in grampian. Health Economics Research Unit Discussion Paper no. 07/94. Aberdeen, UK: University of Aberdeen.

Ryan, M., and J. Hughes. 1997. Using conjoint analysis to assess women's preference for miscarriage management. *Health Economics* 6:261–74.

Schneider, N. G., M. E. Jarvik, and A. B. Forsythe. 1984. Nicotine vs. placebo gum in the alleviation of withdrawal during smoking cessation. *Addictive Behaviors* 9:149–56.

Singh, J., L. Cuttler, M. Shin, J. Silvers, and D. Neuhauser. 1998. Medical decision-making and the patient: Understanding preference patterns for growth hormone therapy using conjoint analysis. *Medical Care* 36 (8): AS31–AS45.

Suzuki, W., and Y. Okusa. 1999. Conjoint analysis wo mochiita kaigo juyo kansu no suitei [An estimation of long-term-care demand]. ISER Discussion Paper no. 486. Osaka, Japan. Institute of Social and Economic Research.

———. 2000. Iryo juyo kodo no conjoint analysis [Conjoint analysis for the demand of health care related to common cold]. *Iryo to Shakai* 10 (1): 125–44.

Suzuki, W., and R. Suzuki. 2003. Jumyo no chokika ha roujin iryouhi zouka no youinka? [Does longevity cause a rapid rise in medical costs for the elderly?] *Kokusai Kokyoseisaku Kenkyu* 7 (2): 2–11.

Tauras, J. A., and F. J. Chaloupka. 2001. Demand for nicotine replacement therapies. NBER Working Paper no. 8332. Cambridge, MA: National Bureau of Economic Research, June.

Tsuji, M., and W. Suzuki. 2002. The application of CVM for assessing the telehealth system: An analysis of the discrepancy between WTP and WTA based on survey data. In *Assets, beliefs, and equilibria in economic dynamics,* ed. C. Aliprantis, K. Arrow, P. Hammond, F. Kubler, H. Wu, and N. Yannelis, 494–506. Berlin, Germany: Springer.

U.S. Department of Health and Human Services. 1988. The health consequences of smoking: Nicotine addiction. A Report of the Surgeon General, 1988. U.S. Department of Health and Human Services, Public Health Service, Center for Disease Control, National Center for Chronic Disease Prevention and Health Promotion, Office on Smoking and Health. DHHS Publication no. (CDC) 88-8406. Washington, DC: Government Printing Office.

———. 1990. The health benefits of smoking cessation. A Report of the Surgeon General, 1990. U.S. Department of Health and Human Services, Public Health Service, Center for Disease Control, National Center for Chronic Disease Prevention and Health Promotion, Office on Smoking and Health. DHHS Publication no. (CDC) 90-8416. Washington, DC: Government Printing Office.

———. 1995. 21 CFR Pt. 801, et al. Regulations restriction of the sale and distribution of cigarettes and smokeless tobacco products to protect children and adolescents: Proposed rule. Analysis regarding FDA's jurisdiction over nicotine-containing cigarettes and smokeless tobacco products. Notice. *Federal Register* 60:155.

———. 1996a. 21 CFR Pt. 801, et al. Regulations restriction of the sale and distribution of cigarettes and smokeless tobacco products to protect children and adolescents: Final rule. *Federal Register* 61:168.

———. 1996b. Clinical Practice Guideline no. 18: Smoking cessation. Public Health Service, Agency for Health Care Policy and Research, Centers for Disease Control and Prevention. AHCPR Publication no. 96-0692.

Van der Pol, M., and J. Cairns. 1997. Establishing patient's preferences for blood transfusion support: An application of conjoint analysis. *Journal of Health Services Research and Policy* 3:70–76.

Wasley, M. A., S. E. McNagny, V. L. Phillips, and J. S. Ahluvalia. 1997. The cost-effectiveness of the nicotine transdermal patch for smoking cessation. *Preventive Medicine* 26:264–70.

World Health Organization (WHO). 1993. *International classification of diseases.* 10th ed. Geneva, Switzerland: WHO.

Contributors

David M. Cutler
Department of Economics
Harvard University
Cambridge, MA 02138

Jeffery Geppert
National Bureau of Economic
    Research
30 Alta Road
Stanford, CA 94305-8715

Akihiko Iguchi
Graduate School of Medicine
Nagoya University
65 Tsurumai-cho, Showa-ku
Nagoya 466-8550, Japan

Tamotsu Kadoda
Department of Economics
Daito Bunka University
1-9-1 Takashimadaiva
Itabashi-ku, Tokyo 175-8571, Japan

Koichi Kawabuchi
Tokyo Medical and Dental University
Division of Public Health—Health
    Care Economics
1-5-45 Yushima
Bunkyo-ku, Tokyo 113-8549, Japan

Makoto Kawamura
Department of Economics
Hosei University
4342 Aihara-machi
Machida-shi, Tokyo 194-0298, Japan

Masafumi Kuzuya
Department of Geriatrics
Graduate School of Medicine
Nagoya University
65 Tsurumai-cho, Showa-ku
Nagoya 466-8550, Japan

Yuichiro Masuda
Department of Geriatrics
Graduate School of Medicine
Nagoya University
65 Tsurumai-cho, Showa-ku
Nagoya 466-8550, Japan

Mark McClellan
Centers for Medicare and Medicaid
    Services
200 Independence Avenue, SW
Room 314G
Washington, DC 20201

Kathleen McGarry
Department of Economics
University of California, Los Angeles
Box 951477
Los Angeles, CA 90095-1477

Haruko Noguchi
Faculty of Social Science
Toyo Eiwa University
32 Miho-cho, Midori-ku
Yokohama Kanagawa 226-0015, Japan

Seiritsu Ogura
Department of Economics
Hosei University
4342 Aihara-machi
Machida-shi, Tokyo 194-0298, Japan

Jonathan Skinner
Department of Economics
Dartmouth College
6106 Rockefeller Hall
Hanover, NH 03755

Shigeru Sugihara
Osaka School of International Public
    Policy
1-31 Machikaneyama-cho
Toyonaka city, Osaka 560-0043, Japan

Reiko Suzuki
Japan Center for Economic Research
Nikkei Kayabacho Bldg.
6-1, Nihombashi Kayabacho 2-chome
Chuo-ku, Tokyo 103-0025, Japan

Wataru Suzuki
Department of Education
Tokyo Gakugei University
4-1-1 NukuiKita-machi, Koganei-city
Tokyo 184-8501, Japan

David A. Wise
Harvard University
John F. Kennedy School of
    Government
79 John F. Kennedy Street
Cambridge, MA 02138

Naohiro Yashiro
Department of Economics
International Christian University
3-10-2 Osawa, Mitaka-shi
Tokyo 181-8585, Japan

Yanfei Zhou
The Japan Institute for Labour Policy
    and Training
4-8-23 Kamishakuji-i, Nerima-ku
Tokyo 177-8502, Japan

Author Index

Subject Index